D1389787

Leslie Aspin is not a hero. He is a crook.

He has never shot anyone, except from behind.

He became a British Secret Service agent, not out of patriotism, or even for money; but because he was blackmailed.

The job was too much for him. After a series of attempts on his life, and an assignment he did not like, he ran scared.

In search of security, he went to Fleet Street's leading investigative newspaper, the Sunday People.

They refused to believe his story.

He produced tape recordings, plane tickets, and hotel bills.

He showed a letter from a solicitor describing a meeting between the solicitor, a Chief Constable, and Aspin himself.

Provisional IRA leaders in Belfast confirmed that the name Leslie Aspin was high on their death list.

Middle East contacts reported that Black September had offered £50,000 for the head of a man named Leslie Aspin.

The British Government was unable to deny the story.

Aspin could not be faulted.

Now he and journalist Trevor Aspinall have written the full story.

Cowardice, treachery, greed, blackmail, and hopeless inefficiency — this is the truth about espionage.

I, KOVAKS

Leslie Aspin

with
Trevor Aspinall

EVEREST BOOKS LIMITED
4 Valentine Place, London SE1

Published in Great Britain by Everest Books Ltd., 1975
ISBN 0 903925 524
Copyright © 1975 Leslie Aspin and Trevor Aspinall

Computer typeset by Input Typesetting Ltd., 4 Valentine Place., London SE 1
Printed and bound in Great Britain by
Redwood Burn Limited, Trowbridge & Esher

Dedicated to
Trevor Aspinall,
the only man in the world
I trust.

Chapter 1

Last Message to Homer
October, 1974

Christ. I wish I could relax. Everything has gone according to plan so far, after all, and there's no way anyone's going to get at me aboard this 747. I should be light-headed with the joy of getting clear, but here I am sweating so much that I can hardly hold my pen as I write.

I'm pretty sure that I've made no mistakes so far. If I had I wouldn't be sitting here.

The danger point was at Heathrow. The Special Branch boys there know me better than most people in my business – my old business, that is.

You see, I'm a newly retired spy, secret agent, agent provocateur, call it what you will. My problem is that my bosses, back there in Whitehall, don't know yet that I've quit. They suspected that I might try to get out, that I *do* know, but I reckon I've beaten them by about two days. At the moment I'm ahead of them and the sundry other organisations I've fallen out with over the last few years. And if only this bloody fool pilot would lift this lumbering great elephant off the Schipol tarmac I'd feel a bit more confident that I'd be staying ahead – and alive.

But I'm so bloody nervous – frightened. It's getting worse. Deep down inside I've got the feeling that I've done something wrong, that I've missed a trick, made a mistake. And if I've done that I'm as good as dead. It might help if I go back over today's movements now. I've got

7

to write it all down anyway, because I want a full written record of my activities just in case my retirement is cut short by what my department would call an "accident".

Getting through the checks at Heathrow turned out to be routine and I'm sure no-one realised who I was at that stage. If they had they'd have held me. Flight BE506, a Trident, had a usual loading of businessmen and tourists — no-one who seemed to take any particular interest in me.

We came into Schipol on runway 0624. Being a pilot myself I always notice which runway we use, it helps take my mind off the things which can go wrong if I take a professional interest in taking off and landing. Anyway, Amsterdam's a favourite staging post which I've used for years and know well.

After we had taxied to gate C36 and the passenger pier had swung round into position, I hung back until most of the other passengers had disembarked and then walked off just behind a very pretty brunette. As we got to the main concourse I fell in beside her, trying to give the impression that we were together. If anyone was watching for me they would expect me to be alone. So far, O.K.

At the end of the moving concourse, where the rest of the passengers went on down the escalator to passport control, I lost my bird. Instead of going on down I turned right and made my way straight through, past the porn bookshop and bureau de change, to the telephone and cable office. There was no-one obviously on my heels.

I knew the guy in the cable office, the one who sits behind his little desk feeding the sparrows which have made a home in the terminal, as he puts through telephone calls and hands out cable forms. He looked up and smiled. He obviously recognised me: "Cable or phone, Menheer?".

I asked him for a cable form and as he reached under the desk a sparrow which had been sitting pecking at crumbs at his left elbow fluttered into the air. We had a little conversation about his pets.

I filled in the form while standing at his desk. This hadn't been part of my plan but it was something I felt I had to do. First, I wrote the message: "GONE, GET STUFFED". Then I wrote in the cable address of my controller in London and his code name, HOMER. I signed it with my own code name, KOVAKS.

8

As I have already said, this was not a part of my plan. It was, however, something that had to be done, a final communication, a breaking of already strained ties. Or, maybe, just a stupid act of bravado in an attempt to prove to myself that I could break away from the department. Anyway it's done now. Kovaks has sent a lot of cables from Schipol. There just had to be a final one.

After sending the cable, I hung around in the departure area and had a few drinks, looking over my shoulder until this flight, KL683 for Montreal and Houston, was announced. We boarded at gate C55. There were no problems there; just a search of my briefcase for weapons by the security guys, but that's routine nowadays and they do it to everyone...

The pilot has just heaved this flying hotel into the air. The whining, roaring screech of the engines has choked back to little more than a whisper. I can feel my neck muscles relaxing as I fight to unlock my back teeth. I am almost ready to loosen off my too-tight lap strap – but not quite. My calf muscles are still knotted from forcing my feet into the floor during take-off.

While I was writing I had started to relax a bit, now it's all gone. Christ, how I hate flying, or rather the getting up and down bits of it. I hate it like most people hate dentists. At least, to be more precise, I hate being flown. If I'm piloting myself it's O.K. You know what I mean. If I'm doing the driving I might be able to fix things if they go wrong, but there's damn-all I can do if that idiot up there makes a mistake. If that happens I can only die.

But that's it. We're in the air. I'm clear. Out. Free. Alive. And with just a little more luck it looks as if I might stay that way for a few years to come.

With at least four efficient organisations keen on putting a bullet into me for one reason or another you can imagine my relief at getting out from under.

We've just reached optimum height and I've undone my seat belt. At last I feel less tense. I can even feel a sort of glow setting up inside me – and I don't think it's anything to do with the four Scotches I put down at Schipol.

So I've declared myself redundant. Kovaks has retired.

Kovaks. What a bloody silly name to give a guy. Why the hell can't they call us Charlie, Bert, Jim or something? We're all ordinary guys — why not give us ordinary names?

If nothing else the names are downright embarrassing. Take mine. I'm fair-haired, pale skinned and you couldn't get to be more conservatively English-looking even if you hailed from Boston, Mass. I could well be a Smith, Jones, Brown or even a Postlethwaite or Ffoulkes. But never, never so long as I've a hole in my ear, could I be a Kovaks. But that's the name I've used in cable offices all over the world for years.

However, I've just used it for the last time. I'd dearly love to see the look on Homer's face when he gets that cable. He's had someone on my tail for weeks now, suspecting that I was going to do something which might well embarrass him. But for the last two days I've been dodging around like a hungry bee and I'm sure that I'm on my own now. At least, I'm as sure as anyone can be in my situation.

I know for a fact that Homer would rather have me dead than retired. I was tipped off about that a week ago by an old colleague who telephoned to tell me the department suspected I was about to embarrass them by talking to a newspaper about my activities over recent years. Of course, I explained that it was all a lot of nonsense but it gave me a fright. Even though they didn't appear to know that the dreadful deed was done, so to speak. For two months I had been having secret meetings with Trevor Aspinall of the Sunday People in London.

I had left with him proof of my activities and a documented history of my espionage dealings, to be published in the event of a fatal "accident". An "accident" which I felt might well be imminent.

But the fact that my old boss might well have a former team-mate of mine on my track doesn't really worry me overmuch. My old department doesn't employ the best for this sort of thing — which is rather proved by the fact that they put me on their payroll.

I am, however, more than somewhat worried by a couple of Black September operatives, a whole host of IRA Provo ·madmen and a handful of Mafia hit-men. And then there is a whole covey of old smuggling colleagues who have now found out that I have double-crossed and triple-crossed my way through the past six years of my life — for my profit and at their expense.

Come to think of it, there's something very secure about being aboard an airliner in these days of terrorist hijacking. It's a pretty fair bet that no-one has been allowed on board with a gun tucked in his knickers. I hadn't thought of that until I was recalling the number of people there are around who want to claim the honour of bringing the career of Kovaks to a sudden and violent end.

Most of the people who want to sail their little plastic boats in a bath filled with my blood are professionals. I'm about as amateur as they come. Oh, I was a good smuggler, could patch up a Perkins diesel quicker than most and smell patrol boats ten miles off, but I was a lousy agent. I was scared to death all the time that someone would find out what I was at. Well, that's understandable. I never ever received any training as an agent, other than the odd tip on how to infiltrate other organisations.

I have, however, learned to cover my tracks pretty well and keep my head down when the shit hits the fan. That's what I'm doing now and that's what will probably keep me alive to spend the money I've saved during my life as Kovaks.

I suppose I'd better explain why I am so concerned about writing this account of my life. After all, it's not a usual step for guys in my ex-business to take, even though I heave heard at least three old colleagues express their wish to do it when they pack it all in. But I suspect they want to grind axes into the skulls of their old bosses. With me it's not that way, I only want to set the record straight.

Recently I have seen a couple of my old mates written off by the Service as criminals after they were caught on department business.

Another has been shot because the bosses would not give him protection and I, myself was asked to "deal with" yet another.

Because I have no intention of ending up being ditched by the Department as a crook, or being quietly "taken out" of things, I am going to tell as many people as I can what it was all about. I want eveyone to know how they conned me into joining their comedy act and how they mismanaged a lot of the business they undertook. I want what I am writing to serve as a warning to other men who may be asked to help them. I want would-be recruits to know that, although the grand patriotic pleas sound great at the time smooth-talking con-men drip them from their sugary lips, it's all so much bollocks once you start work.

I also want the British taxpayer to know how a lot of his money is spent – and wasted – on idiot schemes dreamed up by men who would be better off writing film scripts than running their espionage cells from their mahogany and walnut desks in their plush-carpeted offices.

I don't want to come out of this looking like a hero either. I'm not. Maybe that's the trouble, I never could see myself as a real-life James Bond any more than I could see my old workmates in that role. Everyone I met in the business, apart from the civil servants who sit behind their nice, safe desks in London, or whatever capital you care to think of, was in it for the money. And that includes me.

Oh, I've had the fast cars, my own light aircraft, the birds and a few years of jet-set high life. But at thirty-three I'm a sick insomniac and feel as though I were seventy – and there's not much money left either.

On top of this I've been shot, stabbed and beaten by professionals and become a hunted animal. I've also had to leave my wife and kids for an indefinite period to ensure their safety.

When I work it out that way, the whole fiasco has been anything but worthwile.

My cover was blown by the IRA at the beginning of September. My bosses immediately deserted me and their promised aid "if anything goes wrong, old boy", has been refused.

Within hours of my cover being stripped from me my controller was no longer on the number where I had contacted him for years. The switchboard had never even heard of him, would you believe. His deputy had never worked there either and the Special Branch man, in my own area, whose job it was to ensure that my home remained safe in my absence and to act as a liaison with my big boss when necessary, told me that he too had been "excommunicated" and could only write to our joint boss at the Department. He was no longer trusted with a telephone number.

It is fortunate that I had already established the existence of the whole control set-up by tape-recording conversations with my bosses and ensuring by means of professional witnesses that they were unchallengable. It is more fortunate that I have kept documents and instructions over a long period and also made precise notes of my assignments.

If it had not been for the proof that these documents and recordings provided, I would never have dared write this account. It would have been so easy to write me off as an adventurer trying to make money or stir up trouble for the British Secret Service . . .

It's two days since I was writing on the Jumbo to Montreal and I have now settled into the Hunting Lodge Motel on Highway 34, just outside Patterson, Wayne County in the Mid-West of the U.S.

To avoid embarrassing people who are helping me, I don't intend to explain why I came to this particular place. It is sufficient to relate that after leaving the 747 at Montreal I transferred to an Air Canada flight for Chicago instead of going on to Houston. From Chicago I then took a Delta flight on to St. Louis.

In this way I further covered my tracks and made it almost impossible for anyone subsequently attempting to trace me to follow my movements through the massive amount of paperwork involved in ticket transfers from airline to airline.

From Chicago I telephoned ahead and booked a Hertz car for the two hour drive out here to the motel. For a while at least I feel safe. Only one person from my old life knows where I am and that's Trevor Aspinall of the Sunday People. Somebody has to know in case of an "accident" and I know that I can trust him with my secret. One of my last assignments was to try to infiltrate a situation he was investigating after he had refused to hand over names of informants to detectives who arrested him along with the arms dealers he was about to bring to book. His silence cost him a week-end in jail and a lot of unnecessary aggravation at the hands of the police, but he kept the names of his informants to himself.

But back to my own story. My recruitment by the British Secret Service as a spy was brought about by the fact that I had previously spent a number of years as a smuggler in the Middle East and Europe. This account will be more readily understood if I begin at the time when I was a successful smuggler.

Chapter 2

Mediterranean Market Place
Rome, 1968

I had just arrived back in Rome from a short holiday in England with my family and taken the bus from the airport to the town terminal at the railway station.

It had been my intention to rest up at home for quite a bit longer. In fact, I had promised my wife that I would take a couple of months off. I had spent hardly any time with her during the past year.

But the phone call smashed that plan after only ten days at home. Nearly a million lire ready to slide into my back pocket was too much to ignore. So, row with wife, kiss for kids, taxi to station, train to London, taxi to airport and plane to Rome.

The phone call had been curt and to the point, that was the way of Paul, my contact who had been asked to get the deal moving. It came at 6a.m. and I recognised his voice as soon as he spoke. All he said was "Cigarettes, Leslie – Switzerland to Italy. Bank backing – eight-hundred-thou-for-you, half-and-half. Rome hotel?"

I was hardly awake by the time he had finished but the message was like an electric shock – more than £4000 to arrange the transport of cigarettes from Switzerland to Italy. The money being put up by a bank in Geneva who finance such deals. We would also use boats provided by the bank, and that meant good, fast transport. I was to be at my usual hotel in Rome as soon as possible to do the deal and would recieve my money in two lumps – half before and half after the deal.

14

I told Paul that I would be in my hotel that same evening and that he should contact me there.

It was good to be back in Rome again and I savoured the cooling evening air as I set off on the ten minute walk from the terminal across the Piazza di Cinquecento and through the side streets leading to the Ambascatori hotel in the Via Veneto.

I came up opposite the hotel, turned to cross the road outside the American embassy and paused for a while as I caught the odour of coffee and hamburgers from the Wimpy bar behind me. In the quiet of the early evening, between the end of the working day and the beginning of the frenetic Veneto night life; when the nostrils are no longer affronted by exhaust gasses and the ears by screaming, whining Fiats; when only the junior league prostitutes parade slowly up and down the pavements, the Veneto is a place to pause. A welcoming place.

I also took stock of the situation over at the hotel. Paul was an old and trusted acquaintance, but a man with a gun in his kidneys or a stiletto at his throat is no respecter of friendship. And there were, even at that time, a lot of people who would have liked to have seen me out of business. The pickings were rich, very rich, for the successful – and I was successful.

However, everything was quiet, just a couple of strolling whores and another talking to her minder as he leaned out of the top of his baby Fiat at the kerbside.

I could see the porters just inside the doors of the hotel and recognised one of them as I picked my way through the few cars using the street to the refuge in the centre and then across to the steps of the hotel.

By the time I was up the steps all three doormen were coming out to me. "Welcome back, Signore," one greeted me. There's something awfully elevating about being greeted by the staff of a luxury hotel as a regular visitor. I always look around for the envious glances on the faces of passers-by. I invariably feel badly let down, however, when I see that no-one is taking any bloody notice!

Preceded by a porter carrying my case and once again feeling badly let down, I moved across the thick pile of the reception area. At the desk I was recognised by an under-manager. "Ah. Welcome back Mr.

15

Allen, we have your usual room, you are lucky, we are busy, very busy". The man had used the alias I always used at this hotel, my second christian name, and I had hardly smiled and nodded when my case was whipped up again by a porter who disappeared towards the service lift.

By the time I got up to my room, with yet another porter, the first guy had opened the windows and was on his way out of the door. I gave the one still with me a thousand-lire note as I stood at the open window and looked over at the embassy opposite. He left, making suitable noises.

There's something comforting in the two marines who stand just inside the glass doors guarding their little piece of Italy.

Moving back from the windows I used the ornate antique-style telephone by the bed to order a couple of bottles of mineral water before going through to the bathroom to shower and freshen up after my journey. The long day was beginning to tell – I was tired and more than a little tense.

The water arrived while I was still in the bathroom and I used it to mix a scotch-and-water which I drank as I towelled myself dry. Feeling somewhat better, I shrugged on a bathrobe from my case and sat on the edge of the bed sipping my drink as I reached into the hard base of my soft-sided black leather case for my .38 Smith and Wesson revolver. I checked the action to make sure that it had not been damaged by clumsy luggage handlers – it was in good order – and then loaded it with shells from a compartment also at the bottom of the case, before placing it in the drawer of the cupboard at the side of my bed.

I was lying back on the bed listening to the light drone of traffic noise filtering up to the room as the evening traffic built up on the street below, when the telephone rang, snatching my attention back to the job in hand. It was Paul. "You're in then." It was a statement rather than a question. "No, I'm still twenty thousand feet over the city waiting to land."

"Prat: I'm coming up."

I moved the hardware from the drawer to my robe pocket, lit a cigarette and moved over to the wardrobe, picking up a couple of suits from my case as I left the bed. I hung up the suits just before the knock on the outer door of the room. I opened it, hand in pocket and keeping the door between me and the man standing there. It was Paul. Alone. "Come in, I haven't unpacked yet. What's the hurry?"

Paul moved past me, through the short hall, looking through the open bathroom door as he passed it. Before I had shut the outer door he was through the bedroom opening and had spun round to face me. Christ, what a professional. Not a word until he had checked the room for strangers and possible danger. In five seconds flat he had checked out the whole place.

He came back to meet me in the bedroom doorway and took my hand as I held it out. "Good to see you, Leslie." He dropped my hand and walked over to the corner table by the window where I had left the whisky bottle and, using the same glass that I had, poured himself two fingers. Sitting down in the armchair next to the table, he stretched long legs straight out in front of him, ankles crossed and showing the soles of his near-new hand-made shoes. It was claimed in the business that he wore shoes only until the shine had gone from the instep. He rather played up to this one and flashed the soles of his shoes at every opportunity.

Picking up my pack of Marlborough cigarettes from the table, he lit one with a gold Ronson which he took from the side pocket of his beige Savile Row Lightweight. Every inch the English gentleman was our Paul. Tall — about six-feet-two — and with an impeccable taste in clothing that matched his English public school accent.

Not that he had ever been to a public school. They don't have them in Malta, where Paul, the bastard issue of a matelot's night out with a local lass who drank too much, was born and educated. In fact, Paul had never been to school at all in any regular sort of way. But the back streets of Malta have a way of educating people for survival which is second to none, and his veneer had been acquired whilst working in his Uncle Joe's whorehouse in Soho, where he had quickly picked up the affectations and mannerisms of the upper crust clients, as he had also picked up the viciousness peculiar to Maltese ponces.

I never did find out what brought about his transfer to the smuggling circus but there were stories of a prostitute being found beaten to death just after he returned to Malta and respected officers from London's West End Central police station were certainly heavily entertained by his family on Maltese holidays.

17

He took one sip from the glass and put it back on the table. I lay back on the bed, propped on one elbow. He broke the silence.

"It's two boats, Leslie, and we're buying help from the waterguard. There's a meeting fixed with their man in an hour or so if you agree to go ahead and, as I said on the phone, it's the usual deal with half now and half later – eight-hundred-ells-all-in. You on?"

"What's my end, first?"

"You take it all from here. Meet the waterguard, find the crews, pick up and deliver. Geneva have got the stuff waiting already and you just let them know when and where you want it. They'll handle all prepayment and have a man waiting for the beach money. Usual sort of thing. Oh yes, the boats are in Malta."

It was apparently, as Paul had said, a normal deal. "Waterguard" was jargon for a customs officer, in this case an officer of the Guardia di Finaze, probably the most corrupt law enforcement service in the world. The "prepayment" was the first half of the money due to the shipper by the client and the "beach money" would be the second half, handed to me on delivery for immediate transfer to the bankers via, in this instance, their men on the spot.

I thought for a few seconds. There were one or two rapid calculations to be made. Then I said: "O.K. That'll be an extra skipper at a grand sterling and seven crew at five hundred each, four-and-a-half grand on top of mine. And I haven't had my fare and hotel yet."

"No," he replied. "Greek Charlie will skipper the lead boat and provide the second string man. You do the crew, radios and reception."

"Here's five hundred expenses for fare and hotel." As he said this, he pulled a slim packet from an inside pocket and put it on the table at his elbow. He continued: "Then there'll be five hundred apiece for six crew, half-and-half. The Greek will handle the crew money."

The deal was good. It also had the advantage of being backed by the big boys in Geneva, so the money was safe. "Right, where's the meet and how much are we paying the waterguard?"

He smiled, stood up and unbuttoned his silk shirt at the waist. Tossing a canvas money-belt on to the bed he said: "Four hundred in ells for the guy tonight and the beach-man will pay them the other half

18

on delivery. He's using the name of Mario and will be at the foot of the Spanish Steps at ten-fifteen." He glanced at his watch. "That's in an hour and ten minutes. Your start-money is in there," he said, nodding to the belt, "as well as his."

He took up my pack of Marlborough and tipped out the half-dozen cigarettes it contained onto the table. Then, having torn the packet in half, he took a gold pen from his pocket and wrote on the inside of the top half. It was an old identification gimmick. We had used it before, often. When I took the half packet from him I saw that he had written the letters P and A. By the time I arrived at the rendezvous, the man I was to meet would have the lower half of the packet with the letters U and L written in it. Simple but foolproof.

The customs man would never meet Paul. He would be instructed, by telephone, to pick up his part of the packet which would be left in an envelope in a bar or café. In the event of a double-cross Paul was unknown to the customs man – I was the only one at risk.

I took the belt and emptied the four pockets. The money was all there in high denomination notes. I then counted my start-money and nodded my acceptance to Paul before putting it all back into the pockets of the belt.

He got to his feet, asked if there were any more questions and was told that there were none. He was already moving towards the door as I rose from the bed and he said: "You know where to get me if there are any snags." Then he was gone.

As he slammed the door behind him, I went back to the bed and picked up the belt, quickly removing the money and splitting it into two bundles. It wasn't that I didn't trust Paul, in particular, just that I didn't trust anyone. He would think that I would carry it in the belt and that is just where someone who wanted to relieve me of it would look. From the writing desk I took two envelopes. Into one I put my half of the money and my start-money and the rest I put into the other. I then took both packages through to the bathroom and put them into the cabinet there.

Neither the transfer from the belt or this simple attempt at hiding the money would fool even an amateur thief. But these precautions would give me time to fight off an attacker who, if tipped off by Paul, would be going for the money-belt.

19

As I left the bathroom I pushed in the security catch on the door as an extra precaution and then dressed. I suddenly realised that I had eaten hardly anything all day and how hungry I was. But there was no time for dinner. As I checked my watch I saw that I only had about an hour before the meeting. Anyway, there were things to do.

I picked up the telephone and asked the switchboard to place a call to Malta for midnight. Assuming the meeting at the Spanish Steps was kept, I would need help from there almost immediately.

I had still only half finished my unpacking. So far I had only hung up my suits. I now hung my shirts and a couple of pairs of casual slacks alongside the suits and dropped my underwear into a drawer. From the bottom of my case I took a roll of adhesive medical strapping and, having collected both envelopes from the bathroom, strapped the one for the customs guy to my left forearm, half-way between my wrist and elbow. The other I placed in an inside pocket of my suit jacket, which I then put on. Picking up the half cigarette packet from the bed, I crumpled it before putting it into a side pocket of my jacket, then from the bottom of my case I collected the belt holster for the thirty-eight which I slipped onto my belt. I then transferred the thirty-eight from my robe to the holster.

A final check in the mirror pleased me. I looked a lot more fresh than I actually felt. I picked up my room key from the bedside table, closed the windows and left the room to take the lift down to the foyer.

At reception I asked for and got a large envelope into which I placed the smaller one containing my money from Paul and, having initialled the seals on the new envelope, handed it back to the under-manager on duty for storage in the hotel safe, slipping his receipt into my top pocket before heading for the door. After handing my key to the head night porter, I left through the revolving door as a young porter gently turned it. I checked my watch – forty minutes to go before the meeting.

Happy that I would not have to rush, I set off to walk to the meeting place. I knew the route well and made for the Piazza Barberini as soon as I left the hotel. By now Rome had swung into life and the old dolce vita was getting under way all round me. In the short distance to the Barberini I was accosted four times by smiling prostitutes and twice by ponces. The Veneto was lined by cars with sharp-eyed whore minders

20

at their wheels and others cruised slowly keeping a watchful look-out for likely clients. Two carabinieri lounged in a shop doorway talking with a small knot of whores, no doubt fixing up a little off-duty reward for leaving them to ply their trade unmolested.

From Barberini I strolled slowly up the Via Sistina which led me to the top of the steps above the Piazza di Spagna. With some time still to go before the meeting, I sat at the top of the steps and watched the hundreds of people using them. They are a favourite gathering point for tourists and locals alike – a good place for a meeting such as mine.

Ten minutes before the time set for the meeting, I moved down the steps until I was about ten yards from the bottom before moving over to the side and leaning on the wall there. There must have been a dozen men and half as many women standing or strolling at the bottom of the steps. The tourists were easy to identify, but there were five or six locals, any one of whom could have been my man.

At ten-fifteen precisely I saw a man break away from a group which consisted of another man and two women, and head towards the base of the steps from the fountain where the group was located. He checked his watch as he arrived at the bottom of the steps and looked around him. The others in his party moved round almost behind the fountain, into a position where they could watch him and I moved down to stand about a yard from him, making an obvious show of looking at my watch. As I looked up our eyes met and he nodded a greeting, "Signori." It was a normal polite way of passing the time of day and he might or might not have been my man. I smiled and nodded back. "Good evening." We stood and looked out together over the square. I took out a pack of Marlborough and made a slow job of lighting one, as I held the packet so that he could identify the brand. That did the trick and he moved closer as he said: "You too smoke the Marlborough, eh?" He produced the lower half of a packet and held it out to me. I took it and checked the inside to find the expected letters written in it. "Mario?" I handed him my half which he checked.

With an inclination of his head, he indicated that we should move away from the steps and we walked together round the outside of the square, mingling with the tourists. "You are Leslie?" he asked as we set off. For a moment I thought of denying it. Who the hell did he think I was after all the rigmarole we had just been through? But in the past I had found that my sense of humour didn't go down with latins and this guy looked tough. Small and quietly spoken, but wiry. He was what I automatically thought of as a knife-man – light on his feet, quick eyed, well-balanced as he walked.

Anyway, I nodded and smiled. He then handed me a piece of notepaper which he tore from a spiral bound book and said: "It's all there, Leslie, all there." I looked at the paper. As I had expected it contained a couple of telephone numbers, both in Naples. It also had the name Guido written on it. When I looked back at him he continued: "Two days before you work you telephone these numbers – they are for me and Guido. We will see all is right and give you the times. You must then also give me your frequency for the warning, maybe eh?"

I will explain later how the liaison works between smugglers and bent customs officers. It is sufficient for now to record that I handed him the envelope from my inside pocket. Without opening it, he placed it in his own pocket, smiled again and left to rejoin the people he had left earlier. During our short conversation, the other guy in the party had never taken his eyes off us.

I waited for the party to move away before moving off in the opposite direction, up the Via du Macetti and then Tritone and so back to Barberini and into the Veneto again. Here I sat myself at a table outside a café and ordered a campari-soda, which I sipped as I relaxed and observed the Rome high-life crowd buzzing back and forth from bar to bar and the Rome low-life crowd trying to get their hands into purses and pockets as the jet-setters made such heavy work of having a good time. This had been one of my favourite forms of entertainment on balmy nights in Rome for the past couple of years. I checked my watch – nearly eleven o'clock. I still hadn't eaten and there wasn't time for a decent meal before my call from Malta came in. I set off back to the hotel and was in my room in another ten minutes.

As I passed through the small vestibule, just inside my room, I pressed the bell for room service and, as always, I had hardly got my finger off it when there was a knock at the door. I ordered sandwiches and coffee, shrugged out of my jacket and lay back on the bed. The next thing I knew I was being shaken by the room-service guy who was obsequiously apologising for having to wake me up. I waved him away but called him back to give him a 500 lira note. No sense in upsetting the guy – he might be looking after me for a week or more.

I ate the sandwiches and drank the coffee before stripping and having another shower and had just stepped back into the room when the telephone rang. About thirty seconds of pregos and allos later, I had Endo on the line from Malta.

"Endo, Leslie."

"Yes, Leslie, how you, my lovely boy, how's the business?"

"Good, you want a deal Endo? I'm in Rome."

"Ah, Rome. And the dollies with the big tits, yes?"

"Yeah, O.K. Endo, but do you want a deal?"

"Of course, I want the bloody deal, all bloody deals from you lovely Leslie, all the deals I want. You want boats?"

"No, I've got boats, six men who I'll pick up in Malta and a man at this end with your radio set-up if it's still in operation."

"How much?"

"A grand, dollars all in."

"No, two grand dollars."

There was no point in arguing. I had been ready to go to a thousand pounds, I'd done a good deal. The conversation continued: "O.K., you robbing bastard, Endo. Your man still over here?"

"He's in Rome too Leslie, but it's not the man you know, he's dead, last month. I'll call the new man and ask him to meet you. Tomorrow?"

"Yes, tomorrow. Where?"

"Where are you staying, Leslie?"

"I'm not bloody-well telling you that, as you well know. Fix a place and give him my description."

"O.K., Leslie. Last horse cab on the rank at the Coliseum at exactly noon tomorrow, sorry, today. OK?"

"O.K. See you when I come over."

"Wait a little, Leslie. Half and half?"

"Yep, first half in lira tomorrow if it's on. See you."

"O.K., I'll call him, his name's Rene."

I had hardly got the receiver back on the rest when the telephone rang again. Once more the man didn't have to identify himself. It was Rene. He was the French Algerian field organiser for the Bank. We

23

had worked together several times before and I knew him as an efficient, though ruthless, operator. He would supervise the deal and make any on-the-spot decisions necessary. We arranged for him to call in for breakfast the next morning.

At last, I was able to sleep.

I was woken by a loud knocking on the outer door of the room. It was daylight and, as I had not closed the curtains the night before, I shut my eyes against the bright light. I squinted at my watch – it was eight-thirty – and slid from the bed and into my robe. From under my pillow I took my thirty-eight and held it in my robe pocket as I opened the door a few inches to see who was making such a damned awful racket. It was Rene. I had forgotten our appointment and had not arranged to be woken by the staff.

He carried a glass of orange juice in his outstretched left hand and he offered it to me as he walked into the room. I took it and nodded him through. "Good morning Leslie, late night?" "No, long day, order breakfast while I shower." He moved to the telephone as I made for the bathroom.

When I came out Rene was sitting at the small table with our breakfast in front of him and helping himself to scrambled eggs and bacon. He poured me a cup of coffee and said: "So you've taken the deal, I'm glad. We will work together, yes?" His English was near perfect when he spoke slowly, but he still used the speech pattern of his French Legionnaire father occasionally, when speaking quickly.

I told him that I would be happy to have him along but that I thought he was taking unnecessary risks if we did so. Deals were deliberately set up to avoid the possibility of people like him getting caught. In this instance Paul had been selected to deal with the waterguard and start-money and I had been given the job of providing the labour and organising the shipping end of things.

It was Rene's job to keep in the background and liaise with Geneva. His being with me was particularly dangerous.

Endo didn't know Paul and Paul didn't know Rene. I was the only man who had to know Paul, Endo, the customs man and the crews. If caught, I was the only one who could blow the whole set-up. By working closely with me Rene doubled the risk to the organisation.

However, this was not my business and Rene was a good companion and a first class man to have in a tight corner. He was also bloody good with the radio tranceivers we would be using for the Italian end of the operation.

It was to be a week before I learned of the real reason behind his wish to accompany me on that trip.

From my room I telephoned the airport and booked two seats on the late afternoon flight for Malta, so that we could check over the boats and crew and brief the Greek. Rene called Geneva and arranged for the consignment to be shipped to Dubrovnic in Yugoslavia, where the bank had a bonded warehouse. This stage of the journey was perfectly legal and the cigarettes would have normal clearance papers through to Dubrovnic. It would also be legal to load them on to boats straight from the warehouse. The Yugoslavs, of course, knew that they would be smuggled into another country, but they turned a blind eye to the trade, which at its worst, was only robbing the exchequer of a Western Bloc nation.

Before checking out of the hotel, I telephoned Parletti at his Naples flat. He agreed to act as our radio man and I promised him a briefing as soon as possible.

The job of a radio man in a modern coastal smuggling operation is crucial. It is his task to follow the boat or boats along the coast, keeping in touch with them by means of a powerful two-way radio.

He can observe the projected landing area for police or customs activity and warn off his collaborators in case of danger. In this exercise he would also keep in touch with the corrupt customs men, Mario and Guido and monitor the radios of the customs patrol launches for signs of a double-cross.

Parletti was, and still is, an expert at this difficult and vital job.

I lunched with Rene at a restaurant off the Veneto and we took a cab to the airport in good time to catch our plane for Malta. By seven o'clock we were booking in at the Malta Hilton and at eight we met Endo in Chains restaurant. I introduced Rene as a friend who was helping me, not wanting Endo to know that he was an important man in the Bank set-up and he was accepted at face value.

Endo counted off his crews: "First, Leslie, we have the Englishmen Holland and Sexton, you know both of them and have used them before. Then you have the ginger Aussie for one engineer and Pete

25

Perkins for the second. I knew you would want Big Smith as a gunner and I have got him to agree. He has been sliding in and out of Libya a lot lately and didn't really need the money. The last guy I don't know very well but he has a good history over in Gibraltar and has been hanging around with the right sort of people for some time. He calls himself Bernard Brut and apparently he is from Marseilles. He's O.K., I'm sure. Sure enough to risk my second half on him eh?"

I knew all these men except the last and Endo had put together a good bunch of guys. Holland and Sexton were a couple of adventurers in their late twenties who had been on the Maltese smuggling scene for about five years. They had worked for me on six or seven occasions and were both ex-Royal Marine Commandos and handy with the dinghies we used to ferry goods from ship to shore.

Ginger Aussie was a huge red-bearded Australian who had been in the business for about two years, during which time he had earned a reputation as a first class engineer and an evil fighter. The only weapon he was ever known to use was his teeth. I had twice seen him bite off ears in bar brawls and he was reputed, on one occasion in Marseilles, to have taken a nose as well.

Big Smith was a natural killer and had been working as a mercenary for years. He never cared which side he was on or whether he was part of an army or on his own. He needed to kill and he needed money. He would arrive on board with a light machine gun with which to fight off patrol boats if necessary. From Endo's conversation it appeared that he had been working for Black September recently. If this were true it was a fair bet that the spate of terrorist activities against Israel had had a lot to do with him.

I could only accept the unknown man, I knew nothing about him and didn't have time to check him out thoroughly. Oddly, Rene seemed quite happy about having him along. He seemed to have no misgivings at all.

Since we had arrived I had been trying to telephone Greek Charlie at the flop-house he used whilst in Malta. He had not been seen for two days and I assumed that he was on a drinking jag. Ashore, and between jobs, he was hardly every sober. Rene and I decided to check his haunts. He would have to be briefed pretty soon.

We left Endo in Chains and set off on our search for the Greek. He would be in one of the sleazy bars round the harbour area quite near us. He seldom moved far from this area.

On our fifth try we were successful. We found him slouched over the counter in Charles bar in Spinola Road, with his eyes about six inches from an open oyster shell which he held in his left hand. In his other hand he held half a lemon and was gently squeezing juice into the shell. As we came up behind him he became tired of watching the writhing oyster, put the shell up to his mouth and flicked the oyster in with his thumb. I sat down next to him and put my hand in between the jar of live oysters on the bar and his right hand. As he reached round to take another oyster from the tank he saw my hand and looked back up my arm to see who it was with the temerity to interrupt his favourite meal.

It must have taken him ten seconds to focus his bleary, squinting eyes on my face, but eventually he recognised me. Swinging round to face me he swept a half-full glass of wine over his lap and didn't even notice.

I looked back at Rene who just shrugged. There would be no sensible conversation with the Greek that night. Rene came forward and we took the man, one on each side, eased him off his stool and over to a table where we got him on to a chair and propped his right side against the wall.

Rene called for coffee and during the next half-hour we managed to get three or four large cups into him. Fortunately he was not so far gone that he couldn't recognise me and he understood that I needed him sober. But all he could manage in the way of speech was my name which he slurred out from his grinning face every few minutes.

It was about midnight before we got much sense out of the Greek and he then agreed to let us take him back to his room where he could sleep it off. He understood that we had a deal and that he had to be sober. Rene called a cab and we got him to his filthy bed on the second floor of a seedy dump ten minutes' drive from the bar.

Having thrown the grunting Greek on to the flea-pit of a bed I looked round the room. It was disgusting. The single low-wattage light bulb swung from a dangerous-looking ragged cable in the centre of the room, picking out the wine and spirit bottles which had overflowed from the table in a corner and the top of a chest of drawers, the only other furniture in the room apart from one wooden chair, and lay on the floor, some broken. Food wrappers and newspapers containing half used loaves and cheese were littered everywhere. Even after we had opened the French windows on to the minute balcony the air hung stale and nauseating, reeking of the black tobacco used by the Greek in his cigarettes.

By way of doing the man a favour, I felt through his clothes and found a roll of pound notes and ten-dollar bills in his hip pocket. These I took and replaced with a note asking him to call me at the Hilton next morning. There was no sense in allowing him to lie there and be rolled by other inmates of the stinking flop-house.

I put out the light and we went, leaving the door almost closed. The lock had long-since been smashed off by a keyless tenant or intruder.

Back on the street Rene and I walked towards Spinola Bay until we found a cab which we took to Sascha's nightclub in Ball Street, Paceville.

At the top of the few steps which lead from the pavement to the club door Rene took my arm and held me back. "Hold on, Leslie," he said. "Tanda may be here and if he is I want to collect some money he owes from a trip two months ago. It was a bit of freelancing and not for the Bank, so don't blow anything. You're the only guy who works from here who knows of my Bank connection. O.K.?" I nodded. "How much?"

"Five grand, dollars."

"Let's hope he's there. Why haven't you had it yet?"

"He's arguing, or at least he has been arguing on the telephone."

Down the steps and through the door we were confronted by Max, the owner of the place. He recognised both of us and smiled his welcome, waving us through into his whitewashed grotto. (This was before he turned the place into a darkened dungeon to keep up with the modern trend.) I walked on past but Rene stopped and asked: "Tanda in tonight, Max?" He was told that Tanda was in one of the lower rooms eating. We made our way down.

I had met Tanda on several occasions and worked with him once so I recognised him as we walked through the doorway.

He sat at a small table with an attractive blonde. He was only half-turned towards us and did not look away from his partner as we came in.

Rene drew himself up to his full six-feet-five-inches and walked slowly across the room to the couple. There were perhaps another dozen people there and only a couple of them took any notice of the tall, slim man who walked like a cat. He reached Tanda and stood just over his left shoulder as he looked down at him. The woman looked up and smiled. That was a usual reaction from a woman for the swarthy, handsome Rene. Slowly Tanda looked up and around. His eyes, directed to where he expected a head to be, fixed on Rene's throat. He leaned back and up into Rene's face. "Rene! You bloody man. How you been, eh?" His voice, always clipped, was higher than usual. "Sit down, Rene." He looked round further and saw me. "And Leslie, you too, you bloody man," waving us to the table. We pulled two chairs from another table and sat with him and his girl-friend.

He continued his nervous chatter: "Leila, these bloody men they are old friends. This is Leila, you guys, a new friend, eh, Leila?" She smiled widely and said: "Ello." She sounded French. All I really remember about her is her accent and her big tits under a tight mohair sweater.

Tanda was another expatriate Greek who owned a fast Vosper boat which he used for smuggling. He was known as being straight with his confederates – unless he felt he could cheat them with impunity. A slight and wiry man who dressed well and used expensive and nauseous toilet waters, he was an inveterate coward. He looked back at the door and called "waiter" to no avail. He then got up and left the room, returning very quickly with two extra glasses. Nobody spoke while he was absent and as he came back he said: "Now, let's all drink." He sat down, took up a nearly full bottle of red wine from the table and poured two drinks for Rene and me. "Cheers," he said.

I said nothing and just lifted my glass but Rene looked over his and replied: "To good business."

The Greek put his glass down before it even reached his lips, took out a handkerchief which spread an aroma of femine perfume, and wiped at his mouth. "I was going to call you again tomorrow, Rene. Surely, you haven't come about that?"

Rene sipped at his wine, took a mouthful, swallowed it and then sat swirling the remaining half round and round the glass. He looked slowly from Tanda to the blonde and then from the blonde to Tanda. The blonde had, by this time, stopped smiling and she started to pick at her side-salad to overcome her embarrassment at the obvious discomfort of her boyfriend. Tanda looked at her and nodded towards the door. The message was obvious it was time she went to the powder room. She picked up her handbag from the floor beside her chair and left.

For some seconds no one said anything. Then Tanda broke the silence as he mopped his sweating brow: "I was going to ... I haven't got ... I am trying to get the money from the others, Rene. I can't pay you till then. You know the business Rene, eh?"

"You've been paid, Tanda. I want mine. Now." Rene spat the words rather than spoke them at the frightened Greek. There was an intense evil in the almost whispered demand which made Tanda flinch. He looked at me for help. I just slouched in my chair and looked back at him as I sipped my wine. This was not my battle and if I had to take sides I was with Rene.

Rene reached over the table with his left hand and took hold of Tanda by the left wrist, jerking the arm out straight until the hand was clenched on the table in front of him. With his right hand he picked up his glass, raised it to his lips and drained it in one gulp. I now became nervous. He was going to indulge in an old trick of his and a restaurant was hardly the place for it. However, I knew there was nothing I could do without fighting Rene – and there was no chance of that.

He now took the rim of the glass between his right thumb and forefinger and, with a quick flick of the wrist, broke off a triangular section.

At the same time he wrenched Tanda's clenched fist over and held it back upwards on the table. "If your right hand moves, Tanda, you stinking shit, Leslie will shoot you." He then took the jagged piece of glass and drew it across the back of Tanda's hand about an inch above the knuckles, leaving a thin trickle of blood oozing out where it had passed. "Tell us where to get my five grand, Tanda, or the next stroke will make your fingers useless for life. Now, Tanda."

His voice had still not risen above a whisper. His body and mine hid the scene from the rest of the restaurant. Tanda was helpless, in the grip of the big half-breed and about to lose the use of his fingers.

He began to whine an answer: "I ... I haven't," the glass started to cut into the flesh above his little finger, "I have it at home."

Before letting go of the man's wrist, Rene told him to stand and, as he did so, moved towards him, all the time keeping a wary eye on the free hand. Expertly he frisked him and handed me a stiletto which he took from beneath his jacket. There was no gun.

"Let's go, Tanda," said Rene. Just then the blonde returned. If I hadn't known better, I would have thought that she'd been watching and had waited until the trouble was over before returning. She stood at the table, not knowing whether or not to sit down, as she looked at the half-eaten steaks. She looked askance at Tanda. He told her that he had to leave.

Rene looked at Tanda. "She live with you?"

"Yeh."

"Well, you'd better come along too, my pretty," he smiled, the evil gone and the old charm reasserting itself. "Pay the bill, Tanda."

The Greek threw two £5 notes on the table and we left the club. As we went up the steps to pavement level, I fell in slightly behind Rene and Tanda with the girl. We turned right up Ball Street and found a cab outside the St. Julien Hotel which took us to Tanda's apartment in Valletta.

The apartment was on the first floor of an old block overlooking the sea and was comparativley luxurious. It had a large living area and was well furnished in a contemporary but tasteless way – lots of money and no finesse.

As soon as Tanda had re-locked the door, Rene told the girl to go to her room. By now she was quite willing to accept that Rene was running things for the rest of the night and that she had better just do as she was told. She left us.

In the living area, which led off a short hall, as did all the other rooms in the apartment, Rene kicked the door shut. "Where is it, Tanda?" He now spoke in his normal voice, no longer having to whisper. The menace seemed to have gone from him. Tanda replied: "I haven't got it from them yet." He was standing about four feet in front of the tall French-Moroccan as he said it and had obviously taken heart from the lack of menace in the voice and the loose stance which Rene held.

Just before Rene's toecap crushed his balls, he must have been thinking he could still talk his way out of his debt. He didn't try to do this as he lay spewing all over his marble floor trying to imitate a foetus. I held Rene back as he was about to smash in another kick to the man's kidneys. He shrugged and sat in an armchair. We waited until the Greek had pulled himself to his feet after crawling to a table. Rene said: "The money, Tanda."

It must have taken him nearly half a minute to make his way fifteen feet to a wall safe behind a picture on the wall. When he had got there and pulled back the picture Rene moved over behind him to check on the contents before his hand went in. A lot of over-confident men have ended up with a bullet in their entrails that way. He also, he told me later, made a mental note of the combination.

As Tanda took it from the safe Rene relieved him of a bulky leather pouch and threw it to me. It held a selection of Swiss francs, sterling and dollars – at a glance it was possible to tell there was a small fortune contained in it.

Rene closed the safe and twirled the combination wheel. He pushed the Greek forward and followed him towards me, then pushed him into an armchair and told him to stay there.

Taking the wallet he spent several minutes sorting the notes before taking a selection and throwing the wallet back to Tanda. "Next time, you slimy Greek pouf, you lose the lot – and probably your useless bloody life as well, understand?"

The Greek looked up from the wallet, on the floor where it had fallen when it was thrown to him. He hadn't been able to take his hands from his crutch at the time. He said: "You have your money but it is mine not theirs. I have not been paid."

Rene just smiled: "You have, you lying bastard, but anyway, I couldn't care less. It's mine now. Don't forget tonight, Tanda. I promise that next time you will be a very dead Greek." He nodded to me and as we walked through to the hall he shouted gaily: "Au revoir, mon capitain." Then we were out of the main door of the apartment and it slammed behind us.

It was only when we were in the cab that I realised that during the whole lesson in debt-collection, I hadn't spoken a single word. Rene himself hadn't said all that much, considering the fact that he'd collected five grand from a guy who didn't want to part.

Back at the hotel, I left Rene at his room and went on to mine. There was still a deal to set up and I would have to be at it again in the morning. I showered and dropped on to the bed, just pulling the top sheet up to my belly. I fell asleep immediately.

At eight-thirty I was awakened by the telephone and a husky Greek Charlie: "Leslie? You have my money, yes?"

"Yes, Charlie, you drunken bum, I've got your money. You're lucky it was me and not some alley-thief who took it. When can we see you?" "I come round right now, Leslie. O.K., I come round right now." "Oh no you bloody-well will not, Charlie. We'll meet at the dock in two hours." "But I will come to the hotel, Leslie."

It was just possible to imagine Charlie emptying the dustbins at the Hilton, but only just. The thought of his smelly, unshaven hulk walking through the lounge was too much.

"No, Charlie, at the dock. Where are you berthed?"

"Msida Creek, about ten down from the governor's launch, both boats I see you on the jetty about two hours then, O.K.?"

"O.K., Charlie. See you then."

I got out of bed and shaved with my cordless razor before taking a shower and dressing in shirt and slacks. I wore my shirt outside my trousers to hide the thirty-eight clipped inside my waistband. It was my intention to collect Rene and go on down to breakfast.

I took the stairs the one floor down to Rene's room and was about to knock on his door as a waiter arrived with a breakfast tray. I took it from him as he opened the door with his pass-key and went through into the room to observe my friend at his morning exercises. I have never pretended to be a gentleman, but even I had to raise my eyes from the bed and out across the blue Mediterranean through the open French windows.

There was Rene, arms and legs akimbo and lying on the double bed with a bird going down to him as if she hadn't eaten for a month. At least I took it to be a bird. I didn't think that he was queer. But all I could see was its arse.

So I did what any red-blooded Englishman would do under the

circumstances. I balanced the tray on my left hand, walked over, and goosed the arse and slapped it. It was a bird. Her back straightened, she screamed and looked over her shoulder at me, fear showing in her eyes. I remember thinking that she must be married and probably thought she had been caught by her old man.

As she leapt off the bed and made for the bathroom Rene just lay there looking at me. "You bastard, Leslie. Maria, Maria, you bitch, come back in here, vite, vite, you bitch."

I put the tray down on the edge of the bed as she came back from the bathroom, tucking under her armpits a towel which just about hid her nether-end.

Rene looked at her. "And take off the bloody towel." She looked from Rene to me and back to Rene. "I thought he was a waiter." "No, he is my friend, you silly cow, huh?"

She dropped the towel and let her hands fall down at her sides as she smiled at me and moved round to the other side of the bed. Rene took her hand, tugged her down until she sat beside him and then reached up and began to stroke one of her tits. "Jump in and join us, Leslie."

I must admit that I had more than an inclination to do just that. She was a rather lovely olive skinned brunette of about eighteen with a slight figure and tight arse. Her tits were firm and not too large.

I'd even shared birds with Rene before so it wasn't that which stopped me. It was purely that I can't go at it cold before breakfast. I turned down his polite offer and went out saying: "See you later, we have an appointment in about two hours."

I took a quick stroll round the Spinola point and went back to the hotel dining room for breakfast. It must have been an hour after I had left that I went back up to Rene's room. I knocked. I knocked again. She opened the door about three inches and said; "He's gone to see you." She didn't resist when I pushed the door gently open and walked through. She continued: "He thought he would see you at breakfast."

I decided that we had crossed in the lifts. "I'll wait, darling, if it's all the same with you." She shrugged and returned to the bathroom where, judging by the steam coming through the door, she had been busy when I knocked.

Thinking back to the scene of about an hour before, I moved over to the bathroom and opened the door. She was just getting out of the bath and I stood in the doorway as I watched her drying herself. She was certainly worth attending to. I envied Rene. There wasn't a hint of shyness in her, in fact she deliberately flaunted herself knowing that I fancied her.

She threw the towel at me and said: "You do my back please." She lay forward and placed her hands on the edge of the bath. Her olive tan was all-over and I could just make out the line of fine hairs down her spine. I dropped the towel and ran both hands straight down from neck to buttocks, thumbs meeting over her spine. She groaned softly. I moved my hands back up and round to grasp her breasts, she groaned again. And that was it. Trousers round ankles and at it in the African Krall style.

That was when Rene, the bastard, came in and slapped my arse. I pulled away panting and looked round at him. He grinned: "How you say? Tip for tap, or something like that. Two slaps in one morning Leslie. And you English, you are so very clean, in the bathroom you must do it?" His voice rose towards the end of his sentence and broke into a full throated laugh. "Come Leslie, we have the business. Go when you are ready my pretty and I will telephone you later."

As we went down in the lift I told him of the arrangement I had made with Greek Charlie and we caught a cab at the front door of the hotel to take us to Msida and the Greek.

The cab dropped us at the top of the creek and we walked down the Pieta side until we came to the Governor's launch. About a hundred yards away to seaward we saw a pair of converted motor torpedo boats moored side-by-side. Sitting on the steel barrier at the harbour edge was Charlie. He waved to us and we walked up to him. He had made an attempt at shaving and was wearing clean denim trousers held up by a wide leather belt and a nearly-clean red shirt. He showed no sign of being hung over after his heavy drinking session of the day before.

His moustache bristled as his lips spread in a wide grin, exposing his brown, but even, teeth. "Leslie. I am sorry about last night. I have been waiting for two weeks for the work. There is nothing to do but drink. You see Endo yet?"

I told him that Endo had given me the crew names and then he asked, looking at Rene: "And the Long One, he is with us, yes?"

35

"Yes, Charlie. He is with us. Some of the way anyway. Let's get aboard and check the boats."

The three of us climbed on to the deck of the nearest boat just as Pete Perkins came out of the wheelhouse, wiping his oily hands on a piece of cotton-waste. "Good to see you, Leslie; won't shake hands." He grinned at his filthy engineer's hands.

Perkins was one of the few men in the smuggling business whose real name I knew. All the others, to the best of my knowledge, used names they had acquired over the years they had spent in the business, usually having acquired papers and passports to support their aliases. But I had known Perkins when I was a mechanic with Colin Chapman's Lotus racing team a couple of years previously. He had acquired the name he now used because of his skill with Perkins diesel engines.

I looked round the deck and asked him: "What shape are they in, Pete? Any complaints?"

"Not one, my old cock. Not a single one. Ready for the off right now if you wish!" Pete was the archetypal adventuring Englishman. Slim, fair haired and always smiling, he spoke well and was always polite, even with the roughest of the people he worked with.

We checked the quarters in the boats and Rene looked over the radio and direction-finding equipment. All appeared well. The boats were obviously efficient and mechanically they were reported to be sound. They were smart without being flashy and should not attract too much attention on the trip.

As with most good smuggling conversions, thick steel plates had been attached right round the boat from just below the Plimsoll line to deck height and the inside of the wheelhouse was fitted in the same way. This gave protection against all but armour-piercing shells.

Two long loading hatches had been cut through on each side of the forward section of the hull to facilitate quick offloading and hose boxes had been fitted — large enough to carry a heavy machine gun and a couple of lighter weapons. Special mounting plates were attached for the heavy gun in the bow and for light machine guns at each side of the cockpit.

The inspection over, Charlie, Rene and I went ashore and walked up to a dockside bar, to sort out the details of the trip. There was little to discuss about the actual navigation. We all knew it would take about forty-eight hours to reach Dubrovnic from Malta. Greek Charlie would not be briefed on his dropping zone in Italy until he left the Yugoslav port, for security reasons, and that only left the fine detail regarding armament. Charlie agreed to arrange for two French 756 heavy machine guns to be brought out to us after we had left Msida harbour. Along with the heavy hardware I also asked for two light machine guns and four armalite rifles.

This armament was somewhat heavier than usual, but increased activity by the Italian naval cutters at that time had resulted in at least three boats being blown out of the water. The only answer was to fight back if you didn't want to surrender and spend a number of years in jail.

Charlie agreed to provide the weaponry and we discussed the crewing of the two boats, splitting the available men according to their specialities.

At this stage Rene voiced the opinion that he didn't feel that the new man, virtually unknown to all of us, should be trusted. He would rather not have him along. In fact, he would be happy to provide a replacement, a man well known to him.

The Greek, of course, had no knowledge of Rene's situation with regard to the Bank and looked to me for guidance. Rene was my responsibility, I had brought him along. I agreed to accept Rene's man.

Rene promised to introduce the new man to Charlie that night in the Roundabout English pub near the Hilton. We told Charlie to crew up and be ready to leave at eight next morning and then left him to return to the hotel.

Over lunch in the Hilton, Rene told me of his odd request to change crews at the last minute. The man who he was about to introduce to the trip was known to the Bank and it was they who wanted him on the trip. He gave me the impression that he was helping to break in a new field controller for the area, an impression which turned out to be very far from the truth.

After lunch, Rene telephoned Geneva to issue instructions for the cargo to be in Dubrovnic as soon as possible. He was told that it was already on the road, in anticipation of our go-ahead, and that it would be in the warehouse when the boats arrived.

We both slept during the afternoon and at six o'clock Rene came to my room to tell me that he was going to collect the new crewman and would meet me at the Roundabout pub at eight with the man. Greek Charlie was due there at eight-fifteen so I would have time to look the man over before he arrived. Rene still gave me the impression that there was nothing out of the ordinary in the introduction of this man.

I showered, walked around the point to the Dragonora and then back to the Roundabout, arriving just before eight.

Rene was already at a corner table in the bar and waved me over. He introduced a slightly built Italian by the name of Carlo as an old friend. He was about twenty-five years old, swarthy and probably of Sicilian descent. A not uncommon type in the smuggling business.

As Rene went to the bar to collect fresh drinks for himself and Carlo and a Scotch and American for me, Greek Charlie came in. I waved him to the table. Rene looked over and acknowledged the fact that Charlie had arrived. When he returned to the table he also had an ouzo and a water jug to complete the round of drinks.

I introduced Charlie to Carlo, who explained that he was a dinghy-man and that he had been in the business for only a short time, having gained his experience in handling the rubber craft as a water-ski instructor. Charlie seemed satisfied and Rene told the guy to be at the dock in time for the eight o'clock departure next morning. Carlo agreed and left the three of us to finish our business.

The money had arrived for Charlie that afternoon and he was about to set off for the rendezvous where he would pay three of the crew who wanted the money stashed in Malta before they left. The others would be paid their initial half on the boats after we had set off. With some trusted men it was normal practice to pay the start money the night before a trip, but with most men money was not handed over until craft were clear of the harbour.

Charlie left, assuring us that he would be ready at eight in the morning. Rene and I had a second drink, he drinking his usual straight vodka-on-the-rocks. Then we walked along St. George's Road to Teguilio's restaurant at the apex of Spinola Bay.

We were both in a quiet mood and said little as we slowly covered the few hundred yards to the eating house. There we had a light meal and discussed past experiences and women, anything rather than the trip which would begin in the morning. We both returned to the hotel at ten o'clock and went straight to our rooms.

I arranged a call for six o'clock and then telephoned the Bank in Geneva. A line was always put through to the home of the duty 'manager' at night for such late business.

I checked with him that what Rene had told me was correct and asked him what gave with regard to the new man, Carlo. He, I was told brusquely, was Rene's concern. I was to mind my own business. Rude bastard.

Before turning in I called reception and arranged for my bill to be ready at seven next morning.

Awakened by the telephone operator with my early call, I immediately phoned Rene to make sure that he was awake, ordered a full English breakfast and jumped into the shower.

By the time Rene called to tell me that he was just going down to the lobby, I was dressed in denim trousers and heavy sweater. I pulled on my espadrilles, picked up my lightweight case and joined him at the cashier's desk, where we both settled our accounts.

By the time we had reached the door, the hall porter already had a cab waiting and we drove straight to Msida where we were dropped alongside the boats. It was seven-thirty.

Rene and I had decided to use Charlie's boat and Rene insisted that Carlo was with us. Our engineer would be Perkins and Ginger Aussie would be our gunner. Charlie came out of the cockpit with another man we both knew as we leapt aboard. Rene had never met him, but I knew him as Happy Mike. A carefree ex-US navy man who had been around the Middle East for about two years. He was as good a sailor as was to be found on the smuggling routes. He was to handle the second boat.

The four of us huddled over the chart table in the lead boat and arranged radio signals and code names. We also arranged a rendezvous off Dubrovnic should we get separated. We would cruise at twelve knots and when visual contact was possible Mike would take his lead from our boat. Our route would be up to Sicily, around the "heel of Italy" and then diagonally across to Yugoslavia and up the coast to Dubrovnic. We would pick up our arms one hour after setting out.

At ten minutes to eight Mike jumped onto his boat and the engines coughed into life. The boats were equipped with Perkins diesels and they both sounded in good order. We cast off at precisely eight o'clock, putting out past St. Elmo point and taking a North-East heading for Sicily. It was good to be back at sea and to feel the powerful engines under my feet as we rapidly picked up knots to test the engines before dropping to a steady twelve.

After about an hour, Charlie changed course slightly to come alongside a twenty-five foot fishing boat which had been making slow headway across our bows from the West. It was the work of only a few minutes to take aboard the five boxes containing our armament before we were again under way at low revs while the number two boat did the same. After she had finished her loading, Charlie opened the throttle to cruise at about twelve knots again and both vessels set their bows up for Sicily, regaining their North-East course.

Depending on weather the trip to Sicily would take about ten hours and, with Charlie at the wheel the rest of us spread out on the decks in the sun, with the exception of Big Smith, who began to check and test the weapons. By the time we had been under way for three hours, even he had nothing to do. He had by then pumped a few rounds through each of the weapons, tested their mountings and replaced them in their boxes. There was no need for them until the final stages of the trip.

The solid thrum of the engines had lulled Smith, Perkins and Carlo into sleep and I was almost in the same state myself when Rene came forward and shook my shoulder. He noded back towards the wheelhouse, indicating that he wished me to join him there and moved aft himself.

When I entered, he and Charlie were examining a transistor radio which they appeared to have taken from a frameless rucksack which lay beside them on the deck. Charlie was silently muttering obscenities.

Rene looked up at me and said; "We found this in Carlo's bag. There's not much time – he may wake up at any minute – so I'll explain quickly. This radio is not what it seems, look." He opened the already-unscrewed back and it was obvious that it was not a normal receiver. The tuning mechanism was connected to a very small circuit and the loudspeaker was also small. But beneath these parts the rest of the ten-by-eight inch casing was taken up with complex circuitry and a high-powered nickel cadium battery.

Rene continued: "It's a transmitter and, although I haven't tested it,

I'm positive that when it's switched on it will be on a direction finding frequency used by the Guardia. I brought Carlo along specially, because he was on the boat we lost six weeks ago and said he escaped because he was just putting stuff ashore when the Guardia pounced. Two months before that he was with the one that got blown out of the water – again he was on his way to the shore. He is an agent, Leslie."

Suddenly the whole set up became clear. This was why Rene was along on this part of the trip instead of waiting in Italy. He was here solely to check Carlo.

"What now?" I asked, the tightness in my throat lifting my voice an octave or two. I was already aware of the next move.

Just then Charlie hissed. Rene and I looked forward and saw Carlo moving to the bow where he leaned over the port rail. Rene put the radio back into the rucksack and replaced some clothing which had been on top of it. He threw it back to where it had apparently been placed by Carlo in the bunk area aft of the cockpit.

He took my arm and led me to the stern rail. "He's got to leave us, Leslie. I'll do it but we don't want too much fuss. There's not much time, either, eh?" he was right. If a body was to be dumped the best place was half way between Malta and Sicily; miles from anywhere.

By the time we had returned to the wheel-house after our short conversation, Carlo was again lying on the forward deck, face down on a bunk mattress. Rene shrugged: "Just cover me in case of trouble, Leslie. We do it right away, yes?"

I slipped my thirty-eight out of my belt holster and nodded, my throat too dry to speak. The business of killing, even traitors and informers, horrified me. But Carlo had to be attended to.

I followed Rene around to the front of the wheelhouse where he went and sat next to Carlo, who didn't even look up. He probably never even heard him.

Rene then raised himself to his knees, a stiletto in his right hand with his thumb half over the hilt, pressing on the flat of the blade. Placing the fingers of his left hand across the blade with his index finger touching his thumb he arched over Carlo until the blade was about an inch from the base of the skull. Then, carefully aiming by sighting along his right thumb, plunged the knife home and twisted it as his right hand slid under his left. Carlo was dead.

There had been no sound. I was rooted to the spot as I leaned against the wheelhouse, thirty-eight held in my rigid hand. I had heard of Rene's skill with the stiletto but had never seen him in action. It was sickening. He had dealt with a human being like a matador administering the coup-de-grace to a bull – with the professionalism of a surgeon in the operating theatre.

I heaved myself to the rail and shot my breakfast overboard.

After about a minute, I turned round and leaned my back against the rail. Perkins and Smith were still sleeping. Charlie was still at the wheel looking straight ahead and past Rene, who was standing looking at me. He had put the knife away and his shoulders hunched forward as he licked his lips and swallowed hard several times, his adam's apple bobbing up and down as it does with long-necked men. He smiled grimly: "That's that, Leslie. Wake the others."

I moved forward, turning my eyes from the body that had been Carlo, and kicked Smith's shoulder gently "Wake up Smithy, and you, Pete. We've got work to do." The two men looked round, squinting into the harsh light, and then sat up. "What work?" asked Smith.

Rene went back to the cockpit and brought out the rucksack. The two men still didn't know what had happened but Perkins was looking at the still body of Carlo, apparently left asleep. There was no blood visible. What little there was was hidden by the long hair.

Rene took the radio from the rucksack and went forward to the two men, still sitting on the deck. He opened the back and explained what the purpose of it was. Both of them knew enough to understand that he was telling the truth. He told them of the two previous trips which Carlo had made. "Christ," said Perkins in a low voice, "I knew blokes on both boats. What are we going to do with him, the bastard?"

"It's done, Pete. He's dead." Rene told him. Both men looked back at the lifeless Carlo and then looked away again quickly. But whereas Perkins looked out across the empty sea, Smith looked up at Rene. "Why didn't you let me do it, eh? That's what I'm around for, innit?" Rene not wanting to upset Smith just told him that there had not been enough time to let him know and said: "He laid himself on the chopping block very conveniently, no?"

We went through the few items of clothing in the rucksack and examined his passport. It had been issued three years previously in

Rome and gave his birthplace as Catanzara in Southern Italy. He was twenty-five years old. His occupation was given as "fisherman".

Rene and Smith checked the body, removing an Omega watch and a crucifix and chain. He wore no rings and there was nothing else which might identify him. Smith stripped him and he and I threw him overboard like so much trash. Then, after cruising for another thirty minutes, we threw his clothing and pages from his passport overboard scattering them along our route. At Rene's insistence even the watch was thrown to the fishes. In the almost impossible event of the body being found there would be nothing anywhere near it to help with identification. And as the crews had not been told any details of our trip he could not have contacted his bosses with useful information before he left.

They would, in all probability, know that he had been asked to join a boat for a smuggling trip, but they would never be able to prove anything against the skipper. He would just deny everything and say that he had never seen the man. Anyway, Greek Charlie's reputation was such that nobody would even bother to question him. He had been in the business a long time.

The radio was locked away in the wheel house by Charlie. It would be of great value later in the trip.

The rest of the journey to Dubrovnic was uneventful. We skirted Sicily just outside territorial waters after ten hours cruising, and, in fair seas, made our way up through the Ionian and Adriatic to our destination in a further thirty-four, standing off the harbour until about seven-thirty in the morning. The reason for this was that boats arriving in any port during the night or early hours of the morning always attract more attention from the authorities than at other times.

Charlie and Mike sorted out the paperwork with the customs officers as soon as we tied up at a jetty in the small harbour. Rene set off around the harbour to arrange for a boat to get the pair of us back to Italy as soon as loading was completed, and I made for the Bank warehouse.

Half an hour later we were both back on Charlie's boat. The cargo would come aboard at nine o'clock and Rene had sought out the skipper of a Bank Vosper which was lying in the harbour, having been laid up with engine trouble from an earlier trip. (Altogether the Bank must have controlled some sixty boats at that time and it was not unusual for them to leave them scattered around the various Mediterranean ports awaiting orders. Finding one in Dubrovnic was good news – it would save Rene and me chartering a boat to drop us on the Italian coast.)

By ten o'clock the loading of both boats was complete and the hatches were battened down. The two dinghies on each boat, with their motors, had been brought up and strapped on the decks and wheelhouse roofs to make room for extra cargo. I had given Charlie and Mike their actual and alternative radio frequencies for communication near the pick-up point and the place at which we hoped to collect their cargo about two days later. They were instructed to sail just before dusk and to keep the crews aboard until then to avoid any possibility of trouble.

Rene and I booked a room at a small hotel away from the docks and, after a light lunch of fish, slept until about four in the afternoon. We then joined the Vosper, where the skipper was waiting with a one-man crew, and set off for Barletta. We spent a few hours yarning with the skipper over a couple of bottles of wine and then slept until he shook us awake. It was two in the morning and we were five miles off Barletta. I checked the chart with the skipper and then helped the crewman to get the dinghy ready to put overboard. There appeared to be no nearby craft, so I instructed the skipper to make as if heading to Trani, about seven miles east of Barletta.

After holding this course for some twenty minutes, I instructed him to kill all his lights and then to put about and take a course parallel with the coast to a spot about three miles the other side of Barletta. At low revs we were in position about a thousand yards off the beach at about three-thirty. We put the dinghy over and then handed our cases down to the crewman before climbing into the dinghy ourselves.

As we cast off the skipper followed instructions and slowly put straight out to sea with just sufficient revs to make way. In this manner he would present only his narrow profile to any watcher. In practice it would be impossible to see him.

Rene took charge of the powerful Evinrude 500 motor and ran us in at a speed which would attract no attention. Flat out the powerful motor would have had the whole coast awake at that time in the morning. In minutes we had beached the craft and were ashore – only getting our feet wet when we helped the crewman to turn the boat around. Within a few more minutes we had made our way up on to the main highway and fifteen minutes after that had been offered a lift in a truck on its way into town. We then joined the early morning workmen's bus to Bari where we took a cab out to the airport. At ten o'clock, we were going through Rome airport and before eleven I was being greeted once more by the smiling staff of the Ambascatori.

I immediately telephoned Mario and told him to be ready to help us the next night. I would call him again when I reached Naples with further details.

Tired and dirty, I decided to take a bath and for a full hour I luxuriated in the tub before getting bored with topping up the hot water. By the time I had dressed in a lightweight brown mohair suit, it was nearly time for lunch. I called Rene and he invited me down to his room.

When I got there we discussed the pick-up. The boats would arrive off the Gulf of Salerno some time after midnight, probably at about one a.m. Before then we had to be in the area of the drop and have the trucks standing by to collect the 8,000 boxes of cigarettes they carried. We also had to establish our liaison with Mario and make sure the trucks would arrive on time. Rene had his car standing by and ready to leave as soon as we had lunched so I made one telephone call – to Paul – and told him to have the customer standing by on our frequency from midnight and to have his trucks within an hour's drive of the rendezvous. I also told him the exact location of the drop and gave him a call-sign for use by the trucks.

Again we lunched in the hotel and at two-thirty we were on the autostrada and heading South. At five o'clock we were in Naples and I telephoned Mario from the main rail terminal in the Piazza Garibaldi. Thirty minutes later we met him at the Via Acton public gardens. He had his man Guido with him.

We couldn't leave the handing over of the drop-location any longer if he was to do his job efficiently, so I asked: "What's the situation, Mario? Where are the regular patrols tonight?" "Tonight," he replied, "we are concentrating above Napoli, but there is what you call a flap, we think. They seem to expect something and the navy are very active out of here. Now, where is your place?"

45

I told him that we intended to drop near Sessa, about twenty miles from Salerno. It was a good area for our business, with long beaches and several dirt roads leading down to the sea. We could get our trucks right down to within a few yards of the shoreline.

"O.K., Leslie. I have a tip-off about a drop right round near Terracina tonight, eh? That will keep them clear."

I gave him my frequencies for the ship-to-shore operation but not for the trucking organisation. There was no need for him to know that. In return he gave me the customs frequency for that night. We parted.

Rene and I then drove around the coast to Amalfi where, after a search of the bars, Rene found a guy by the name of Guiseppi. He had not discussed the matter with me before, but I now realised why he had kept Carlo's radio.

Guiseppi had a high-power ski-boat capable of some forty knots. At midnight he would take the radio to a point about ten miles off Naples and switch it on. If the signal was picked up by the navy he would then play hide and seek with them for an hour or so before ditching the radio over the side.

Having left Carlo's radio with Guiseppi we drove on round the coast to Salerno, where we had a leisurely dinner. After strolling round the town for a while, we set off for the lower tip of the Gulf of Salerno. An easy drive took us to a point near Castellabate just before midnight.

There, using the pre-arranged call-signs, Rene put out his first call: "Egg calling chicken . . . egg calling chicken. Come in chicken."

We waited for five minutes and then Rene repeated the call. This time, after about thirty seconds, we received a reply: "Chicken calling egg, chicken calling egg." From the strength of the signal the Greek was pretty close. The staccato voice went on: "Ee Tee Aye thirteen-thirty-five, repeat, thirteen-thirty-five."

All was well. Charlie had been briefed to add eleven hours and thirty-five minutes to his estimated time of arrival off the beach. His call meant that he would arrive at about two a.m. His timing was perfect.

The weather was ideal for a drop. There was sufficient cloud to cut out the moon and the sea was pretty calm. If Mario did his job and the Carlo trick worked all would be just perfect.

Our next contact with the Greek would be by light signal from the beach, unless things went wrong before he got there. We set off back towards Salerno and made the turn onto the half-made service road after about forty minutes. By one o'clock were parked just above the beach.

Rene, who had been monitoring the police, customs and navy patrol bands as I drove switched over to the boat frequency once again: "Egg ... egg." The reply came: "Chicken ... chicken." All was still going well and there was no change in the arrival time. Rene switched back to the waterguard bands, flicking from one to the other by using pre-set buttons. There was still no unusual activity.

He then switched over to transmit and, on low power, called the collection party in fluent Italian using the call sign I had given Paul. He ordered them in right away.

At precisely two o'clock we left the car and stood at the top of the beach. I took with me a six-volt torch with a cardboard extension taped on to the front to direct all the light forward and allow no side-spread to be observed further along the beach. With this I gave three one-second flashes straight out to sea, and soon we heard the rumble of trucks coming in along the road to the beach.

Rene left me and moved inland to meet the trucks, returning after a few minutes with two men I did not know. They stood with us and looked out to sea. After about ten more minutes we heard the quiet throb of a high-powered outboard motor at low throttle and, two minutes after that, I was shaking hands with Big Smith. He had come ashore empty to double-check before calling in the cargo.

He took my torch and flashed it out to sea using a signal that had not been agreed with Greek Charlie until just before he had come ashore – a standard safety procedure. He then told me that the boats were lying off at about a thousand yards and would now come on in. They did this and became just visible a short way off shore. Smith set off for the boats and by the time he was half way back the other three rubber boats were nearly at the beach, each piled with boxes.

One of the truck men whistled and about a dozen men ran from behind us to the dinghies. The landing was under way.

For about an hour the four dinghies ferried back and forth from boats to beach as the shore party calmly and quickly rushed the boxes up to four high-sided cattle trucks parked just behind the beach.

Rene, who had returned to our car to monitor the radio as soon as the first boat came in, told me later that the Guiseppi diversion had worked and that there appeared to be three patrol boats involved in looking for him after they had been pulled away from Terracina.

The transfer completed, the boss of the truck party handed me a leather brief-case, which I took to contain the balance of the money due to the Bank, before taking the last truck back up the road. I immediately handed this over to Rene. We didn't check the money it contained. It was enough for the people who had ordered the consignment to know that they would die if they bilked the organisation.

We set off straight away for Rome. By seven a.m. I was back in my own bed at the Ambascatori after accepting the knowing looks from the lobby staff who obviously thought that Rene and I had been tom-catting all night. Some tom-catting!

Both Rene and I slept right through until evening and then met for dinner at Salvino's, lower down the Veneto. We were both subdued after the excitement of the previous few days and, despite having slept all day, were both still tired.

Rene opened a mild flirtation with a couple of expensive-looking whores on the way back up the Veneto but it came to a rapid close when two swarthy ponces came to take over the negotiations. We both returned to the hotel where there was a message for Rene to call Geneva. He left me to make my way to the bar and went up to his room to make the call. Within ten minutes he had joined me and ordered a double vodka-on-the-rocks and Scotch and American for me. He spoke as soon as he sat down: "Leslie, we are in business again. The Bank are, how-do-you-say, overpleased with us because of that Carlo and such a good trip. We both go to Geneva tomorrow for more business. They will now meet you."

This was good news. Although I had worked for the Bank for some time I had never been invited into their inner sanctum, so to speak. They were obviously prepared to take me right in now. We decided to go to bed early and catch an early morning flight to Geneva.

The next morning we were at the airport before nine to collect the tickets, which had been arranged by the Bank, from the Alitalia desk and we were in Geneva just over an hour later. By eleven we were sunning ourselves at a boulevard table overlooking the lake and drinking over-priced Scotch and vodka.

After one drink Rene used the bar telephone to call his bosses and came back to tell me that they would see us at noon in the suite above the bank itself. We both had another and then set off up the west bank of the lake on foot to walk the half-mile or so to the business area of the city and so to the bank itself, which turned out to be only a few hundred yards from the Notre Dame cathedral.

I was surprised to find that the bank was not all olde worlde as I had imagined, but a modern stainless steel and glass block. Rene led me through the swing door into the air-conditioned interior and straight through to the far left-hand corner and a small private lift with a uniformed guard standing in front of it.

The guard obviously knew Rene and acknowledged this by smiling and nodding to him before opening the door of the lift and letting us through. But, knowing Rene or not, he wasn't about to trust me. Before I had time to turn round to face the door, he was in behind me and had run his hands over me in an expert display of frisking. He relieved me of the thirty-eight, which this time I was wearing in a shoulder holster. "When you come out, you have him back yes?" What could you say?

The lift silently shot us up to the top floor, where the guard opened the door by re-inserting his key in the control panel and we were confronted by a lounge-suited heavy, who also recognised Rene and tried a half smile on him, showing his gold-capped front teeth.

By instinct, I looked around for the stair-well, but could only see one door, the one to which we were being ushered. It appeared that the only way out of this place would be to play birds – and it was a high building.

The only furniture in the hallway we were then in was a straight-backed chair, obviously for the bodyguard. He ushered us straight over to the door and, after pressing a buzzer three times, opened it to let us through to a beautifully furnished salon, all Louis something furniture and pictures. A beautiful blonde sat at an elegant desk in the far right-hand corner and she rose as we were shown in: "Rene!" She ran forward, mincing over the thick pile of the Persian carpet and flung her arms round his neck before planting her lips on his

49

as he lifted her from the floor to bring her up to his level. He made a bit of meal of her before pushing her gently off and saying: "This is Leslie, my pretty. Leslie, this is Lisette. She is lovely, yes?"

I smiled at the lady but didn't get the Rene treatment. Bloody Frenchmen. All I got was a butterfly tickle across my right palm which might, I suppose, have been described as a handshake.

She returned to her desk and pressed an intercom switch: "It's Rene." Then, after some five seconds, the reply came: "With friend?" "Yes." "Show them through please, Lisette."

Smiling, she opened a door just to the left of her desk and waved us through.

I had thought the outer room elegant, in a spindly-legged sort of way, but the one in which we now found ourselves was incredible. I'm no sort of connoisseur but it was obvious even to me that the furniture in this room was worth more than the proceeds of my last four trips put together. It measured some twenty feet by twenty and was carpeted with two matching Persian rugs, which filled the whole area. The elegant desk, chairs and other furniture were again of the Louis-what-have-you type and the whole thing was set off by beautiful dark red drapes in velvet. Through the panoramic window, the only compromise with modernity, one looked out over the city and into the clear blue sky.

As we entered a short, balding fat man walked round the desk and came towards us, holding out his hand. Rene held back and allowed me to move in front of his as he said: "Doctor, this is Leslie Aspin."

The man beamed and took my hand, reinforcing his grip by taking my forearm in his left hand: "I have heard much about you, Mr. Aspin ... Leslie ... and now we meet. It is good. Please sit down." He indicated a chair at the front of the elegant desk.

He then released my hand and shook Rene's, waving him to another chair. He himself moved round to the back of the desk and sat down, hand flat on the table in front of him and eyes riveted on mine. We sat like this for some thirty seconds before he said: "First, both of you, I must thank you for the trip you have just done ... and the special service in particular. You have saved us much inconvenience. There is a bonus of five thousand dollars for each of you."

His English was clipped in a teutonic way, but near perfect. As he finished his little speech he obviously wanted us to say something and we both thanked him. He continued: "Lisette has the money and also what you are both owed for the original deal. You must collect it on the way out."

Again he paused for quite a long time, looking from one to the other of us. Then he continued: "I have asked you both to come here for a special reason. You, Rene, have worked for me for a long time and when you leave you have our full permission to tell Leslie about the way we organise things and who are our friends.

"And you, Leslie, must tell me now if you don't wish to join us and wish to carry on as a freelance. If you wish to carry on as you do now we will still use you in the same way as we have in the past. But, if you join us as a virtual staff man, there is no going back on it. You will learn many things which you must keep to yourself and there is only one penalty for a double-cross with us. Should you double-cross us I will have you killed. I do hope you understand that, Leslie. Now, what is it to be?"

His voice never rose above a quiet conversational tone throughout his entire piece. Here was a guy telling me that he would send me to the bottom of the sea just as another man would have asked after my mother. And, looking him straight in the eye, I believed him. But, what the hell. This was the real gold mine of the smuggling business. I could put up with his threats.

"I'm in," was all I could muster by way of reply.

He then spent ten minutes explaining that things were changing in the business and that his "investors" were looking for new ventures. "We will be moving into new fields and there may well be more risks for you. Commensurately the rewards will be that much greater for all of us, especially for you.

"I see from the look on your face, Leslie, that you are pondering on the type of business we will be doing. I also note from your file, which I have here, that you have never shipped drugs. You may rest assured that you will not be asked to carry drugs or even organise their transit. We too dislike that sort of thing.

"For the time being you will both carry on as usual, with the exception that you will work as a team and will both be responsible to me – and only to me.

"Paul will no longer be used and, in fact, will leave the business permanently. And I am afraid that you two will have to bring about his early retirement when you return to Rome."

He paused again as he took in our reaction to this bland statement before continuing: "You see, we think that Paul was in some way connected with Carlo. And anyway, even if we are wrong, he has been getting on altogether too well with his customs friends. We have watched him and he is either freelancing or selling us out now and again. He is finished."

I remember thinking that this smooth bastard was sitting there in his luxury office, insulated from the real world by millions of dollars and quietly issuing a death sentence on a man against whom he had no real evidence.

What I didn't think of until later was the fact that I was going to be connected with the execution.

After another pause he ended the interview by standing up and moving round his desk as he said: "I am sure we will all profit greatly from our new arrangement. Remember, both of you, that you communicate only with me, or, in my absence, with whoever is on the special number.

"As I have already said, Rene, you may tell him everything that we have told you of our operation. Now, good-day gentlemen, don't forget your packages from Lisette." As he finished he opened the door and ushered us through, closing it behind us.

Lisette came over and took Rene's left hand, leading him over to her desk and taking two packages from a drawer. One she gave to Rene and the other to me. Neither of us bothered to open them there and then. A man who could order a death as an ordinary person would order breakfast at the Hilton was hardly likely to short-change us. Have us killed – but never short-change us.

Still holding Rene's hand she smiled up at him, having to half break her neck in the process, and asked: "When are you coming back, my Rene?"

He scowled down at her. "Coming back? We now have the holiday here I think, for a few days with Lisette, eh?"

She stopped smiling. "In you packets there are your tickets for a flight," – she paused – looking at her watch "a flight in one hour. He should have told you."

Rene made to move back to the door into the inner office but Lisette held him back by his sleeve. "No, Rene, he will not change his mind." He allowed himself to be restrained and she stood on tip-toe to kiss his chin. He shrugged: "O.K., my pretty, O.K. For us it is the next time around once more." She let go of him and pressed a button on the underside of her desk before taking us over to the door and opening it to usher us into the presence of the big ugly out in the hall. He shunted us into the lift and we were shown out of the building by the man at the bottom.

As we walked on to the pavement, a chauffeur opened the door of a Cadillac and the bottom guard indicated that we were to use it. The Bank certainly laid things on. I began to enjoy my new job. The lift-man even held the door open as he handed me a buff envelope which I realised contained my hardware. It wasn't until then that I remembered handing it over – I had been so overawed by the whole business.

In the Caravelle back to Rome Rene began to fill me in on the background to the Bank.

Firstly, contrary to the belief I had held until then, it was not an actual bank, not in the real sense of the word. It was, in fact, an organisation which dealt in precious metal and commodities. Also, I was surprised to learn, it had a strong British and American connection, with agents in London and New York, along with many Middle Eastern countries. It was a huge, international, and eminently respectable concern, on the surface.

Rene also explained that, judging by trips he had made to the U.S. on Bank business, the Mafia held a strong interest in the operation which he considered to be financial rather than active.

He explained that, through sub-companies and usually undiscoverable links, the Bank had access to some sixty boats such as those we had used on the last run into Italy and several coasters and cargo vessels. They also had access to a fleet of refrigerated container lorries working all over Europe and a number of bonded warehouses such as that in Dubrovnic. The only thing they did not seem to have was a moral code.

The one thing which he did not mention, but which I was to learn later, was that the Bank also owned, or controlled, a cigarette factory in Switzerland where they would turn out any brand of cigarette, properly blended and packaged, for any client who would order more than two hundred boxes (one million cigarettes.)

Back in the hotel Rene and I talked over the question of Paul and his pending "resignation" from the Bank organisation.

We decided that it was best to get it over with as soon as possible and we both knew that Paul was no fool and would cover himself wherever possible. After a hell of a lot of discussion Rene finally decided to act the next day and there and then put the first phase of the plan into operation.

To get the wheels turning, Rene telephoned the Bank and asked them to brief Paul with a fictitious assignment which he was to hand on to me. They were to tell him to contact me the next morning and to brief me as soon as he could. They agreed.

He then telephoned a man who I had never heard of before by the name of Henri and invited him to meet us at the hotel as soon as possible. We both moved down to have dinner in the hotel dining room.

Just as we were finishing our meal, a bell-boy came to the table to announce that a visitor was waiting in the lobby. Rene went off and came back with a stocky, well-built man, who spoke with a French accent. He introduced him as Henri and he joined us for coffee. Quietly, Rene outlined his plan to bring about Paul's "resignation".

The three of us then left the hotel and walked up through Barberini and the Via Macelli to a bar near the main post office and the La Stampa newspaper office. Here Henri found Angelo. He was a middle-aged Southern Italian with a sinister lop-sided grin which had been smashed into his face by a rifle butt during the war.

Angelo was a weapons man. It was laughingly said in Rome at the time that he could equip an army within ten days if someone offered him the right price. Our price was only fifty thousand lire, just enough to buy Henri a brand-new 9 milimetre Beretta, smuggled from the factory in pieces and assembled to order when required. Such a gun would be totally safe and untraceable — ideal for a quick, one off, killing.

We left the bar shortly after Angelo, who stopped for one quick glass of wine, and walked to another about two hundred yards away. Here we set up a couple of drinks and watched a couple of young American sailors being prepared for fleecing by a pair of extremely expert whores. It was so obvious to anyone just sitting back and observing, that the two guys sitting a couple of tables away from the laughing girls and the drunken sailors, were just waiting to roll them on the way to the next bar.

We had two drinks each and watched the two couples leave, just ahead of the two muggers, before going back to the first bar to meet Angelo again. We gave him his money, which he counted out there and then, and he handed Rene a manilla envelope which contained the ordered gun.

Back in my room Henri checked over the Beretta and cleaned it thoroughly before inserting the six rounds which had come with it into the clip and slamming it up into the handle. He wrapped it in a handkerchief and tucked it into his hip pocket. He arranged to meet Rene and me in the morning for breakfast and left with Rene. I turned in after showering and flicking the security catch into the doorknob and did not wake until Paul telephoned at about eight-thirty the next morning. I listened quietly as he told me that he had a job for me. He asked to be allowed to come on over to the hotel. This wasn't part of my plan and I told him: "No. I've got company and will have all day if I can manage it. I've been going a bit short and she's lovely. Piss off!" I hung up.

He then telephoned Rene and told him that he must see us that same day because the job was urgent. Rene agreed to meet him in the Wimpy bar over the road from the hotel at seven-thirty. He agreed to this and was asked to sit at a table somewhere near the door so that Rene could find him easily. (The Veneto Wimpy bar is very continental in style, has waiter service and produces a very fair meal at reasonable prices. The lighting is subdued and it is a popular place with young Italians and staff from the U.S. embassy next door.)

I passed nearly the whole day with Rene, either in his room or mine, talking over old times and discussing the probable trends of the new business which the Bank had told us of. Neither of us ate after breakfast, which we had in my room, and neither did we drink any

55

alchohol. We were only apart when Rene left the hotel for half an hour at about three o'clock to return with a bundle of clothing – something we had been asked to get by Henri. Henri himself came to the hotel about an hour later.

Henri had asked for a lightweight white jacket and some sort of hat for himself. Rene went a bit overboard with the hat and provided a pretty Tyrolean job, but the jacket was a fair fit. For himself Rene had provided a long lightweight raincoat and a beret.

At six-thirty we left the hotel together. Henri wore a matching casual outfit of black slacks and cashmere polo-necked sweater. The Beretta, he tucked into his waist band above his right thigh. Rene was dressed in a light brown gaberdine suit with shirt and tie. He carried his extra clothing, along with Henri's, in an addressed parcel under his arm.

From the hotel we walked down the Veneto and into the back street behind the Barberini until we found what we were searching for – a whole batch of Lambretta scooters. They were parked along the kerb and against the walls near a café which was obviously popular with young people.

Rene and I walked briskly past the two dozen or so scooters while Henri held back at a slower pace. Past the café, and with no-one taking any obvious notice of him, Henri quietly walked up to the second machine from the end, found that it had the key still in the lock, picked it off the wall and rode on up the narrow street. Around the next corner Rene hopped on to the pillion seat and they rode slowly away. I turned back for the hotel.

At a few minutes after seven-thirty Rene drove up to the kerb outside with Wimpy bar just on the corner of the Via Boncompagni. He was wearing the long coat which hid his extreme height as long as he was on the machine. Henri rode pillion. Across the wide street people were eating and drinking at the pavement tables outside the cafés. The prostitutes and their minders were after early business and throngs of people strolled along the pavements. Scooters were buzzing up and down the street like angry hornets around their nest and baby Fiats farted back and forth. It was a warm and therefore a busy night on the Veneto. Unless it had been the plan would have had to be put back.

Wearing the Tyrolean hat pulled low, but not low enough to appear sinister, Henri calmly walked across the twelve feet of pavement to the open restaurant door and made his way down its left hand side past the ice cream kiosk which serves both the restaurant waiters and passers-by from an exterior window. I had by this time moved from the lobby of the hotel to the edge of the road outside the Wimpy bar.

Paul was sitting with his back to Henri in the first cubicle past the kiosk. He was in the outside seat of a table for four and hunched over something in front of him.

Henri walked slowly towards him, head down but still able to see the dozen or so people in front of him and beyond Paul. They were all busy with their eating, drinking or talking.

He stopped about a foot from Paul's back and pulled the Beretta from his waistband in his left hand. As he did this he started to turn as though to leave the restaurant and, facing across the victim's back, put the gun to Paul's head and pulled the trigger.

Before the crash of the shot had even registered with the waiters and customers, he had turned for the door. All around him screams and sounds of cutlery crashing to the floor from dropped trays, mixed with scuffling feet as people from the other side of the restaurant ran for the street. Henri hurried through the door with them, relying on their shock to prevent anyone identifying him as the killer.

Three steps and he was across the pavement and on to the back of the scooter. Ten minutes later they had left it in a street running parallel with the one in which we had found it, thrown their top clothes over the top of the paling fence into a shop construction and were walking back to the hotel. Twenty minutes after the shooting they stood with me in the crowd outside the Wimpy bar and watched the police activity.

The technique of such killings was developed by Chicago mobsters in prohibition days. The principle is simple. The shock of hearing the shot blanks off the minds of most people within earshot. Following this shock their first reaction is either to duck or run. Whichever of these courses they take they don't bother to take a good look at the guy who has blown off some other guy's head. It's an old and well-tried device.

The three of us walked back over the street to the hotel where Henri and I waited in the bar while Rene went to his room. He returned after about five minutes and handed Henri a buff envelope. I was never told how much Henri was paid but assume it would have been the equivalent of £500 – about the going rate for a professional job at that time. Henri left us.

I am not proud of my involvement in this and other killings and the only attempt I can make at justification is that if I had either backed out or informed, I too would have been killed.

Everyone in the business knew that there was only one end for an informer and Paul had been judged as such. I personally have never killed except when certain that someone else was about to kill me.

At about midnight, I telephoned the Bank and told them simply: "There has been a change in the Italian organisation structure." The bastard on the other end simply replied: "Yes, we know, thank you."

Obviously they had been keeping Paul or me, or both, under surveillance.

We both stayed on at the hotel for a couple of days before we were contacted by the Bank and it was suggested that we might like to take a holiday. This was good news. Things had been hectic for some time and I needed a rest. We both returned to our homes.

The "leave" must have lasted about ten days before I received a call from Geneva instructing me to meet up with Rene in Rome. From there we worked on seven or eight shipments out of Dubrovnic over a period of a couple of months. Usually on these trips, under our new organisation, I would sail with the goods and Rene would handle the landing arrangements. We did not involve crooked customs men at this time as the Bank had been tipped off that there was likely to be a sell-out.

Certainly things were hotting up on that front. The patrols were getting much too close for comfort and, on one journey in particular, brought about total disaster.

We had left Dubrovnic with a full consignment of cigarettes for a drop in the Gulf of Salerno, having left that area alone for the last few trips. Rene was once again handling the shore arrangements and I was to join him after the drop for the return trip to Rome.

Everything proceeded as arranged and we made radio contact with Rene before picking up his light signal just before two-thirty in the morning. We took the boat right in to about a hundred yards off the beach and set to with the unloading. There was no moon and we had offloaded about half the cargo, when we were suddenly blinded by a searchlight beam from a boat about three hundred yards along the shore and about a hundred yards to seaward of us.

One dinghy was loading at the port side, nearest to the shore, and the other had just set off for the beach. Our lookout and gunner, a Dutchman, screamed a warning just as we heard the powerful motors of the other craft roar to full throttle as it leapt forward.

Our skipper, another Dutchman, known as the Hollander, slammed in his throttles at almost the same instant and we leapt towards the other boat.

I had been leaning against the front of the wheelhouse when the action had started, and as we gathered speed I threw myself to the deck. In seconds the two boats had passed each other and we were heading out to sea. I groped my way back to the cockpit to join the skipper. From there, as he brought the boat up to her top speed of about twenty-five knots, I watched the waterguard vessel sweep round in pursuit, her searchlight seeking for us, switched the radio over to their band and picked up a staccato coversation giving the location of the encounter. She would soon have reinforcements.

We kept a straight course for the open sea, hoping to outrun the following boat, but after about ten minutes we saw the lights of another vessel closing with us from a point to the left of our port bow.

The Hollander swung the boat to veer away from this new threat just as one of our engines began to cough and splutter. With half our power gone we would be sitting ducks for the two customs launches. The Hollander screamed at the engineer, who by this time had made his way to the cockpit and he went down to the engine room. The faulty engine did not fail completely but was still coughing badly. The Hollander eased back on both throttles and cut our speed to about eighteen knots. This he managed to hold.

This speed was not enough to outrun the searching boats and we watched as the newcomer switched on his searchlight to pick us up.

The first boat was about 400 yards behind us when she opened fire from her bow cannon and tracer shells flew across the water at us. The Hollander took evasive action, swerving our boat from side to side, but this slowed us down as the second boat came at us. Our bow gunner opened up with his 756, pumping out tracer at 400 rounds a minute towards the second boat. She took evasive action and also opened fire.

Fortunately all three boats were making too much way and throwing themselves about too much for accurate shooting. There were no early hits.

The engineer came back up an gave the thumbs-up sign to the Hollander, who immediately threw the throttles in again.

I don't know if the thought crossed his mind, but at those speeds it would be only a short time before we ran out of fuel. I recall that that was my main worry. Having opened fire on the waterguard we would be shot to pieces if we hove to.

We then swung round to face the second boat and flashed past her at about fifty yards, as tracer arced over our heads. This meant that she had to lose way and get a turn in to continue the chase. It put both boats behind us by several hundred yards.

We then set out in a wide circle for the open sea. By this time we were well out of the coastal territory of Italy, but the patrols took no notice of that. They both came on at our heels, occasionally spitting tracer over our wake. One lucky burst raked our stern and ricochetted off the starboard side. All this time I had been listening in to their radio and the activity was increasing. I flicked over and called Rene. I asked him to hold on near the drop zone as long as possible. He told me that he was already heading back for home. By this he would mean Naples. I told him to listen out for more messages and signed off.

Suddenly rain started to hit the windscreen and in seconds we were in a squall. We had a chance. I went out on deck. The gunner was huddled over the bow-mounted 756 and the two crewmen who had been offloading were crouched low against the front of the wheelhouse. I slipped the lashings on the reserve dinghy, which was roped to the deck between the hatches on each side of the boat, and heaved it to the port side before returning to the wheelhouse.

There I told the skipper that I intended to leave him to it and take off in the dinghy. He didn't question this. I was important to the organisation and there was no sense anyway in more men being killed or captured than was absolutely necessary. He agreed to heave to for a second or two to let me off.

The sea was pretty choppy and the rain squall, while assisting our getaway, also prevented us from seeing our pursuers.

We were again throwing the boat through a series of curves, but keeping a line out to sea. We must have been about seven miles off shore.

Suddenly the skipper looked at me and put right about in a tight half circle, heading back to the beach. I hadn't expected this and asked him why. He replied: "You will have a better chance in the dinghy and, anyway, it's a trick that's often worked before."

We saw nothing of the patrols as we crashed through the small waves towards the shore, and were about three miles out when the Hollander hove to and let me off, after the other three guys had helped put the dinghy over. As soon as the gunner had thrown down the rope which had been holding me to the side, the Hollander opened up again and put back out to sea.

I started the engine and was just getting under way when both patrol boats roared past from the rear, one on either side and each about fifty feet away. Neither made signs of putting about immediately and they had obviously missed me in the rain. They were, after all, looking for the big boat. I cut back my engine and listened to the roar of the searching boats as they crashed on towards the coast.

When I got under full way again I had to decide what to do about getting ashore. Anywhere along the coast of the gulf I might bump into the beach patrols which were bound to be out searching for stragglers from our landing party. There would certainly be a watch at the harbours also, but I couldn't sit out there until daylight and just wait to be picked up.

Assuming that the patrol boats had headed back out to sea, I gentled my dinghy towards the beach about a mile-and-a-half from a dropping zone. I rowed in the last couple of hundred yards, keeping low in the boat. It was still raining and visibility was well down.

Holding the boat in a situation where I could pull the motor into life and shoot out again if necessary, I sat quietly for about ten minutes. There was no sign of activity on the shoreline. I decided to land.

There was no sense in leaving the boat up on the beach as a give-away that someone had landed, so I rowed out another hundred yards or so, threw out the sea anchor and slipped over the side. I swam ashore.

Lying in the shallows, I again waited to make sure that there were no patrols and, after about five minutes, ran up the beach and straight inland.

In the area where I had landed I knew there were a number of tracks leading up to the main coast road and I set off obliquely until I found one. Keeping to one side of it I carefully made my way up to the road. There was no sign of any activity at all.

I was soaked after my swim and there was still a light rain falling. I was certainly in no shape to seek a lift, even if there had been any traffic. I huddled down behind a wall to take stock and wait until dawn, when I could make my way inland and seek a lift further away from the scene of the drop.

I waited until the sky lightened and then set off across open country to the main Sapri – Salerno road, a distance of about four miles which I covered at a quick jog, managing in some small way to warm myself up a little.

From there I just had to take a risk. My sweater and slacks were not too obviously wet now and I did what I could to tidy myself up by running my fingers through my hair and wiping my face on my damp handkerchief. After about ten minutes at the roadside, I saw a Volkswagen van coming up from the South. From a hundred yards away I could see the British number plates. It was an almost unbelievable stroke of luck. I stepped into the road and flagged it down.

As it stopped a large guy in the driving seat slid back the window and asked what was wrong in a strong Australian accent. There was a girl in the passenger seat and apparently no-one else in the van, which I now realised was a camping truck.

I explained that my boat had broken down out in the Salerno bay during the night and I had beached it an effort to make my way into town to get help. They agreed to help me and I climbed in beside the girl. In half an hour, we were in Battipaglia and I had telephoned a local beach-man with whom I had worked in the past. He collected me about an hour later and took me to his home in Salerno.

There he gave me dry clothes, about two sizes too small, and I bathed and shaved before telephoning the Ambascatori in Rome and asking if there were any messages for me. The message clerk there gave me a Salerno number which I then called. Rene answered the telephone and started straight into a tirade of abuse about his sleepless night. I arranged to meet him at a nearby bar as soon as he could get there. I badly wanted out of that area and back to the safety of Rome.

He arrived in his Renault 16 just as I walked up to the bar and I dropped in beside him. We just grinned at each other until he asked me, as he put the car into gear, how I had got ashore.

I filled him in on the chase and my landing. He was furious that I had lost the dinghy and motor, but said that there was no reason why it couldn't be picked up later by a local who could just happen across it – assuming that the police didn't get at it first. I told him that I couldn't bloody-well care less about the boat. I was safe, alive and free. He hadn't been shot at and chased half-way round the Med.

From Salerno Rene faced the car for Battipaglia and when I asked him why he was going in the wrong direction he explained that he had to check on how much stuff we had got ashore and how many men had been arrested. The Bank would want to know, and we ourselves had to know if there was the possibility of a leak which might involve us. I could only agree with him.

We drove on round Battipaglia and down towards Sapri for about fifty miles, before turning up into the hills and making for a villa owned by the beach man who had been operating for the buyer.

As we pulled up in the horseshoe driveway a man came out to meet us. He recognised Rene and was introduced to me as Umberto. He was obviously happy to see us and took us into his unpretentious home. It was apparent that it was used very little. The furniture was sparse and, when he took us into the kichen to give us coffee, the crockery in the cupboards was too orderly to have been used every day. There were several cups on the table and nothing else.

The three of us sat around the table, steaming cups of coffee in our hands, and Rene asked Umberto how things had gone. He replied that not a single box had reached his trucks, but that after Rene had fled the scene as soon as the trouble started, he had managed to get both his lorries and all his men away before the police arrived from inland. All that had been lost were the few boxes on the beach. He didn't know what had happened to the dinghy which we had abandoned, complete with the crewman, when the boat first took off from the shore, but he had checked with a police informant and there had been no-one arrested. The man was either still at sea or had put in well away from the scene of the drop. He would have had enough fuel for nearly a hundred miles if he took things easy and he could be anywhere by now.

The unfortunate drop was, after all, not the disaster we had feared. There was no more to be learned from the guy and, promising to contact him later, Rene and I set off to make our way down from the mountains and back to Rome.

We said little on our way down the narrow mountain roads. In fact Rene was the only one who spoke, and all he said, over and over again, was: "Merde."

We must have been some five miles back along the main road when Rene pointed over his shoulder with his thumb. I looked back and saw a police car with three men in it right on our tail and making no attempt at passing, in spite of the fact that we were only doing about fifty miles an hour.

I was wearing my thirty-eight, in a belt holster and there was no way a copper would take kindly to that. I quickly slid the whole outfit off my belt and, after wiping the case with a windscreen cloth, slipped it all up under the dashboard, above the wiring. Unless they were really suspicious they wouldn't search the car.

Rene, in the meantime, quickly changed the frequencies on the automatic selector buttons of his radio.

The car followed us for about five miles and then swept past, siren wailing, as the front seat passenger put his arm through the window and waved us over.

We looked at each other and Rene said: "Play it cool, Leslie, they have nothing on us. We are tourists and slept rough last night somewhere down near Scalia, O.K.?" I shrugged.

Two guys got out from the car, loosening off their revolver holsters as they came back to us, one on each side of our car. We waited until one of them, the one on Rene's side, indicated with his thumb that he wanted us out of the car.

With both of us out and covered by one of the nasties, the third guy, the one who had been driving came back to join us. He and the one not waving his hardware leaned into the car. They were back in about two minutes. One of them rattled away at us in Italian. I only knew enough of the language to get by if it came over slowly, but Rene has a natural linguistic gift and Italian is one of seven languages he handles very well.

He entered into a long conversation, or rather argument, with two of the policemen. There was much swinging of hands and what were obviously lengthy explanations by Rene.

He then reached into his jacket pocket and brought out his passport. "They want our passports, Leslie, have you got yours?"

For the first time since I had seen them I was really worried. My passport was aboard the boat – and Christ alone knew where that was. In the excitement of the escape I had completely forgotten my case.

I shook my head. "Tell them it's at my hotel in Rome, I've forgotten to bring it with me." he handed over his own passport and entered into an explanation about mine. All three men looked at me as if they knew that I'd just killed the Pope. The guy who was obviously in charge rattled on at Rene for a couple of minutes and Rene nodded. He then looked at me and said: "They're taking us into Naples for questioning. I'm to drive my car with one of them as passenger and you're to go with them. I don't think they speak any English. Stick to your story if you meet anyone who does, and I'll do all the talking if we don't. They seem more suspicious of the radio than of your having no passport."

It must have been just before noon when we arrived at the main police station in Naples. We were kept under guard in the windowless room for more than an hour before an obviously senior guy came in holding my gun. There wasn't much conversation after that and what there was was in Italian.

Rene was taken from the room and when he returned he told me that we would both be detained and that he had told them that he knew nothing of the gun. They had allowed him to call a lawyer who we both knew worked for the Bank and the local Mafia.

We were then taken to a detention centre, as opposed to a prison, and banged up in a cell on our own.

Late in the afternoon the lawyer arrived and was allowed in to talk with us. He spoke good English and had obviously taken advice from the Bank after receiving Rene's telephone call. He told us that we had better keep on denying knowledge of the gun and asked where my passport was. He would have to get it to prove my identity. I told him about the boat and the battle of the night before. He looked worried but told us that there were unlimited funds available and he would have our stay made as comfortable as possible. We would be able to have food and wine brought in to order and he would have the Bank chase up the passport. He left us.

He was as good as his word and meals ordered by us arrived from a local restaurant regularly. He also sent in cigarettes. For two days we didn't see him, but then he returned to tell us that the boat had arrived in Malta, somewhat shot up, but, along with the crew, intact. My case was being flown over to Rome and would be driven down to his office as soon as it arrived.

That night we ordered our dinner as usual and it arrived at about nine o'clock. However, this time the routine was broken. Instead of the usual two waiters handing it over at the door it was brought by two attractive girls who were allowed by the guard to bring it into the room.

Rene and I looked at each other. It couldn't be true. But it was. The guard locked the girls in the room with us and we heard his footsteps go back up the corridor to his desk at the end.

When the lawyer had said he would make us comfortable I hadn't for one minute expected this sort of thing. I had heard in the past that anything was possible in Italian jails and here was the proof.

One of the girls spoke rapidly to Rene and smiled. He looked at me and said: "They're here for half an hour and she just asked if we wanted cold food or cold women." He took the girl who had spoken to him by the hand and led her to his hard bed, ignoring the trays which they had placed on the table against the wall and between our two beds. The other girl moved over and sat on my bed.

Quite honestly, I was more interested in the food and, anyway, a stinking prison cell is hardly the place for a quick turn-on to a double sex act. I just couldn't make up my mind what to do.

I looked over to Rene's side of the cell just in time to see his trousers drop on top of his girl's dress. He had obviously made up his mind. He slid on to the narrow bed alongside the girl. I looked away and back to the slim brunette with the large brown eyes who was just unfastening

66

the belt of her button-through mini-dress. It fell away from her well-made body, illustrating the fact that she didn't believe in swim-suits on the beach and revealing one of the finest pairs of tip-tilted tits I'd ever seen. I pulled her on to my bed. Within a couple of minutes I'd stopped noticing the grunts and groans from the other side of the cell as I went through the sexual athlete's race card.

The cold veal chop which I didn't enjoy half an hour later gave me indigestion, but it was worth every nauseating mouthful of it.

The next morning we were arraigned before some sort of examining magistrate and, after producing my passport and engaging in a noisy verbal battle, our lawyer informed us that we were to be bailed to appear at some future date. The court had accepted that the gun must have been placed in the car by one of the many people who, we had told the judge, might have used it when Rene was out of the country. They accepted a plea that the radio equipment was to do with Rene's hobby – amateur radio – and that his French amateur licence would be produced at the next hearing.

Later the lawyer also told us that the judge had accepted a million lira along with the evidence and there would be no trouble over our leaving the country. I became one of the thousands of men who have bought their way out of Italian jails and who will never face trial. There are so many men who have done such deals that it is almost impossible for the police and immigration authorities to keep a check on them. However, I have never returned to Italy via the "front door".

Having the backing of the Bank and their lawyer, with his "brotherhood" connections, had enabled us to get out of trouble. We were lucky. I have known guys rot for as long as two years in stinking jails awaiting trial when they haven't had money or influence behind them.

Chapter 3

Arms for the Love of Money

From Italy, after our narrow escape, Rene and I returned to Malta. The Bank sent us £10,000 each and suggested that we lie low for a while and work up new contacts to work as skippers and crews for the new market they had spoken of on our visit to Geneva.

For a couple of months we loafed around and serviced the local girls and tourists, paying the odd visit to Gibraltar to check out the crews working from there.

We were just beginning to think that the Bank had dispensed with our services when we were both called back to Geneva to be introduced to a Libyan.

The night before the meeting Rene, Lisette and I ate dinner in a quiet lakeside restaurant before returning to her flat, where we spent the night. We had travelled a day early in order that Rene didn't miss out with Lisette. This meant that the next morning Rene was by no means at his best and I had to handle most of the arrangements at the Bank.

Once more we went through the security routine and were ushered into the inner sanctum by Lisette, who looked even more tired than Rene.

With the manager, we found the Arab who was introduced as a major in the Libyan army at present in Geneva on diplomatic business. During the conversation it emerged that the "diplomatic business" amounted to an arms deal. At the time there was an arms embargo in being to prevent the Libyans buying weapons. The Bank were fixing to break it. The Libyan gave us the names of two men, one being a colonel, who would liaise with us in Malta; and his own name and address in Geneva. He then left and the Bank manager gave us the details of the first cargo.

Lying back in his elegant chair he told us: "We have fifty tons ready to be shipped out of Rotterdam for a legal destination. I want you to arrange for their arrival in Libya as soon as possible. You can have anything up to a 500-tonner to ship the stuff. Just let me know what you want a week before the pick up is due. You get ten thousand sterling each and we look after the crewing. Be careful of these Arabs, they are dangerous men."

He told us that Lisette had our tickets and trip money before pressing his buzzer and showing us out at about twelve-thirty. At one o'clock we lunched with Lisette in a local restaurant before taking a cab to the airport and flying back to Malta.

After the comparative cool of Geneva the heavy, dusty air of Malta was less then pleasant, and we both went straight to our rooms to shower when our cab dropped us at the Hilton.

Feeling cleaner, and adapting to the heavier atmosphere of Malta, I telephoned Endo after leaving the bathroom and asked him: "How are things for off-shore collections and transfers?"

"O.K. Leslie," he replied. I arranged to meet him at the Roundabout pub at eight the same evening.

Over dinner in the Hilton, Rene and I discussed the deal in hand. We had never worked into Libya and the shipment would present new problems. In fact the whole set-up was the reverse of our normal procedure. On this trip the landing of the goods would offer no problem. The real threat was from patrols out at sea and information leaks which could bring fully armed frigates down to us.

We met Endo as arranged and he agreed to provide a small trawler, as and when we required it, to switch the cargo from the mother ship to the blockade runner which would be provided by the Bank. We left him and called the local Libyans who agreed to meet us at ten o'clock in Sacha's.

The two were already at a table when we arrived at the club. They were known to Max who showed us to their table when we asked for them. The colonel, apparently in charge of the operation, did all the talking on their side and explained that they wanted the consigment dropped at the small port of Zuara, just along the Libyan coast from Tripoli and about thirty miles from the border with Tunisia. He then added: "I want also for you to be there when the cargo is landed so that you can check it over with our experts. We must be sure that it is all good equipment and you must be there to know first hand if we are not satisfied."

It had not been our intention to be anywhere near the cargo so I told him that we would have to take advice from our boss and we left after arranging to telephone him the following morning.

Back at the hotel I telephoned the Bank and told them of the colonel's request. I was told: "If you think it is unsafe you must not go. This is the first time we have dealt with these people and we know little of them. You must make up your own mind about the situation. That is what you're paid for."

I relayed this message to Rene, who was with me in my room. We decided that the colonel had a point but that we would under no circumstances go on the boat. There was also little point in both of us being over there and after a lot of discussion we made up our minds – I would make the trip and Rene would stay in Malta to keep in touch with the Bank. We then turned in, both tired out after our long day.

The next morning I telephoned the colonel and informed him of our intentions. He was quite happy that only one of us should be there and asked if he could call on us at the hotel later in the day. I agreed to see him at noon in the lobby and then showered before ordering breakfast. At about nine-thirty, while I was still sitting at the open window finishing off the last of the coffee, Rene arrived at my room with Endo.

As they settled into chairs, Rene said: "I have been talking with our Endo about the Arabs. He has done some small business with them and knows their methods.

"They want you over there in case anything goes wrong with the plans. If they lose the consignment they will kill you. They have had much trouble with informers and agents. The Israelis have all their eyes on them all the time, especially here in Malta."

That was all I wanted. I hadn't given a thought to that side of things. In the cigarette business one only had to worry about the waterguard, police and the odd pirate, but with this new traffic we had the full James Bond bit.

I told Rene: "I don't like this at all and I think we're better off out of it. I can see us both getting our heads blown off."

"But that is why we get so much money, Leslie, no?" Rene replied. "We must not be too damned quick to back out. We must talk, yes?" Not wishing to go into details in front of Endo I told Rene that we would talk later and asked them to push off while I dressed. I arranged to meet them in the bar after about half an hour.

By the time I went down Endo had left and Rene was sitting alone drinking his usual straight vodka. I joined them but declined his offer of a drink. He took up the conversation again: "I think that if we back out we're finished with the Bank, Leslie. I also think that the Arabs, they will shoot us anyway. They will certainly think that we are on the other side."

There was obviously a lot of sense in what he said. We had reached the point of no return as soon as we learned of the liaison between the Bank and the Arabs. It was now just a matter of who might shoot us for what — the Arabs because they didn't trust us, or the Israelis because we were helping the Arabs. We decided that we would go along with the Arabs and take a risk on the Israelis finding out.

We also made up our minds to tighten up our security and keep our mouths shut in public places.

Foregoing lunch, Rene and I took a long stroll round the Dragonara point as we discussed the arrangements for the deal and decided that, bearing in mind the interest the Israeli intelligence service would have in the deal, not to communicate with the Bank by telephone. We would lay on the transfer for eight days from then and I would return to Geneva to brief the Bank direct.

We walked back round the point along the footpath at the rear of the Hilton. This led us into Spinola Road, where we found Endo in Charles' bar, drinking wine. We joined him for one glass and told him that we wanted to fix precise arrangements for the transfer. He agreed to take us to his office so that we could study charts and co-ordinates for the rendezvous and we all left the bar and climbed into his battered Mercedes outside.

He drove us to a garage he owned in the back-streets of Sliema and ushered us into a partitioned office area at its rear. From a wooden filing cabinet he took a bundle of charts and a half-empty bottle of wine, some of which he poured into a dirty cup on top of the cabinet. He offered the cup to Rene and me, but we both refused.

Shrugging, he sat himself on the only chair in the cramped cubicle, swept some papers to the back of the table and spread out his charts, securing them at the top with the wine bottle. Then, with Rene and me looking over his shoulder, he ran his finger round the Eastern side of the island and then out to sea, before taking up a pencil and putting a small cross on the chart in a position which was probably about twelve miles offshore. He then took a letter from the jumble at the top right hand corner of the table, glanced at it, and wrote a series of co-ordinates on a blank space at the bottom.

After tearing the bottom off the letter, he handed it to me and I checked his figures against the chart. I nodded my acceptance of the rendezvous points and told him that we would expect his trawler to be there at 2 a.m. eight days hence and, after that, every morning at the same time until the transfer was made. We then discussed call signs for radio and light signals and decided that on the first night the trawler would use Alpha-Bravo, the mother ship would use Charlie-Delta and the collection vessel would use Echo-Foxtrot. On subsequent nights, if necessary, the codes would be advanced to begin with Charlie-Delta and Echo-Foxtrot respectively.

Rene and I had decided that it was better for us not to meet with the skipper or crew of the trawler. In the event of trouble we wanted as few links as possible with the deal. We therefore turned down Endo's offer to brief the crew.

That only left one thing to be sorted out – the finances – and after a short bargaining session we agreed to pay Endo £1,200 for the first night and £200 for each extra night. Rene would pay him half on departure and the rest on completion. Endo then drove us back to Charles' bar and left us there.

Rene and I were both hungry by this time and between us we knocked off a couple of dozen oysters with a bottle of light wine before I moved over to the telephone behind the door and called the colonel. He answered almost immediately and recognised my voice when I asked: "Is the colonel there?" This was just as well because I had no intention of revealing my identity. All telephones in Malta are systematically tapped on a random basis and suspect calls are referred to the police. My earlier calls to the Arabs and Geneva could well have been picked up and it was too late now to worry about that, but I had no intention of taking further risks.

The man of the other end of the line said: "Yes, this is the colonel, is everything all right?" I said: "I don't wish to talk now. We will meet you in the same place tonight at the same time." He agreed and I replaced the telephone.

Back at the bar Rene had ordered another bottle of wine and was still at work on the oysters. I, however, had had enough – both of wine and oysters – and Rene acquiesced when I suggested that we should leave. We paid our bill and went back out into the harsh afternoon sunlight.

During the five minutes it took us to walk round to the Hilton, via Church Street, which runs off Spinola Road, we discussed our next moves. With the rendezvous set in eight days we didn't have much time to kick our heels. We decided that I would fly out that same evening to brief the Bank and then move on over to Tripoli to await the drop. Rene would keep his eye on things at the Malta end and in case of delay, for whatever reason, he would communicate with the Bank via Lisette's address using a simple code which would mention that her uncle Pierre had died and the funeral would be in a given number of days' time. The number of days stated would be added to the date of the message to give the new transfer date.

Back at the hotel, I collected my case and booked out before taking a cab to the airport. The next flight out was for London and was fully booked, but a £5 tip to the booking clerk ensured that I was at the top of the standby list. This got me on to the flight and after a quick transfer at Heathrow I was in Geneva just before midnight.

I telephoned Lisette from the terminal and she invited me to spend the night at her flat. Fifteen minutes later I was relaxing in her elegantly modern lounge and drinking coffee as I admired the considerable amount I could see of her tight little body as she curled up on a sofa opposite me.

She was wearing an ankle length, near-transparent white negligée which was about as effective as a cobweb if the intention was to conceal anything.

As she unwound herself and moved over to collect my cup to give me more coffee I couldn't take my eyes off her gently bobbing boobs. I was still looking at them when she took my cup from my hand and, as I tore my eyes away and looked up into her face, she was smiling coyly. "Does this gown upset you, Leslie?" she asked. Well, what the hell could a guy say?

Me, I just said: "You might say that. What about the coffee?"

She moved away towards the door to the kitchen, her buttocks just as fascinating as her boobs had been. I squirmed in my chair and made myself more comfortable, loosening my collar.

She returned and handed me my coffee, stood back about four feet and shrugged the cobweb down on to the floor. "If the gown upsets you I'll take it off, yes? Anyway, it's time for bed." She smiled impishly and moved off to the right of the room where a door led to her bedroom.

I put my untouched coffee cup down and followed her through, but by the time I got there she was already in bed, lying on her back under a silk sheet which did little more to conceal her than the gown had. She held out her hand from the side of the sheet. I shrugged out of my clothes and was about to climb in beside her when I realised that I was sticky and dirty from my day-long journey. Changing my mind, I walked over to the en-suite shower room and turned on the water, cleaning my teeth while the temperature adjusted itself. I spent about ten minutes under the hot shower before turning it over to 'cold'.

As I walked back into the bedroom towelling myself, she just lay there, apparently not having moved. She watched all the way across the room, never taking her eyes off mine. I climbed in beside her and lay back on the pillow.

Suddenly, she was all over me, chewing, biting gently, licking, sliding, panting, groaning. I just let it happen.

When I woke up Lisette was already out of bed. I could smell coffee and hear the clink of crockery from beyond the bedroom door. I didn't feel as tired as I considered I deserved. I joined her in the kitchen. "Good morning, Lisette." I patted her rump.

She pulled away. "Today it's business, Leslie, O.K.?" That was me put in my place. I looked at the clock on the wall. It was eight-fifteen. I just nodded and smiled. As if I'd wanted anything else.

After breakfast we took a cab to the Bank but I had to wait downstairs until she had told her boss that I wanted to see him. I went up after she had telephoned the guard at the bottom door.

It was a short meeting. I simply told the manager of my fears and that we had arranged the drop for seven days from then. I gave him the details. He agreed to have the mother ship and the delivery vessel at the co-ordinates I had given him at the right time, pressed the buzzer and asked Lisette to show me out. As I passed through the door he said: "You are doing well, Leslie, have care for your life."

Lisette closed the door behind me and moved over to lean against her desk. "Yes, Leslie, do be careful. And give my love to Rene – tell him I miss him." She smiled and looked me straight in the eye. I just said: "O.K., be seeing you."

I cabbed back to the airport and caught the next flight for Amsterdam where I lunched at the airport before sending a cable to Rene in Malta with the simple message: "Pierre is very well." I then caught the next flight out to Tunis where I arrived in the early evening.

At Tunis airport I hired a Hertz Mercedes before driving into town to the Carlton Hotel on the Avenue Bourguiba, where I booked in for the night before going out to eat at the Café de Paris.

I then amused myself with a stroll up the Souk el Grana and through the red light area. The night with Lisette had left me in no mood to take advantage of the endless offers of vice in varying forms, but there is an air about such areas which always stimulates me.

I turned in early – it must have been about ten-thirty – and was up and on the road before eight in the morning for my drive to Zuara.

On the way out of town I picked up a couple of extra cans of fuel and one of water. I had no intention of being caught out if the car broke down on the 400 mile trip through into Libya.

As it was I made it through to Zuara before dark and decided to push straight on for Tripoli – about 120 miles further on. With a few days to spare there was no point in hanging around a stinking Arab port when I could amuse myself in a stinking Arab city.

As usual Tripoli was packed out with oilmen and their families,

75

either coming in for a tour of duty, or on their way home on leave. The best I could do in the way of a hotel was little more than a pension, but it was clean and reasonably central. Anyway, after the long slog up from Tunis I was in a state where I could have slept in a hole at the side of the road. I turned in and slept through until about ten o'clock, when I woke up in a heavy sweat. Even with just a sheet over me the temperature in the room had turned my bed into a Turkish bath.

Out of bed and shaved I felt better and, after using the shower down the corridor, almost human. I went to the lobby to call the number the Colonel had given me to make contact with his organisation in the city. Ten minutes later I had a scruffy, unshaven major with me and five minutes after that we were drinking thick black coffee at a café round the corner.

The major was somewhat brighter than his appearance would have had one believe, and he seemed to have his end of the delivery plans well in hand. He was horrified, however, at the hotel I had booked into and, after we had finished our coffee, he accompanied me back to my room and, while I packed and settled the bill for my night's stay.

We then drove in my car to the luxurious Libya Palace Hotel where he negotiated with the reception staff before collecting a key and taking me up to a two-room suite which, judging by its sumptuous furnishings, must have been kept for visiting Sheiks.

I unpacked my case while the Major waited in the sitting room of the suite and, when I returned, he had coffee all ready on a small table between two armchairs. Thick, Turkish-type coffee has never been a favourite of mine and I declined his offer. Against the background drone of the window-mounted air-conditioning unit he began to talk.

"We want you to be as comfortable as possible while you wait for the delivery, but we also want to retain our security. The Colonel will not be happy if you mix with other Europeans in the city. For this reason we are providing you with a guide. He will see that you are comfortable and have everything you need. He speaks good English and has orders to look to your every comfort."

He moved over to a wall table and picked up the telephone and asked for a number in Arabic. He was obviously connected because he then held a short conversation with someone at the other end before replacing the instrument in its rest. He turned back to me and said: "Our man will be with us in just a few minutes. I will then leave you to your own devices until the delivery. Alfred, your guide, knows that you are arranging a shipment for us but he does not know what it is. Please do not discuss the matter with him." He picked up his cup and sipped the dark liquid before lying back in his chair and looking at the ceiling. I told him I was going to shower and went into the bathroom after collecting my robe from the bedroom. It was obvious that conversation was at an end for the time being.

When I came out from the bathroom there was another man in the room. He was about five-and-a-half feet tall and had the sallow yet handsome features of the Anglo-Arab. He was standing looking out of the window as I entered the room and the Major rose to join him as he introduced me: "This is Alfred — Leslie Allan." He held his hands, palms upward as he metaphorically handed us over to each other. He had introduced me by my middle name, which I was using at that time on my business trips.

The Major then excused himself and promised to contact me if there was any alteration in our plans.

Alfred broke the uneasy silence which the uniformed Major had left in his wake. In almost perfect English he explained that he was the outcome of a marriage between an English oil-man and the daughter of a Beirut merchant. He had been educated in England and at the Sorbonne in Paris. He now worked as in interpreter for the Colonel.

He was, of course, on the intelligence staff of the government and I bloody well knew so, but there was no point in taking the matter any further. I was not, after all, trying to screw them. I was on their side.

For the next few days, with nothing to do but wait around, I let Alfred show me the sights of Tripoli. We spent hours in the Souk, a warren of miniature shops dealing in almost every known craft and vice. We visited the fortress of St. Gilles, which stands high above the town and looks down over the fruit groves and the sapphire sea below. We were even allowed the privilege of watching the Dervishes as they circled round and round in self-induced trance.

We also spent many hours in our suite being fed from massive platters of Lebanese hors d'oeuvres by an assortment of beautiful Arab girls. And, of course, I spent many hours in bed, sometimes alone.

During our first day I was walking near the hotel with Alfred when we were accosted by a young boy, maybe about eight years old, but with the wisdom of many lifetimes in his large brown eyes. He held out a flower which I was about to take when Alfred cuffed his ear, sending him spinning against a wall. I rammed my elbow into Alfred's gut and, as he doubled over, I moved to pick the lad up. He cowered against the wall, obviously frightened that I was going to hit him again. I stood back and let him get to his feet on his own. He was a typical street urchin and I had well known that if I took his flower he would consider himself my official guide and helper during my whole stay in the city. It would cost me a few quid, but so what. In the past I had found such kids good fun.

His flower lay on the ground, I picked it up and nodded to the lad to come forward. Alfred came over and started to explain why he had cuffed the lad and I told him to mind his own business. I reached into my back pocket and gave the kid the equivalent of a couple of quid, ruffled his hair and sent him on his way.

For the remainder of my stay the boy was on our heels at whatever time we left the hotel, always ready to dart forward to open a car door and ever ready to offer mute head-shaking, nodding, wide-eyed advice if I so much as paused to look at goods in the Souk. I nicknamed him Ali and he even managed to ingratiate himself with the surly Alfred by the end of the first day. Even when we were being driven through the city Ali would somehow keep up with us by taking short cuts and even clinging precariously to the fenders on the back of cabs. He became a sort of mascot.

On the third night at about seven o'clock the Major telephoned to tell me that he was coming round to the hotel. At the time of the call Alfred and I were discussing what we might do to amuse ourselves for the next few hours but, when he arrived, the Major immediately told Alfred to report back to the office.

After Alfred had left, the Major told me that the delivery was to be the following morning. He would pick me up at seven o'clock and would travel with me, in my car, to Zuara. There we would check the cargo and I would then be allowed to leave.

The plans I had been making with Alfred went out of the window as the Major insisted that I remain in my room for the rest of the night. I started to protest, but he nodded me to follow him and moved over to the door. When he opened it I saw that there were two Arab heavies sitting on chairs opposite the door — obviously hard-men from the hems of their djelabas to their scarlet plant-pot headgear. He shut the door and we moved back into the room.

He left after repeating his request that I be ready at seven the following morning.

I ordered a meal by telephone and spent an hour or so picking at it as I downed about half a bottle of arak. I showered and turned in after booking an alarm call for six a.m.

By seven the next morning I was packed and down in the lobby of the hotel trying to settle my bill. A somewhat sleepy night cashier was trying to explain that it had already been taken care of when the Major came in with his uniformed driver. The driver picked up my case and the Major took my elbow to steer me out to my Mercedes, which somehow had found its way to the hotel door from the garage at the rear.

As I walked towards the car I felt a tug at my shirt tail and, looking round I saw Ali. "O.K., sore?" His eyes were worried and I've realised since that he probably thought I had been arrested. I slipped him a handful of local notes and scrubbed his head before going across to the car.

After ushering me into the driving seat and the Major in next to me the driver put my case in the boot of the Merc and moved off to a Cadillac which was parked behind.

The Major guided me out to the main road, then I hit the throttle pedal more than somewhat and we were in Zuara and at the dockside by seven-thirty.

Just after eight a small cargo ship nudged its side up to the dock and almost immediatly half a dozen sand coloured trucks pulled alongside. The Major and I moved over to the lead truck where he spoke in Arabic to the driver. He then waved to a man I took to be the skipper, and who was leaning over the side, before moving on up the gangplank with me behind him.

I waited on deck while he and the skipper went down a ladder into the hold. I looked down into the darkness and saw the Major and two other men prising the tops off crates and checking their contents. In about five minutes the first pallet was slung out and on to the lead truck. Half an hour later the trucks had all gone and the hold was empty. The Major had examined about every fifth case and was satisfied that all was well.

As we walked back to my car the Major stopped and turned towards me, saying "You are an honest man, Mr. Allan. Will you please contact the Colonel when you return to Malta. We are pleased with your planning." He shook my hand and walked off towards his own car, leaving me to walk to mine. Ten minutes later I was heading back for the Tunisian border and home. The deal was done.

I drove back to Tunis and returned to Malta via Amsterdam. At eight o'clock the next night I was sitting with Rene in the Hilton bar drinking Scotch. All that was left was to pick up our share of the money from the Bank.

Two days after I had returned to Malta, I contacted the Colonel as requested by his colleague in Libya. Once more I used a pay phone and arranged a "casual meeting" in the Dragonara Casino for the same evening. There, as we strolled through the gardens, the Colonel made a proposition which was to change the whole course of my career. He asked me to work for him direct —to cut out the Bank. He pointed out that it was somewhat stupid for him to be paying inflated prices for weaponry to the Bank when he could arrange for purchase direct from suppliers if he could arrange the shipping privately.

He was right. But the reason for the Bank being able to charge their high prices was that they had people like me to arrange deliveries. They wouldn't be at all pleased to find that I had defected and moved into business on my own. I only promised to give the matter some thought.

Over a late dinner with Rene I passed on the Colonel's offer. He was of the same mind as I was. If we double-crossed the Bank we just wouldn't live to spend the extra money we would earn. There was only one way to work such a deal. We would ask permission from the Bank to do a couple of freelance deals.

So next morning, we both flew to Geneva, via London, and set up an appointment with the boss for the following day.

It wasn't an easy session but eventually the manager agreed that we could work for the Arabs on condition that we bought the arms indirectly from the Bank and, if possible, used their vessels. During this negotiating it became apparent that we had given the Bank a way out of a problem which had been worrying them. They were not happy to be dealing with the Arabs, in spite of the vast profits they stood to make. Politically they were playing with dynamite as they used Jewish money from all over the world, and particularly London and the U.S., to maintain an Arab supply route.

With Rene and me apparently working on our own they would have the best of both worlds. They would sell to us, with no obvious knowledge of the destination of their arms, and we would sell to the highest bidder. This would give them an "out" in the event of exposure.

Immediately we left the Bank we telephoned the Libyan office in Geneva and asked that the Colonel should meet us in two days' time at the Amsterdam Hilton. We had decided that if we were to enter into serious business for the Arabs, Malta could no longer be used as our H.Q. Israeli intelligence was too well established on the island for the safe operation of such an exercise.

We then flew to Amsterdam and booked in at the Hilton and, after enjoying an Indonesian meal down in the dock area, set off on a tour of the fringe bars, spending a lot of time renewing old friendships. Amsterdam was, as it still is, a gathering point for mercenaries, smugglers and sundry international opportunist groups. A quick tour of the bars of the city can always produce half-a-hundred international adventurers ready to work at anything to produce a quick and large profit.

It was after ten o'clock the next morning before we returned to the Hilton to drop into our beds and I slept through until Rene called me on the internal telephone at seven in the evening.

I joined him in the bar at eight and we spent a couple of hours around the bars before picking up a couple of girls, eating, then parting company as we took them back to their apartments. All I remember about the rest of the night is that the girl I ended up with was called Helga and that she was something of a sexual athlete, but then, aren't most of them?

When I arrived back at the hotel at about eight the next morning, tired and unshaven, I dropped straight on to the bed and fell asleep. At ten the Colonel was on the phone from the lobby. I invited him up and immediately called Rene's room. no reply. He was still tucked up with his bird.

The Colonel arrived as I was just coming out of the shower and I let him in. He was dressed in a well-cut grey suit and appeared fresh. He explained that he had arrived the night before and was booked in at another hotel.

I ordered breakfast to be sent up and continued dressing. By the time I had finished the Colonel had let in the breakfast waiter and had poured two cups of black coffee. He asked: "You have decided to work with us?" I nodded, drinking my coffee and snapping off a corner of toast without taking the bread from the rack. He smiled and sat back in his armchair.

"Good," he replied. "We will now be serious about our business. Where is your partner?" I couldn't quite answer that one right then but I was able to assure him that Rene was coming.

I smiled as I thought that I was more than probably one hundred per cent accurate in my prognosis. But where he was coming and how quickly he might be with us remained something of an imponderable.

In fact, after about half an hour Rene telephoned me from his room to tell me that it was time to be up. I asked him to come along to me right away.

When he arrived we got right down to business. The Colonel had arranged for all the arms he needed in the immediate future to be in a Rotterdam warehouse during the course of the next three weeks. We could take over from there.

All I could say to that was: "Bollocks."

The Colonel sat forward on his chair: "You can't do the business?"

I then had to explain that we were all ready to go but that he had to buy through us. We would provide a full deal. What he wanted, where he wanted it and at a fair price – our price. I concluded: "We are probably the best there is in the business and we have proved it. We will come in at a price about twenty-five per cent lower than your last supplier. If that's not good enough you can shop elsewhere."

The Colonel smiled. From his inside pocket he took some folded sheets of paper which he handed to me. Rene moved across from the bed, where he had been sitting, and looked over my shoulder as we read through the four foolscap pages.

Starting off with two thousand pounds of "plastic" it ran on down to armalite rifles and ammunition, including enough war machinery to capture a small country. It was a showstopper as far as I was concerned. There must have been a quarter of a million quid tied up in that shopping list. We couldn't begin to stand in the middle if we had to put up even a tenth deposit.

I asked him if we could keep the list and call him later in the day. He agreed, and asked us to call a number which he wrote down for us before leaving.

After he had left Rene and I just sat and looked at each other for about three minutes. He broke the silence: "Leslie, we can't do it. The Bank will never trust us for this amount."

I thought for a few minutes before replying: "Why not? They know who we are dealing with and they know us. Let's try." He then pointed out that there was some £50,000 profit for us in the deal and that the Bank would know that. They wouldn't allow it!

We discussed the matter for about an hour before agreeing that he would fly to Geneva as soon as possible to try it on with the boss. That was all we could do. He flew out just after lunch, taking the list with him.

By three the next afternoon he was back in my room. The Bank had agreed to underwrite the operation on the understanding that their man had the first stage payment of half the money for the arms at the dockside immediately after loading. They would trust us just that far. And the money had to be in cash – Deutchmarks or Swiss francs.

We were in business. I called the Colonel, invited him to the hotel and, while we waited, Rene and I went over the list and checked out the prices the Bank had put against the various items. We came up with a total figure of something under £200,000 and decided to stick out for a cool quarter of a million from the Arab.

When he arrived he came straight up to my room and Rene let him in as I was sorting out the lists on a table near the window. Rene moved over to my side and the Arab sat in an armchair in front of the table. "You are ready with your deal?" He looked confident, lips parting in a thin smile under his military moustache.

I tapped the sheets of paper under my right hand: "If you have the money we have the goods and the means of getting them to you. This little lot will cost you one quarter of a million – sterling – on your doorstep. We want half as the ship leaves and the rest on the dock at your end. Yes or no?"

We had expected the man to haggle and I realised that I had probably underpriced the deal when he merely nodded and said "Good. When can we have the delivery?" I could have jumped straight out of the bloody window but it was too late to up the price then. I told him that we would call him the next day and arrange the details.

Over the next couple of hours Rene and I made our plans. The Bank had told him that they had no ships available for the deal over the next couple of weeks. That presented our first problem – but not for long. Rene telephoned a contact in Hamburg, a man who had done charter work for the Bank on a number of deals organised by Rene. It was as simple as that. The guy could have his ship in Rotterdam in two days. A call to the Bank assured us that they could have the goods in one of their bonded warehouses in the same port within three days and their manager there would accept the first stage payment after he had loaded the ship.

It couldn't have been simpler. Overnight we were in the big-time arms business.

And simple it remained. Rene set off by car that same evening for Rotterdam, while I stayed on to recruit a few of the guys we wanted to guard the ship on the trip from Rotterdam to Zuara. I found three old acquaintances that same night on a tour of the bars. Two were veterans of three or four mercenary wars and the other was a new guy on the scene who had turned killer in Vietnam before deserting the U.S. army. They all agreed to drive through to Rotterdam with me two days later.

The next morning, more than a little hung-over after my night out with the mercenaries, I telephoned the Colonel and asked him to come round. Within five minutes of his arrival we had agreed that he should meet me at the hotel at noon the next day and drive in convoy with myself and my heavies to Rotterdam. He and I would stay at the Euro Motel and the heavies could fend for themselves in a more modest establishment around the corner. At about eleven Rene called to tell me that both ship and goods were in Rotterdam and that he could start loading as soon as we were ready. I filled him in on my arrangements and suggested that he move from the Hilton, where he was staying, into the Euro. I also told him to sort out rooms for myself and the Colonel. We would meet sometime before two the next day at the Euro.

In fact, we arrived at the hotel at about one-thirty after we had driven down in a pair of Hertz Mercedes. Rene had fixed our rooms and the three of us were lunching in the hotel dining room well before two.

In the afternoon the three of us set off for the warehouse and checked over the consignment to make sure that it was all there. It was. The Colonel and I then went back to the Euro while Rene set off to find the skipper so that he might bring him along to discuss final details. The man had already been briefed by Rene and all that had to be decided was the exact timing of the trip.

The pair arrived at about five and we all sat around the table in my room to finalise details. The skipper, a burly German with a splendid full-set blond beard, was a long-time adventurer and blockade runner by the name of Hermann. He convinced us quickly that he knew his business. His only reservation was about my insistence that we put our own private army aboard to protect our investment. He seemed to take this as an insult, thinking that it was he whom we did not trust. He insisted that his own crew could well handle the light cannon and heavy machine guns which he carried for protection. Eventually, however, he agreed that my men were probably better trained than his and that, in the event of piracy, they would be of some use.

It isn't well know outside smuggling circles that there is a great deal of piracy still going on in the world. Illegal cargoes are the fair game of well-armed and fast cutters which operate on information gathered in the bars and whorehouses of the smuggling centres. Millions of pounds worth of goods fall into the hands of these modern buccaneers every year. The authorities couldn't give a damn – they are quite happy for smugglers to shoot hell out of each other in these skirmishes.

We all agreed that the loading would take place at first light the next morning and that the ship would put out on the first tide. It would arrive at Zuara two weeks later and be escorted in by two of the Colonel's gun-boats after contacting them by radio on a pre-arranged frequency. The skipper went off to organise his paper-work, the Colonel went back to his own room and Rene and I went off to find our "army" at their dockland hotel.

After meeting up with the three guards and briefing them on the next morning's plans, Rene and I returned to the hotel for dinner. It was then that we decided that Rene too would travel with the consignment. I would fly over to Tunis, as I had on my previous trip, and meet up with him and the three guards when they arrived.

This plan pleased Rene. He was never happier than when he was at sea, and his status as organiser of the trip would put him on an equal footing with the captain.

We turned in early and were at the docks next morning in time to check the consignment aboard with the Colonel. It took about two hours to ship and stow the cargo and the ship pulled out almost immediately we had finished.

I gave a last wave to Rene and the three guards and walked back with the Colonel to his car. From the back he took a black leather executive case and, after fiddling with the combination locks, handed it to me. I opened it on the bonnet of the car. It was packed with bundles of high denomination Swiss francs. I nodded the Colonel back over to my Merc and he climbed into the front with me.

It took me some ten minutes to count the money. It was all there – slightly over £125,000. Placing the brief-case on the seat beside me I thanked the Colonel and he left me to return to his own car. The deal was half completed.

I waited until the Colonel's car had left the dock before driving straight to the Bank warehouse where I found the manager and handed over the £100,000 initial payment to him, as agreed with the Bank. He gave me a receipt and I left. By eleven o'clock I had the remainder of the money stashed in the bank and had checked out of the hotel. Two hours later I had taken my car back to Amsterdam and was on my way to Schipol where I caught a plane to London to spend a week with my family before making the trip over to Libya.

It was the first time I had been home in months and for four days I luxuriated in just having the family around me. But then, as always, home comforts began to pall, and I was anxious to be off and finish the deal with the Colonel.

I managed, however, to contain myself for the whole week I had promised my wife. And anyway, there was nothing to do in Libya until the ship arrived. I remember thinking, as my wife drove me to the airport at the end of that week, how it was getting more and more difficult to relax at my home. The increasing pressures of my smuggling activities were becoming part of my life. It was like driving a car in low gear, for a long period. I had become so used to the high revs that I was uncomfortable when I couldn't hear the engine whining. Then there was my wife. She knew very little of what I did but she was certainly aware that I suddenly came into possession of large sums of money and spent most of my time away from home. She has since admitted that she was afraid to ask what I really did and was happy to believe the story I had told when I had first met her – that I dealt in light aircraft on the Continent.

From London I flew straight out to Tunis and again made the road trip to Tripoli. This time I telephoned the Colonel's office as soon as I arrived and a man from there picked me up at the door of the Libya Palace and organised my rooms for me. I did not have the same suite as the time before but he did manage one almost as well appointed.

I had arrived at the hotel at about six in the evening. By seven the Colonel had joined me and informed me that, now that they trusted me, he would not insist on the guards as before. I would be free to wander at will in the city. He did, however, warn me to be on my guard against involvement with other Europeans. He informed me that he wished to show me something the next day which he thought would interest me and then left.

I showered for the second time since my arrival and, deciding to take a stroll before finding myself a late dinner, made my way down towards the Souk after leaving the hotel. Before I had gone ten yards I was confronted with the cheeky faced young Arab I had been involved with the time before. He looked up at me as he danced up and down: "You want girls, sights, boys, what you want sore? I am your guide again sore?" I smiled and rubbed his tousled head. "Yup, you're my guide." I gave him the loose change out of my pocket. "But no girls tonight, we'll just walk through the Souk, eh?"

He smiled up: "Okay, okay. You say — we do." He took my sleeve and pulled me forward.

We must have strolled through the Souk for about an hour before I felt hungry. Just the mention of it was enough to find myself just about dragged into an Arab eating house and a dozen words from the kid ensured that I got the full treatment. I don't know what the little bastard told them, but from the service I got he must have dropped a hint that I owned an oil field or two.

He himself didn't fare so well, however. As soon as they had got me settled at a low corner table with a good view of the belly-dancer they kicked his arse out of the place.

For an hour or so I picked at the delicacies they put before me on an endless stream of trays and suffered a bit of harmless leg stroking at the hands of a young woman I took to be a trainee dancer. But by that time I had had enough. The carressing had only raised half a hard and, anyway, I was dog-tired after my long drive up from Tunis. I left.

Young brown-eyes was sitting on his haunches by the door when I got into the still-busy alley outside the eating house. He leapt to his feet with his eyes wide and questioning: "Now what, sore?" I playfully clipped his ear and told him: "Now bed," adding when I saw an extra gleam shoot into his bright eyes, "my own bed. Let's go."

We wandered our way back to the Palace and he left me at the door as I made my way up the steps and into the cool interior.

On my way past the porter's lodge I sent a lad off to collect a couple of bottles of cold water from the bar before making my way up to my room. He arrived just after I had come out of the shower and I took the tray from him and put it down by the bed.

The spicy tit-bits I had consumed at the eating house had raised something of a thirst and I lay on the bed sipping the water as I wondered what the Colonel had planned for me the next morning. I woke up shivering. I had fallen asleep whilst lying naked on the bed and with the air-conditioning turned to zero. I danced around the room for a couple of minutes to get my system back into operation before climbing back on to the bed and pulling up the top sheet and a light cover. There was no sense in turning the conditioner up, for by the time I awoke I would need it back at zero.

At seven-thirty I got up, showered and dressed and had breakfast sent up before setting off for a stroll through the fresh streets of the town. Ali, of course, was with me, having picked me up on the hotel steps.

I don't know when the kid ever went home, or even if he had a home to go to. As far as I could tell, he camped on the hotel steps. I never left the place without him at my elbow or on my heels.

I was back in my room at about nine when the telephone rang. It was the Colonel. He had come to pick me up for our trip.

Down in the lobby I found him and his Major, both dressed in combat uniforms and with 45's at their hips. They both bade me good morning and the Colonel took my arm and led me out to a sand-coloured Land Rover parked by the kerb. The Major took the wheel and the Colonel climbed into the back after putting me in the front passenger seat. We set off.

From my knowledge of the town, gleaned from my conducted tours of the last trip, I soon realised that we were heading inland. We passed through Azizia and, after crossing the Gefara Plain and sweeping trhough Giado and Nalut, turned off the metalled road on to a good, if rather bumpy track.

After about twenty miles we arrived at a fair-sized tented military camp. Within the high perimeter there must have been about three hundred tents and a small hutted headquarters section. We entered the camp through a gate guarded by four men with two entrenched and sandbagged heavy machine guns. The perimeter was patrolled by more guards carrying self-loading rifles.

We drove through the tent lines to a flat area at the Eastern end of the camp and then pulled up. All around us men were doing battle-drill in small squads under the command of white NCOs.

In the centre of the area, a dozen men were pushing a Piper Commanche from under a camouflage netting. The Colonel led us towards it.

Five minutes later we were in the air and heading inland across the desert. The pilot, who, from his accent, I judged to be a German, held a straight course for about forty-five minutes before putting us down on another desert strip alongside about fifty tents. As we had come in to land I had seen a number of long narrow hut structures which did not look like either living quarters or offices and when we climbed down from the Piper, the Colonel led me over to the nearest one.

We entered the hut through a door at the side, the Colonel going in first, followed by me and then the Major. In fact the Major bumped into my back as I stopped just inside the door – halted in my tracks by what I saw. I was in what appeared to be a DC 10 airliner. It was a complete mock-up of the real thing – it could have come straight out of Hollywood.

At the front of the "plane" half a dozen men were being lectured in French by a combat-suited instructor with a grenade in his left hand. The Colonel looked round at me and nodded me into the mock-up. He smiled: "Here we train our sky-jackers. It's good, yes?" I nodded and the Colonel led me through to the front of the "plane" and opened a cabin door on to a mock-up of the flight deck – no instruments but with all the seating arranged as in the real thing. We turned off to the side through another door and were back out on the sand.

It was almost unbelievable. Certainly I would never have believed it if I had not seen it with my own eyes. And the guys under instruction were not all Arabs. Two were white and one of these even had red hair. I learned later that the instructor was Algerian.

From the first mock-up the Colonel took me over three more – a BAC 111, a Trident and a Caravelle. There were others which I did not see but men were moving in and around all of them. There was also an old Dakota body being used to train parachutists in jumping procedures.

Later, in a mess tent which was being used by about a dozen officers, five of them white, the Colonel told me: "I wanted you to see this, Leslie, because you must know that we are not playing at toy soldiers. Here we train people who will strike fear into the very heart of Israel and anyone who helps them.

"We need more trained Europeans to help us with our training programme and I know, because I have checked up on you, that you have many friends who fight for money – mercenaries. I will pay you £1,000 for every man who comes to us for one year."

He walked over to a huge paraffin refrigerator in the corner of the tent and came back with three cold beers. As he opened the cans and handed one to me and one to the Major he said: "Our camps are a pretty open secret, but their location and their exact nature are known to very few people. We trust you to keep things that way."

Who was I to disagree with him? Just imagine what would have happened if I'd said that I wouldn't keep his cosy little secrets.

After the beer the Colonel led us out to the Piper and we headed for the coast, landing at the Nalut camp. Three hours later I was in my room at the Palace and almost ready to believe that I had been dreaming. I stripped and took a cold shower to wash off the dust of the long day as I thought the matter over.

Those guys were in real business. The thought crossed my mind that someone ought to do something about them – but it didn't hang around long. There was no sense in being chopped for annoying the Arabs, it wasn't my war, and anyway, if I didn't provide them with their training cadre someone else certainly would. And why shouldn't I earn from them? When the current deal was over, I decided, I would be sending a few old friends to see the Colonel. I towelled myself and dropped on to the bed for a nap.

The rest of the day and evening I spent in the hotel, eating in the dining room and only popping out to the front for a quick chat with Ali when I told him to push off as I was staying in for the night. He believed me and dashed off with the handful of change I gave him.

At about midnight the Colonel telephoned and told me that the ship was due in the following day at about noon. Could he pick me up at eleven the next day to take me down to Zuara? I agreed and turned in for the night.

Before the Colonel arrived next morning I ran the hired Merc round to a garage and topped up with petrol and water – making sure that the emergency petrol cans in the boot were still in good order and that the water containers were re-filled. I got back to the hotel just after ten o'clock.

I then asked Ali, who had travelled with me on my trip to the filling station, to take me down into the Souk to a shop where I could buy a brief-case. Fifteen minutes later we were back at the hotel, Ali happy at having been of service to me and I happy with the purchase of two new and identical executive brief-cases. I placed both the cases in the boot of my car and re-entered the hotel. The Colonel and his side-kick arrived about five minutes later.

Turning down the Colonel's offer of a lift to Zuara, I followed his staff-car to the dock, where we waited until about twelve-thirty for the cargo ship with the consignment to nudge in and berth.

Rene was almost jumping up and down to get ashore after two weeks plodding about the ocean as the ship zig-zagged its way to its destination. He ran down the gangplank and hugged me as soon as the crew secured her.

He, the Colonel and I walked back up to the deck and the skipper welcomed us all. The Colonel, however appeared agitated and at his insistence we declined the offer of drinks in the captain's cabin and moved straight to the hatch covers. By this time the crew had thrown the sheets back and were stacking the hatch planks to the sides of the ship. The derrick was still swinging over as the Colonel and I climbed down the ladder into the hold to inspect the cargo. This time the Colonel opened every box before he allowed it up in the nets and it took a couple of hours to clear the hold into the trucks which had arrived just after the ship had docked.

When the last box was gone we returned to the deck to find Rene and our three guards sitting on the hatch-covers and obviously angry. They had spent a long time at sea and understandably weren't happy at the delay. It was then that I had the idea which was to earn us a quick three grand sterling.

The Colonel was happy that his cargo had arrived intact and he relaxed somewhat. I told him that I had a deal for him and invited him to join me at a local bar for a drink. He agreed.

I then had a word with the skipper and Rene, and suggested that they follow the Colonel and me to the bar and then go straight on to the next one they could find. They also agreed.

I joined the Colonel and the Major in their car and we set off for a bar to which the driver had been directed. We were there in a couple of minutes. Only a few hundred yards away I saw another bar and my Merc, complete with Rene, who was driving, the boys and the skipper, pull up outside of it. I saw the five of them running for the entrance as the Colonel, the Major and I walked to a pavement table at the place to which the Colonel had taken us.

I ordered three beers and, after they had arrived, I asked for the second stage payment. The Colonel and I walked over to his car and he picked a brief-case from the back seat as he climbed in with me following him. He dialled the combination before handing it to me. I counted the money and, in so far as I could calculate the exchange rates, it was all there. I thanked him and got out of the car carrying the case.

I then told him I would see him in a short while and moved over to the Merc, which was on the other side of the road. Rene saw me arrive and came out. I asked him for the keys, unlocked the boot and transferred the money from the Colonel's case to one of those I had bought in the Souk. I then walked back to the Colonel and the Major at the other bar, returning his case as I sat down. He said: "There's no need to give me back the case, Leslie." I replied that he might need it again and we all laughed.

I finished my beer and asked the Colonel to excuse me yet again before going back to the bar at which Rene and the boys were killing a second bottle of arak. Quickly I told the three heavies that the Colonel could offer them soft, well paid posts as instructors if they wanted to do a deal with him. They were interested.

I took the three of them, leaving Rene with the skipper, back over to the Colonel and, reminding him of our trip the day before, asked him to talk to them about it. He smiled, realising that I was trying to earn myself a quick three grand. "O.K.," he said. He invited the men to join us.

While he was propositioning the guys I strolled back to the Merc and called Rene over as I told him of the training deal the Colonel had offered us. Then, at the car, I took from the boot the second case I had bought in the Souk – the one I had not put the Colonel's money in. With this in my hand I walked back over to the other group.

As we reached them the Colonel stood up and smiled widely as he said: "Leslie, you are the best recruiting officer a general could want. Your friends have all agreed to come in and help us." Then I smiled. Not only would I not have to pay the return fares of the three guys, I was actually going to make three grand out of them. I took the three of them on one side and paid them the £500 each we had agreed for the trip and sent them over to Rene to get their luggage.

They returned to our bar along with Rene and the skipper and I offered to run the captain back to his ship. He agreed right away, probably because I still owed him half his trip money. When we got to the dock I gave him his £7,000 and bade him farewell. He told me he would put out as soon as he had re-fuelled. It was the last I was to see of him on that trip.

Back at the bar Rene and the three gunners were boisterously drunk. The Major was getting that way but the Colonel was holding himself aloof and was looking down his nose at the whole party. I took him over the road to the other bar and ordered coffee. I wanted to know about my three grand.

He told me, reasonably I thought, that he could not pay me until we had got the men out to his camp. Would I accept payment in Malta?

Well, why not? If he let me down he was losing out on both an arms dealer and a recruiting officer. I agreed.

I then told him that I thought we should leave his three new recruits and Rene to enjoy themselves at the bar and asked him to give me a lift back to Tripoli. He agreed and we moved back over to the other bar.

There, taking Rene by the arm I led him back to the Merc. He didn't argue when I told him that the money was in the boot and that as soon as I left the area with the Colonel he was to take the Merc and, leaving the lads to their own devices, head over into Tunis, check the car in and then shoot off to Amsterdam where I would meet him in the Hilton in a few days.

With Rene briefed and my team paid off there was nothing to keep me hanging around in Zuara any longer. I told the Colonel that I was ready to leave as soon as he was. He nodded and sent the Major over to collect his car. We all set off for the city, the Colonel and I sitting in the back of the car with me clutching the empty brief-case.

During the journey I told the Colonel that I intended to set off for home the next day and he asked me to be in Amsterdam and in touch with his office a week later. They dropped me off at the Palace where I went straight up to my room to clean up after the long, hot day. I showered and then slept for a couple of hours before leaving the hotel at about eight-thirty to stroll up through the Souk with Ali. I was feeling relaxed and particularly pleased with the way things had gone on the deal we had just pulled off.

Ali took me through the Souk to the same eating house I had been to a couple of days before where I settled into a dark, cushioned corner to watch the belly dancer and wait for the meal.

As on the previous occasion, I had hardly settled in when the nubile young bird glided over to settle alongside me on the cushions. When the food arrived she proceeded to feed me the delicately spiced morsels and I remember thinking that it was a pity that knives and forks had ever been invented – to say nothing of Women's Lib. Her total subservience as she fed me with one hand and caressed me with the other, would have had Germaine Greer in a state of apoplexy. Me, I just enjoyed it.

After a couple of hours or so the girl took me gently by the hand and pulled me to my feet before leading me through to a room off a corridor behind the eating room. Here, she quietly eased me back on to the cushions which covered most of the floor and, using the just audible rhythm filtering through from the other room, started to dance. As she danced she slowly discarded her flimsy clothing. Apart from the fact that she only had five articles to drop off as she swirled between the cushions, I was treated to my own dance of the seven veils.

She dropped the last flimsy veil from her hips as she undulated only about three feet away and then, holding my eyes fixed on hers, settled down beside me and started to unbutton my shirt.

I quickly hefted my thirty-eight from its belt holster and slid it under the large cushion at my back. She didn't even notice me doing it. One button at a time, and with much caressing, it must have taken about ten minutes to ease my shirt off, before her hands moved on to my trouser belt.

She had just pulled the end from the retaining loop when the door burst open and young Ali raced in shouting in his falsetto voice. I only caught the odd word as he gabbled but what did come through, snatched me right back from the cloud upon which I was floating. What I heard was "Men ... coming ... asking boss." He stood with his back to the door, panting, trying to get his breath.

Then the world blew up. The door crashed open a second time, throwing Ali forward towards me and the girl, who was by this time cowering against the wall and holding a cushion across her breasts. I quickly pulled my thirty-eight out from under the cushion and cocked it as Ali careered towards me. Hard behind him came two men in Arab dress who paused as their eyes tried to adjust to the dim lighting. Ali spun round to face them and, crouching low, tried to dart between them for the door. He stopped on the end of a long curved knife which the one on my left thrust at his chest. For a fraction of a second his light body hung on the blade before sliding to the floor. The girl screamed. By now I was in a kneeling, double-handed firing position and the man to my right shouted as he spun round for the door. As the bullet crashed into the back of his neck it threw him forward, slamming the door shut with his body.

The other man then leapt for the drapes to his left, apparently going for the window. He was just grasping at them when my second bullet smashed into his spine. He flattened against the wall and then slid to the floor, bringing the curtains down on top of him. Behind them there was no window anyway – they were there purely for decorative effect.

Grabbing my shirt, I moved over to Ali – he was very dead, a trickle of blood coming from his mouth as his head lolled over when I examined him. I knew by instinct that the other two were the same way and took off through the door after pulling the Arab in front of it away by his ankle.

The whole incident had only lasted a few seconds but as I made my way into the corridor the proprietor of the place and one of his henchmen were coming through the door from the eating room. They eased aside, trying to force themselves into the walls of the hallway, when they saw the hardware in my right hand. I ran past them, through the main room and on out into the Souk.

Ten minutes later I was back in the Palace and opening my room door. The place looked as if a bomb had hit it. The mattress had been ripped to shreds, the fitted wardrobes had been torn from the wall and even the facia panel on the bath had been prised away. My luggage was scattered all over the room and the black brief-case lay open on the floor. Someone had been after my money.

As quickly as I could, I threw what clothing I could find into my suitcase and quit the room, hurrying down to the desk to check out.

The doorman got me a taxi and I bolted into it as he held the door open for me, telling the driver to take me to the airport. Then, after being driven for about three minutes I told the guy to stop, paid him off and waited until he had disappeared before making my way down to the dock area on foot.

Once there I felt better, safer. Ports all over the world are much of a muchness. In this respect they are rather like airport lounges – the experienced traveller can find his way round without having a close knowledge of the exact layout. I made my way to the deep-water berths and the half-dozen or so vessels there.

Within half an hour, after two abortive attempts, I had arranged with the skipper of a German coaster to ship out with him at first light. I told him that I had got into trouble gambling in the Souk and had to leave in a hurry. The $1,000 I offered him for protection overnight and passage to his next port of call – Malta – convinced him that my story was true and he gave his own cabin over to me, placing a couple of crewmen on guard outside the door.

True to his word he sailed at dawn and, as soon as we had left coastal waters, he came down and invited me up on to the bridge. I spent the rest of that day lazing in the sun on the hatch covers and drinking cold beer. Next morning we arrived at Sliema. From there I took a cab straight to the airport where I booked a ticket through to Amsterdam. By nightfall I was bringing Rene up to date on the robbery attempt.

We came to the conclusion as we talked that the only people who could have known that I was worth robbing would be the Colonel and his aides. Somewhere there had been a leak.

It was highly improbable that the Colonel himself would have sold me out because that would have meant finding new delivery boys. But, whoever it was, he would have to be rooted out in double-quick time. We decided to throw the ball into the Colonel's court and telephoned his Geneva office right then to tell them that it was imperative that we should meet him at the first opportunity.

Two days later he arrived in Amsterdam and I filled him in on the attack and attempted robbery – not, of course, telling him that Rene had already left with the money beforehand. He reacted with massive fury and, using Arabic, cursed for a full two minutes. He then told us that he had heard of the attack and my involvement in it within half an hour of its taking place. He had even arranged for the disposal of the bodies – much to the satisfaction of the eating-house proprietor. However, he told us, he had thought that I had fallen foul of local gangsters in some sort of side deal – probably drugs – and that his men had been trying to get a trace on me ever since and he was half-convinced that I was dead when he got the message that we wanted to see him.

We told him that no way were we going to work for him until he weeded out his informant and he left after promising to let us know when he had dealt with the man, or men, responsible for the attack.

This let-up in the arms business came at just the right time. The next night Rene and I bumped into Ginger Aussie and we took in a few bars after dinner – he was in the City looking for help with a couple of cigarette shipments from Dubrovnic to Italy. He had been offered the deal by a small time operator in Naples, and being known only as a 'heavy', couldn't find a skipper prepared to trust him. He offered us half the profits on the deal if we could organise things for him.

Eventually we agreed on a three-way split on the profits and by noon the next day we had two boats standing by in Malta and Endo was looking for crews. By the time we joined Endo in Malta that same night the whole deal was fixed.

The boats Endo has found for us were well-converted ex-Royal Air Force launches and their skipper and crews had been on the scene long enough to know their jobs. At a conference in the Roundabout pub it was decided that I would travel on the lead boat and that Rene would be on the second boat.

It was not possible for Rene to operate the radio in the landing zone because of our recent run-in with the Italian authorities. He briefed the Aussie on the codes instead and sent him off to Naples the next morning to instruct the pick-up party and keep a general watch on that end of the operation. Before he left Rene also gave him the name of a man who would provide the equipment for the radio link and help him set up a monitor to listen in on the waterguard chatter.

Left with three or four days to spend in Malta, Rene and I took advantage of the time to renew old acquaintances and it was while we were doing this that we learned of a three-boat delivery which would be leaving Dubrovnic at about the same time as ours. The trip was being organised by a couple of Americans who had come to Malta especially to recruit their crews. Their boats had been brought over from Gibraltar and the whole crowd were virtually unknown to the locals.

Someone, however, had told them that Rene and I might be able to advise them and they came to us for help. We agreed to help them only if they delayed their trip until after ours, which they did not know about. They agreed to hold back for a couple of weeks in return for advice on landing areas and radio links and we would be paid £1,000 if the trip came off.

It was a good deal, they had no local help apart from transport and warehousing and they intended to market the goods themselves when they got them into Italy. They stood to make a huge profit.

The day after we had passed on our suggestions and tips for their operation Endo told us that the Yanks intended to set sail for Dubrovic in three days' time, and once there, to make the trip as soon as possible.

He did not know that we had come to a deal with them over timing and we never told him. After he had left us we decided to take action against the Yanks which would teach them a lesson, and, at the same time, make us a few grand.

We worked out the approximate landing time of the three boats to within about a day and then sent a cable to a friend of Rene's in Italy with details of the whole trip, including the radio frequencies they would use. Our man would tip off the waterguard and pick up a few million ells which we would split between us later on.

We also sent an urgent cable to the Aussie and gave him the date and time for our drop. This, we had decided, would take place on the same night as that of the Yanks but fifty miles further up the coast. While the waterguard were busy with the other boats we would be left alone to work in peace.

Two days later, as the Yanks were preparing their boats to set out the following day, we set off for Dubrovnic just before dusk. We arrived at the Dubrovnic berth in mid-afternoon two days later and had loaded both boats and re-fuelled before dark.

At first light Rene took his boat out again to cruise at minimum knots for Sicily. I remained in port after moving my boat to a situation well away from the warehouse where the Yanks would load up.

They arrived at about ten o'clock and started loading all three boats after about an hour. I walked back up the harbour to the dock office and discovered from a friendly Slav I had met on a number of previous trips that they would be putting out within an hour or two. As soon as I was back on board I had the skipper head out and make course for Sicily. At cruising speed and using the radar we came up with Rene at about five in the evening. Two hours later our radar picked up the three boats which were running on almost the same course as we were.

All through the night we cruised ahead of them, making sure they remained at about the same distance behind us. We had decided previously that they were unlikely to suspect vessels in front of 'tailing' them. They were by no means experienced smugglers and in any event no one would interfere with them in international waters.

We came up on Sicily during darkness after about 36 hours fair cruising and made as if to head straight over for Malta, reducing speed as we watched our screens until the other three boats cut back to the West around the point at Pachino.

We then put over to the West and North ourselves and allowed the Yanks to get well ahead. We now knew that they would make their drop the next night. All we had to do was pass them at distance the next day and make for our drop-zone as soon as we heard the fracas begin when the waterguard pounced.

During the whole of the next day we cruised slowly up the West coast of Italy and hove-to just after dark just above Naples. At about one o'clock in the morning all hell suddenly broke loose on the radio as the waterguard pounced on the Yanks. We made straight in for our drop, radioing the shore man as we went. Half an hour later we were off the beach with both our boats off-loading. The radio was still alive with the troubles the Americans were having and we felt confident as the dinghies purred back and forth from ship to shore. The whole drop went like clockwork and Ginger Aussie came aboard my boat as the dinghy came back for the last time. He had collected his second payment and we had no more business in Italy.

We must have been about half a mile off shore with about the same distance between our two boats when trouble hit us. Although there was virtually no moon, it was possible to see a few hundred yards across the shimmering, light swell. I was at the wheel while the skipper got his head down after the long, boring, trip up the drop-point. Suddenly, dead ahead, a searchlight came up at us from low in the water at a point about three hundred yards away. Within seconds a fast fourteen foot launch had swept past raking us with her searchlight. It was impossible to see much of her, blinded as I was by the light, but I was certain that she was up to no good as far as we were concerned.

100

I quickly assessed the situation. We had nothing to fear from the waterguard, having dropped our cargo, and could probably talk our way out of trouble if stopped. But I suddenly realised that I had not switched on the lights after putting out from the dropping area. That would provide extra suspicion for any customs man. At the same time I realised that, if taken ashore for questioning, the authorities would soon check up and find out about my last escapade. I smashed the throttle in and put the bows up to the sky. We would have to try to outrun the launch.

I looked back and saw the wake from the launch curving round in a tight circle as she came back round at us with her searchlight sweeping in a wide arc. There was no doubt she was after us and with the throttles full out we were making about twenty-five knots straight out to sea. She had a good ten knots on us and slowly overhauled us about fifty yards to port as her light attempted to hold us – a very difficult feat with two pitching and bouncing boats going flat out.

Over the noise of the engines I heard the chatter of machine-gun fire as tracer floated towards us, passing just over our bows. We were in serious trouble. Ginger Aussie was firing back from the port gun point but it was unlikely that he could home in on the other boat – she was so low in the water and presented almost no profile.

She started to pull ahead and across our bows. We had a chance. I yanked the wheel over and headed for a point where I reckoned our paths would intercept.

Much too late the helmsman on the other boat realised that we were almost on him and tried to pull away from our bows. We crunched into him on his rear starboard corner and his engine must have been wrecked immediately – we ploughed on through the boat, unable to stop even if we had wanted to.

As I looked back into the wake there was nothing to be seen and I swung round in a tight circle to the approximate spot where the collision had taken place and throttled back. There were four guys swimming in the water, one of them clutching a chunk of wood from the smashed boat. I pulled away and told the skipper to throw a dinghy over when we passed them again but to take the engine off first. As I put about again he and the Aussie unlashed one of our shuttle-boats, took the engine off and threw it over the side. I made out to sea again at cruising speed and headed for home. We were back in Valletta to be greeted by a very worried Rene by nightfall.

On the whole it had been a good trip. With the reward money from the Italian end and our share of the Aussie's take, Rene and I were well funded and didn't need to touch our earnings from the Colonel. We decided to take a break and flew back to Amsterdam the next day.

From Amsterdam I telephoned the Colonel's Geneva office and asked for them to get him in touch with me. Two days later the Major arrived at the Hilton to see me with a message that the men behind the double-cross had been found and dealt with. The Colonel would arrive the next day to pay me for the three mercenaries and offer me a new deal.

Rene had moved on to Geneva to spend some time with Lisette and I tried to contact her at the Bank office, but was told she was on two weeks' leave. She and Rene had gone away. I would have to deal with the Colonel on my own.

When he arrived he came straight to my hotel from the airport and called me from the lobby where I joined him before moving through for a drink in the bar.

I had never seen him looking so happy. He explained why: "Leslie, we have the very good news. The embargo is not operating against us any more and we can now get all the guns and explosive we want from our friends. What we want now is more men for our training cadre and someone to organise their travel to our camps. We want you to do this. Will you help us?"

I didn't realise it at the time but I was about to start work for Black September.

I agreed to help him.

He then gave me my instructions, which were to send likely men to his recruiting office in the Rue Cabler in Paris where they would be vetted. If possible, I was to send them in groups of five or six. Then, if suitable, the groups would be sent to Tangiers and shipped by boat to Tripoli.

This route remained the main method of sending the instructors through to Black September for at least two years. It may even still be in existence.

During the next few months I sent him about sixty recruits at £1,000 a head and, on two occasions, travelled with them. In Tangiers I learned that the recruits are mustered in one of three hotels, the Kabult, the Amhindra or the Blue Garden. When he had ten or more assembled they would be shipped out for Tripoli and taken by truck from there up to the training area at Hammadah Al Hamra. It was this camp to which I had been taken by the Colonel very early in our dealings.

At the time I saw nothing wrong in helping the Colonel provide the training facility for his army. Now, of course, I realise that he was training the very men who were to bring terror to the whole world with their hijackings and urban warfare.

I did not even give too much thought to the matter when I was offered £2,000 to escort six Southern Irishmen from Dublin all the way to the training area using my own route through Tunis.

At the time everyone considered the IRA as some sort of political nuts. In fact, in my party there was a prominent young Irish politician who I was to meet several times in the years to come.

Chapter 4
Creation of Kovaks

In February, 1970, after a particularly busy couple of months ferrying arms from the Colonel's growing stockpile into Spain for Basque terrorists, I decided to take a long break at home in England.

Flying direct from Rome, where I had ended up after my last trip, I arrived at Heathrow airport just before noon to find myself confronted by a posse of Special Branch men at the immigration control desk. Politely, but firmly, they asked me to accompany them to an office in the administration section of the building and, being certain that I had committed no crime in Britain, I agreed with some confidence. There was nothing they could confront me with which could worry me unduly. Or so I thought.

When I was shown into the room there were already four men there, three sitting around a desk and one sitting to one side. I was offered the fifth chair.

The man behind the desk opened the conversation: "We know all about your business in the Middle East, Aspin – or Allen, or whatever you wish to call yourself. You've been up to a lot of no good for a long time."

Then, taking it in turns, the other men outlined the major stages of my recent career with almost complete accuracy. I said nothing until they were finished and then said: "I don't know what you are talking about and, even if what you have said is true, you have no reason to hold me in this country. I deny everything you have said."

For fifteen hours the men took turns at questioning me about specific trips and kept firing names at me — names of people I had worked with or for. They did not mention the Bank, Rene, the Colonel or the training camp.

I denied everything. One thing puzzled me, however. They never once mentioned anyone dying while I had been around. I felt sure they were trying to trap me into a situation where I would admit to an offence which would allow a foreign power to have me extradited.

During the interview no one raised his voice and the whole business was conducted in a gentlemanly manner. They questioned and I denied knowledge of the whole affair.

In the early hours of the morning, after some fourteen hours of interrogation, a tall man, well spoken and immaculately dressed in a blue pin-stripe suit, came into the room. He nodded the others out.

After settling behind the desk he leaned forward onto his elbows and said: "Leslie. We obviously know what you have been up to and all we want you to do is help us. We are not in the least concerned with what you have been doing — apart from the fact that you can be of great assistance to us. We only want you to tell us who you have been dealing with and where their meeting places are.

"You are in a position to help your country in the fight against terrorism. You know these Arabs are a bad lot and are training all sorts of undesirables to create dreadful havoc internationally.

"There is a worsening situation in Ulster and we think that the Arabs are helping extremists over there by providing training and arms — to say nothing of explosives. You can help us nip all this in the bud. It is your duty to help your country.

"Now come on, be sensible and help us."

I replied that I was sorry but that I had no information which could help them. I had now become certain that they were trying to trap me. The mention of Ireland had frightened me — that was getting rather close to home. I remember thinking that it was time I took a long holiday.

The man behind the desk shrugged and told me: "You will be given time to think things over. Remember, it is your duty to help us. Go straight home and do not attempt to leave your own locality. You will be kept under close observation from now on. We will contact you later."

He pressed a button on the desk and one of the others returned to the room to be told to hand over my luggage and take me out of the building. This man took me with him to another room where I was handed my two cases and then ushered me out into the passenger area where he left me to make my own way.

I boarded an airport bus into London and then took a train out to my home town.

My wife and the kids were still in bed when I arrived and I moved quietly through the house so as not to wake them. I needed time to think and made myself a pot of coffee as I pondered on what the SB people had said. I lay back in an armchair to think things over.

The next thing I knew I had one of the lads bouncing up and down on me and shouting to his mother that dad was home. I had fallen asleep before I had even started to work things out. I decided to try to forget the whole thing. Maybe they would leave me alone and their parting words had only been an empty threat.

During the next couple of days I settled back into family life and thoughts of the airport incident came less frequently. I had decided that I would almost certainly give up the smuggling business, collect my money from the various deposits I had used round the world and buy into a respectable business.

But on the third day at home, the well-dressed guy who had concluded the session at Heathrow arrived at my door. I invited him in and, as we sat in my lounge, he again put forward his plea that I should help my country. I again refused.

I explained to him that my reasons for doing so were not that I wished to be unpatriotic, or even unhelpful, I knew damned well that most informers ended up very, very dead and I had no wish to retire in that way.

The guy then came back with the offer I couldn't refuse, so to speak. He said: "Well, Leslie, much as I hate saying this, we think that having your help is so important that we are prepared to blackmail you. If you don't help us we will leak the information to your old contacts that you have helped us. We and our friends abroad have just sufficient knowledge to act against a few of the people you have worked with and that will convince your old pals that we are telling the truth. They will be convinced that you have betrayed them. That will put you in the same situation that you would be in if you actually did give us the help we require.

"Why not, then, join us and be paid for your help?"

So I agreed.

The man stood up, shook my hand and moved to the door of the room. As I showed him out of the front door he turned and said: "We will arrange a meeting very soon. Thank you."

That same evening I received a telephone call asking me to be in a coffee house just off the high street of my home town at eleven the next morning. I would be met there by a man who would explain precisely what was required of me.

I turned up at the coffee house at the appointed time to find the man who had called the previous day sitting at a corner table. He nodded and stood to place a chair for me.

Already on the table he had an extra cup and he smiled as he poured coffee into it for me. He said: "I do not wish to talk business in here, it's a nice day and we'll take a stroll when you have finished your coffee. We are very pleased that you are going to help us and I've been asked to thank you by a very senior person."

I was nervous and just nodded my reply.

After a couple of cups of coffee the man paid the bill and we left the building. As we went through the door two men, who had been sitting at the tables on either side of us, followed. They remained about fifty yards from us during the rest of our meeting.

As we strolled around the town the man gently extracted from me all the key names in my dealings with the Arabs over the past year. I told him of the Colonel and his side-kick Major and gave him the addresses and telephone numbers for the pair and their associates throughout Europe. I gave him details on Rene, the Bank and its managers and of the Irishmen I had helped into Libya. I also gave him the names of skippers and boats I knew to be involved with shipping Arab arms throughout Europe.

He made very careful notes of all that I told him and after some forty minutes, apparently satisfied with my assistance, he left me in the town centre and made for the railway station with his watchdogs still on his tail.

I had been given no further instructions by the man and as I made my way home I convinced myself that I had seen the last of him. What a bloody great mistake that was.

Exactly a week later I received a telephone call from London and immediately recognised the voice as being that of the man I had given the information to. He asked me to travel to London the following day on the morning train. He would have me picked up at the station on my arrival. He had, he explained, one or two more questions to put to me. I agreed to go. There was nothing I could now do to back off from the deal at any event. I was already in over my head and at the mercy of the guy at the other end of the line.

When I arrived in London I was approached as I passed through the ticket barrier by a mousy individual who said: "I've been asked to collect you and take you to the guv'nor." I smiled. It was like something out of a bad spy novel. He led me out of the terminal to the cab rank where, after queueing for some ten minutes, he ushered me into a taxi, telling the driver to take us to the Cumberland Hotel.

Once at the hotel the man took me up to a room on the fourth floor and knocked on the door. It was opened by a man I did not know, who nodded me through and followed me in.

The man I had been dealing with previously was sitting at a small desk against the window and he waved me to an armchair in front of it. The other guy sat on the edge of the bed.

As I took a cigarette from the pack in my shirt pocket, the man behind the desk opened a file and said: "We've checked out most of your information and, somewhat to our surprise, have discovered that you have been absolutely straight with us.

"Now look, old boy, you can be of much more use to us than we at first thought. I want you to think very carefully about what I am going to say.

"It appears to us that you are in a situation where you can infiltrate yourself into the worsening Irish situation and become one of our most valuable men in that field. We are prepared to pay you very handsomely to do this and do what we can to guarantee your safety while you are doing it.

"We do not think, anyway, that you will be in much danger, dealing, as you will be, with people whose trust you have earned over a number of years. Now, should you agree to join us — and we are using no pressures such as those we had to employ at first — we are prepared to pay you £1,000 for the information you have already given us and similarly generous sums for your help in the future.

"We will pay all your expenses in retaining your contacts and making new ones on our behalf and we will also provide money with which you can set up any arrangements we should ask you to make."

I didn't have to give the matter much thought. The thousand pounds was there for the taking and, if future payments didn't come up to scratch, I could always quit. Besides, the idea of being on the side of the angels appealed immensely.

I replied that I was their man. The man behind the desk smiled widely. I got the impression that he had expected a battle with me. He said: "Let's get things sorted out, then. My name is Homer, Mr. Homer if you like." he consulted a piece of paper in the file before him and continued: "Your name, your code name for when you contact me, will be Kovaks, K-O-V-A-K-S."

He then wrote down a number of things on a small piece of paper which he handed to me. When I read it I saw that he had listed code names for a number of men, including Rene and Endo and also alternative names for arms, ammunition, explosives, missiles, and launchers, the IRA, Ireland, Dublin, Libya, Tunisia and, as an afterthought, grenades. I list them in that order because that is the order in which he wrote them. I still have that piece of notepaper and on the reverse side is an address in the Home Counties and a cable address in London. There is also an instruction not to send telegrams or express communications to the Home Counties address — this, I later discovered, was because it was nothing but a 'dead-letter box'.

Deliberately I have not given the code names for the people and articles above, or the addresses, because it is not my intention to compromise my old firm, much as I now feel they have let me down.

Homer waited for me to read the writing on the piece of paper and then said: "You are now working for what is popularly known as the

109

Secret Service. Here", handing me another slip of paper, "are two telephone numbers where you can contact me at any time in an emergency, or when requested to do so to receive instructions. You will also be in touch with a Special Branch man in your own area who will act as a liaison between you and us. He will also see that your family are looked after in your absence and keep a fatherly eye on you when you are on your home territory. Now, to business."

He went on to explain that, although I had a few links with the Arabs and the IRA I was only in as far as the shallow end. There were others well established in the field and an increasing amount of gear was finding its way into Southern Ireland and on to Belfast.

He continued: "I want you to get in to the big league on our behalf. I don't care how you do it, but we've got to get a man inside to feed us with information. You have all the funds you need and you will be allowed to make whatever deals you consider necessary to establish your cover in this field.

"Here are the names of people at foreign embassies who we suspect are helping the IRA."

He gave me a list of Arab and Continental embassies. Against each was at least one name. I raised my eyebrows at him and he went on: "Yes, we do seem to have a lot of non-friends in our camp, don't we, dear boy?"

He then produced a slim grey tape recorder and told me that I was to contact as many of the people on the list as possible, especially the Arabs, and talk over with them the question of helping their smuggling activities. These conversations I was to record on the tape machine. He explained that I would have the machine fitted to my body by one of his men before meeting any of the men in Britain. For meetings abroad I would have to rely on my recollection after leaving the person concerned.

After telling me to contact him as soon as I had made reasonable headway Homer gave me an envelope which, I later discovered, contained £1,500 and stood up. Obviously our meeting was at an end. I left the room and was escorted downstairs by the same guy who had collected me from the station. He had, it appeared, been hanging around in the corridor during our talk.

I returned home and immediately put through a call to the Colonel's office in Geneva. He was not there and I asked that he should telephone me on a safe line as soon as possible.

I spent the evening watching television with my wife. Over the years she had learned not to ask about my business and, apart from the kids, this left us damn-all to talk about anyway. We went to bed at about ten-thirty.

The Colonel called me back at about three in the morning, having just got my message. He had been trying to contact me for some time, he said, explaining that he wanted some work undertaken. I asked him when we could meet in Amsterdam and he agreed to meet me there the next afternoon — about thirty-six hours later.

I slept through until lunchtime and then left for London to catch an evening flight to Holland, getting to the Hilton in time for a quick sandwich before turning in for the night.

The Colonel arrived just after two the next afternoon and came straight up to my room after calling me from the lobby. Firstly I asked him what deal he had been needing me for. I was amazed when he replied that he wanted me to concentrate on getting things organised for the Irish, with whom, he explained, he now had a closer liaison. He was playing right into the hands of my new bosses.

I didn't leap straight at his offer of Irish business. Homer already knew about him and his Irish link. He now wanted to find out about other supply sources for IRA arms.

I told the Colonel that I intended to base myself on London in future and that I was trying to cut Rene loose from the business. He was being too greedy, I explained. Used to intrigue on the grand Arabic scale he appeared to understand that he was only to deal with me in future and gave me the names of two men at his London embassy who would take over from him if I insisted on working in the capital. He also gave me contact men in Paris, Rome and Germany. Already in possession of the addresses in Malta, Amsterdam and Geneva, I now had a complete list of his European offices.

The Colonel then told me that he was supplying arms and explosives free to the IRA and that all they had to do was organise the shipping. He asked me to liaise with them over this and I then received from him the names of two men in Dublin with whom I should deal.

In all, our conversation lasted about two hours. After the Colonel

111

had left I packed my bags and set off for London.

By eight that evening I was back at the Cumberland hotel and talking with Homer. I had called his office from the airport and been told to make my own way to the hotel. At the time I thought that the Cumberland was a sub-HQ for my new boss but later I realised that, along with other large and impersonal London hotels, they just booked rooms to suit their requirements.

I told Homer of the whole conversation with the Colonel and he was delighted, telling me that he had never expected such rapid progress. He then suggested that I should move into the Tara hotel in Kensington and that I should wait for him to call on me there the next morning. I asked him who was to pick the bill up and he explained that ALL my expenses were down to them from that time on.

I took a cab to the Tara and booked in, hopping into bed as soon as I had showered.

At nine-thirty the next morning Homer was in the lobby of the hotel and asking if he could come up. I had just finished my breakfast and felt pretty well rested. This was unusual for me. It was at that time that I first noticed that I was waking frequently during the night and was getting out of bed in the morning feeling all washed out.

When Homer arrived at my door he had his number two with him – the man who had been at our first interview in the Cumberland. He introduced him as Frank Abbott. He appeared to be to Homer what the Major was to the Colonel. I remember thinking that they were all playing the same game, by the same rules and with the same teams. I later discovered that Frank Abbott was a cover name.

The first thing Homer did when he sat down on the bed was to throw an envelope across to me. I was standing at the window at the time and caught it as it thumped against my chest. When I opened it I found that it contained £500 in five pound notes. "Expenses" said Homer, holding out a slip of paper to me. I took it and read it – it was a bloody receipt.

I took the pen which Frank held out and scribbled a signature of sorts on the piece of paper before handing it back to Homer. He smiled and placed it carefully in his inside pocket.

Homer then set to and briefed me to call on all the men whose names the Colonel had given me, as soon as possible, with the exception of the Irishmen. They would have to wait a while. I agreed to do this and Homer suggested that I should start there and then.

From a brief-case which he had brought in with him, Frank took one of the small tape-recorders and asked me to lift my shirt. When I did so he place the machine in a specially constructed belt and strapped it round my waist – the machine being at the back. From the recorder he ran a wire round my body and taped the mike itself to my chest.

With my jacket on the whole assembly was invisible and could only be detected if I was properly searched or had my back patted over-enthusiastically. I was happy that I could avoid trouble over the gadget.

Homer continued his briefing by telling me that I must draw from the contact I was to make as much as possible about routes and actual weapons and also get them to name as many of their compatriots as possible. Such information, he explained, could well be invaluable from a political standpoint in the future.

He suggested that I do one call a day and that I should liaise with Frank, who he was then calling "the Major", about being fitted with the recorder before going on my meetings.

I pointed out to him that I was wary of going about his business unarmed. I had not brought any weapons back into London at the time I was picked up by his Special Branch colleagues and had resisted the temptation on my last trip.

He agreed that I could arm myself, but explained that he could not provide the documentation to cover it. If, however, I found myself in any embarrassing situation whilst working for him, I would only have to telephone his number to have the matter sorted out.

I agreed to go along with this assurance and asked if Frank could come back to the hotel in the early afternoon, about two-thirty, to wire me up before I set off on my first mission. They agreed to do this.

After they had left I finished dressing before leaving the hotel and setting off by cab for Earl's Court and the Zambesi Club.

At the club, a much-favoured haunt of mercenaries and Anzac adventurers, I found an old friend from Malta. We had a couple of drinks as I explained my need to "tool-up" and he took me over to the Colehearn pub, just over the road, to introduce me to a raving queer who squeezed my hand rather than shook it. My old mate, Jimmy, held a quick whispered conversation with the queer and turned back to me: "A good thirty-eight – not hot – one ton." A hundred quid was too expensive but I was in no mood to haggle and it was all down to Homer anyway. I agreed to take it if I could have it within the hour and got thirty rounds thrown in.

Another quick whispering session with the queer and the deal was done. We went back to the club as the other guy (gal?) set off up the road.

Well, within the hour the queer came into the club with a brown manilla envelope which he handed to me as we all three stood drinking at the bar. I took the package to the toilet and examined it. It was O.K.

Back in the bar, I handed over the bundle of fivers to Jimmy, who proceeded to peel four off before handing them on to the odd-one. I laughed. Not a bad reward for a quick introduction. However, it was no skin off my nose. We had another drink and I left them, getting back to the Tara just before the Major arrived.

As arranged I called at the Libyan embassy that afternoon and, after being well quizzed by a couple of flunkeys, was ushered into the office of the military attaché. The Colonel had already briefed him and I merely went over the same sort of ground with him that I had with the Colonel. During conversation it emerged that the consulate itself held a pretty big armoury which included a large supply of plastic explosive in a London store. He even offered to allow me to draw from his store should I have immediate requests for supplies in London.

I left him after about an hour and returned to the Tara to telephone Frank. He instructed me to meet him in St. James's Park near the restaurant and, when I met him about half an hour later, he took the tape machine from me, giving me another.

I arranged with him to meet at the airport the following morning to fly out and make contact with the Continental end of the Colonel's operation.

For the next three weeks I moved from place to place, always under the watchful eyes of either Frank or Homer, as I gained the confidence of the Arab terror organisers and committed them to tape. Never once did I fall under suspicion and I was able to pass on to my bosses not only names of Arabs but names and addresses of local people who ran arms dumps for various anarchist groups. I was introduced to these people by the Arab contacts as an alternative source of supply should the Arabs not be able to assist for any reason.

Homer was more than happy at the way my infiltration had gone and I was beginning to enjoy the whole thing. Intrigue had always fascinated me, almost as much as money, and here I had a bag full of both. The next step, Homer decided, was Ireland.

I took a week off and returned home to my family before setting out to meet the Irish. During this period I noticed even more how badly I was sleeping. Over recent weeks I had been able to blame my restlessness on the worrying I was doing over my visits to the Arab suppliers. Now I had no such excuse and, if anything, I was sleeping hardly at all. I visited my wife's doctor but all he could tell me was that I was apparently very fit and some people did not need as much sleep as others. He did not consider that my insomnia was harming my health, but he gave me a prescription for sleeping pills.

I have never liked taking drugs and never did get round to trying them. It has always struck me that it's plain bloody crazy to drug yourself to sleep in my job. Just think how easy it would make it for the guy who wants to creep in and slice up your liver, for instance.

So. Off to the Emerald Isle and the Tara Tower hotel, from which I made a couple of phone calls to the men mentioned by the Colonel. I reached one of them and he agreed to come and see me with some friends that night.

When they arrived, about an hour after I had had dinner, there were four of them. One I had met before – he had been on the party I had taken over to Libya. The others were strangers.

Because of my previous connections with them and their politician friend, they set straight in to explain their problems to me. They were, they said, recruiting and training large numbers of men for a concerted attempt to wrest the whole of Ireland back from the English. The Arabs had been helping with training and weapons and had offered to carry on doing so.

However, they did not trust the "wogs" and suspected that at the end of the day they would have to pay a very big bill in the way of support in one way or another. They would rather set up their deals with me – could I help them?

In my turn, I explained that of course I could help them – I had a big organisation behind me (I grinned as I said that) and could lay on whatever they needed.

At this time I, and many other people, thought that the IRA was a bloody great joke – a lot of idiot Irishmen playing at insurrectionists. I never thought for one minute that they would start slinging real bombs all around Belfast and even England.

They asked me if I could begin supplying them with plastic explosive. So far the Arabs had not given them any of this and they were desperate to start training men on its use. They had the men to train them as these had been trained in its use over in Libya, but they had no actual stuff.

I immediately offered them 500 lbs of the stuff for delivery within the month. This seemed to worry them. The man who knew me from Libya said: "We have heard of people being conned over 'plastic' before. How do we know that you have the genuine article?"

Now, that was a problem. It hadn't crossed my mind to con them. So far as I was concerned they could blow their silly selves to pieces practising with the stuff. I replied: "I will take one of you to the supply port to take a small amount from the consignment, seal the cases and come back here to test it. The man can then return with me to make sure that the cases have not been interfered with in his absence. The shipment will then be sent over."

They agreed with that and also that they would pay me £5,000 for fixing the deal on top of the going rate for the stuff and shipping. I bade them all good night and they left with my promise that I would telephone one of them when the deal was under-way.

Plastic was a commodity which Endo always had to hand in his Maltese warehouses and first thing next morning I telexed him to make sure that he could supply. He could.

The same afternoon I was on my way to Malta, via London, with Sean, the man selected to check out the deal. We were in Malta by eight o'clock and booked into the Hilton.

I had arranged to meet Sean in the bar after we had cleaned up and, as I made my way in, I almost bumped into the tall, gangling frame of Rene, who was just leaving. He gently pushed the willowy blonde on his arm to one side and threw his arms round me: "Leslie, you bloody man. I thought you were dead, no?"

I replied that I was not dead and that he was a bloody soft fool who should stop hugging me PDQ.

I was delighted to see him, however, and we made our way to the bar with his popsie sort of hanging on to his coat tails.

At the bar he turned to the girl and said: "Jenny, this is my old friend, Leslie, we have much to talk about and you must have dinner alone and then come back, yes?" She spat fire at him with her eyes but pecked him on the cheek and was gone right away.

I was pleased to see Rene because I had already thought of contacting him to help with the shipping of the plastic. Now that he was here in Malta he could come in on the deal from the outset. I was just starting to fill him in on the whole deal when Sean came across to the bar. I introduced him to Rene and we all moved over to a corner table, drinks in hand.

I explained to Sean that Rene was going to help us with our deal and that he was an old and trusted friend and colleague. Sean just shrugged – he was in no situation to be suspicious anyway. And Rene, being an old hand, didn't let on to the fact that he didn't even know what the deal was.

I left the two together and went through to the phone booth in the lobby to call Endo. It took three calls to locate him but I finally found him at his garage. I arranged that he should meet us half an hour later at the Roundabout pub and went back to the others.

Rene had to go through to the dining room to tell the blonde, who turned out to be a young American he had picked up earlier in the week, that he would have to miss out the whole evening and then we left for the Roundabout.

Endo was already at the bar when we arrived and he joined us at a table away from the knot of people near the bar. He looked at the Irishman and then to me, only starting to talk after he received my nod indicating that the guy was O.K. He said: "The whole lot is ready for shipping as soon as you like."

I asked Endo if we could pop over to his warehouse the following morning and take a couple of samples before sealing his cases ready for collection in a week or so. He agreed with this as it was a not unknown practice in the business. We had one more drink and left him to return to the hotel.

We all turned in early. Or at least, Sean and I did. Rene went off to keep the American bird happy.

As soon as we had finished breakfast together in the hotel dining room next morning, I took a cab down to town and bought two giant, economy size tubes of toothpaste at a chemist shop. These I took back to the hotel and up to my room where, having opened the crimped seals on the bottom ends, I shook all the toothpaste from them, making sure I did not squeeze the sides together.

Having done this I then washed them out thoroughly with hot water, put them in my brief-case, locked it and telephoned Sean and Rene, asking them to meet me down in the lobby. As an afterthought I telephoned Endo to make sure that he would be ready for us and then went down to join them.

We all took a cab into Sliema where, after stopping off for a couple of minutes to buy a couple of sticks of sealing wax from a stationer's, we drove on to the warehouse. When we arrived Endo was lounging in the doorway waiting for us. He took us through his dry-goods section and into a partitioned area reserved for the storage of fresh fruit in a cool condition.

Against one of the walls were stacked hundreds of cases of oranges. Endo walked up to the middle of this pile and pulled at a box which was identical to all its neighbours. It came free, leaving a gap, the box above it being supported by a thin strip of hardwood. He then pulled out the three boxes beneath it and this made a gap some two feet wide by five feet high. He nodded to us and walked through the gap.

As he disappeared into the darkness we followed him, me going first and then Sean and then Rene. just as I passed through the gap Endo switched on a battery-powered lantern hanging on the wall, about six feet in front of us. This revealed that we were in a 'room' measuring about twelve feet by six by eight. The top consisted of boxes supported on steel bars and the end and outer walls were merely orange boxes. The wall on which the lantern hung was the brick outer wall of the warehouse.

Endo was a past master at concealing his shady wares and he moved his 'caves' so regularly that, short of stripping out the whole place, they were virtually undetectable.

To a height of some four feet, most of the room was stacked with boxes and crates, some under tarpaulins. He led us down to one end of the room, lifted a tarpaulin and revealed a heap of stout 'plastic' boxes. prising the lid off the top one he took out two packets of the stuff and handed it to me: From touch alone I could tell that it was good and fresh so I nodded to the Irishman who knowing nothing about the stuff, could only nod back.

Handing the two packets to Rene for safe-keeping, I asked the Irishman if he had a Yale key with him. He handed over his whole key-ring, which had four on it.

Selecting one of the keys, I removed it from the ring and, taking one case at a time, turned them on to their backs, ran sealing wax over the joint between the lid and the front and impressed the notched end of the key into it. I then re-stacked them.

This is an old and useful sealing method and is just as efficient as the old ring seal. When the cases finally arrived in Dublin our man Sean would be able to match his key up with the seals and be left in no doubt at all that they were the same cases he had seen in Malta.

Rene pocketed the two packets and we all left the room, Endo replacing the orange boxes before taking us back to his office and handing over four detonators for the plastic. We then left him and walked back towards Sliema centre until we were able to hail a cab to take us back to the hotel, Rene handing me the plastic as we drove.

Leaving the other two, Rene to return to his room and book us out on the next available flight and Sean to settle the bills, I returned to my room removed the two empty toothpaste tubes and placed them on the desk. Then, after working each lump of plastic in my hand until it became malleable – something like kids' Plasticine – I fed the softened material up into the tubes, removing the tops first to let the air out. I squeezed about half an inch of paste from my own tube into the tops before replacing the caps.

Having filled both tubes, I re-sealed the bottoms by folding them back into their original positions and squeezing them in a drawer. The detonators were easier. I simply slipped them into the lining of my suitcase beneath the zip edging.

Rene telephoned to say that we were booked on an afternoon flight to Dublin, but that he had to book first class because of limited space on the tourist class. So what, the Irish were paying.

Before leaving the hotel I gave one of the two plastic tubes to Rene and we both threw our own toothpaste away.

By ten o'clock that night Rene and I were both booked into the Tara Tower and Sean was back in the bosom of his family. He had promised to telephone us the following morning to arrange a further meeting with his friends.

Sean called as promised the next day and told us that he was bringing his committee round to the hotel that afternoon.

They turned up at about three o'clock, Sean and three others.

Sean had already briefed them on the Maltese end of the deal and they were suitably impressed. One of the Irishmen asked to see the stuff we had brought back with us and I opened up a tube to show him. They all crowded round and two of them expressed their firm belief that they didn't see how the "bloody putty" could do the damage claimed for it. They demanded proof before going ahead with the deal.

Rene, who could not stand the Irishmen by reason of their amateurish approach to our business, lost his temper. He said: "If I bloody demonstrate now, right now, you do the deal, yes?" The four smiled and Sean said: "Of course we do."

"O.K." said Rene. "Give me two detonators, Leslie." I moved over to my suitcase as he left the room and by the time he returned I had taken two of the four detonators from their hiding place. I handed them to him.

Moving over to the table he took a battery and a small kitchen timer from a jacket pocket and a roll of thin wire from another. Quickly and expertly he connected up the wire to the timer, which had already been adapted as a time-switch, and then connected one of the detonators to the other end. He then cut the wire somewhere in the middle and inserted the second detonator, and tied the battery into the circuit. In three or four minutes he had rigged a safe and efficient delayed action detonation circuit.

Taking one of the tubes and throwing the other to me he started rubbing it between his hands — I did the same. As soon as the plastic had softened slightly we ripped off the lead tubes and then kneaded it into pliable lumps.

Satisfied, Rene left the room and returned wearing his raincoat. He picked up the plastic and placed the two lumps in one pocket and then,

s Passport contains 32 pages
passeport contient 32 pages

PASSPORT
PASSEPORT

UNITED KINGDOM OF GREAT BRITAIN
AND NORTHERN IRELAND
*ROYAUME-UNI DE GRANDE-BRETAGNE
ET D'IRLANDE DU NORD*

. of passport)
, du passeport)   **P 812059**

me of bearer)   *Mr Leslie Alan*
m du titulaire)   *ASPIN*

:companied by his wife)
MAIDEN NAME
:compagné de sa femme)
NÉE

{ and by   children)
{ et de   enfants)

:ational Status *Nationalité*

ritish Subject :
itizen of the United
ingdom and Colonies.

Tá 32 leathanach sa phas seo.
This passport contains 32 pages.
Ce passeport contient 32 pages.

**ÉIRE
IRELAND
IRLANDE**

PAS
PASSPORT }   **H 316974**
PASSEPORT)

Ainm an tSealbhóra   *Leslie Alan Aspin*
Name of Bearer
Nom du Titulaire

Agus a bhean chéile)
lena chois
(Sloinne a hathar)
Accompanied by his
wife
(Maiden name)
Accompagné de sa
femme
(Née)

maraon le   )   (leanbh.
and by   )   (children.
et de   )   (enfants.

Náisiúntacht   )   SAORÁNACH d'ÉIRINN
National Status)   CITIZEN OF IRELAND
Nationalité   )   CITOYEN d'IRLANDE

This page: Some of my passports.
My rapid exit from Malta (chapter 9)
is shown by the visas on the right.

Overleaf: The map I prepared for
British Intelligence showing the
location of Libyan terrorist training
camps.

VISAS

MALTA IMMIGRATION
DEPARTURE
25 JAN 1974
BY AIR - 9

Business Visa

ፍቃድ:
አዲስ አበባ፡ በኢትዮጵያ፡
እንደቀ፡ ተፈቅዷል፡
No.   3035/64

Permitted to stay for *THREE MONTHS*
in Ethiopia
LONDON *March 27th 19 73*

MALTA IMMIGRATION   IMMIGRATION ACT 1970
ARRIVAL   DECLARED PURPOSE: TOURIST.
23 JAN 1974   Leave to land granted for a
period not exceeding three
BY AIR—13   months under tourist
conditions

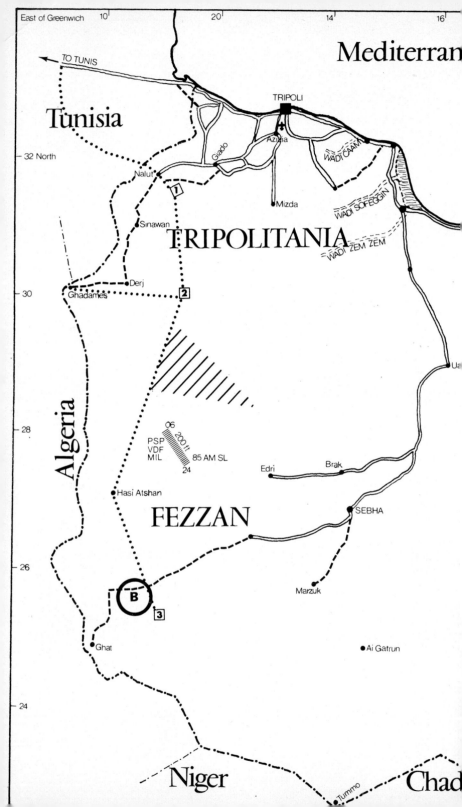

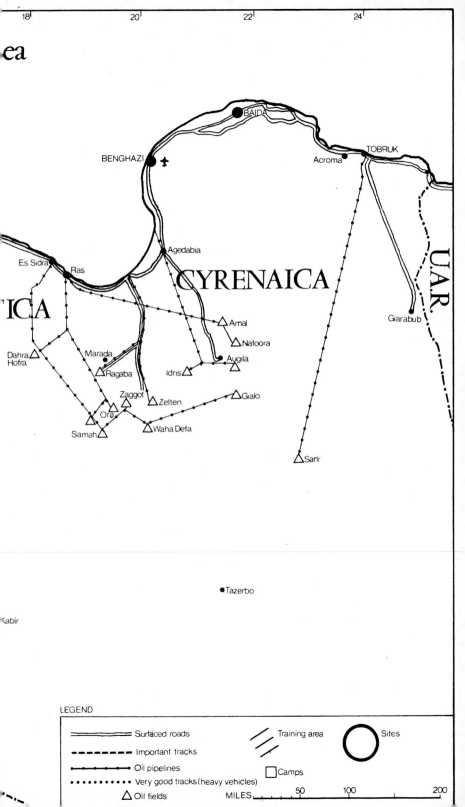

Name _Leslie Aspin_
Address _▬ ▬ Rd_
_▬_.

The above named attended the Accident and Emergency Department today.

Diagnosis : _Infected wound ℞ Shoulder._

....

Wet X-ray films show : ....

....

....

You will be notified if the Radiologist's Report differs from this.

Treatment given : _Cephaloridine (allergic to plaster_
analgesic & penicillin)

....

Given—A.T.S./Initial T.T./Booster T.T./Already immunised
This patient is attending the Accident and Emergency Department again on....._4/7_.

This patient has been referred to... Clinic

First Certificate given/not necessary dated ....

Would you arrange :—
        Further Dressings :
        Removal of Stitches :
        Further active immunisation for Tetanus

....

....

Yours sincerely,

UNH 62

                           Casualty Officer

Above: Treatment
for the knife
wound in my
shoulder after
the Brussels
incident.

Right: One of the few
existing photographs of
me. I'm afraid I couldn't
take the risk of showing
my face to the world.

carefully coiling the wire and removing the battery, he put the detonation circuit into the other.

Looking out of the window into the dark and rainy early evening he pointed across a strip of land separating the road from a railway station which ran almost on the seafront. A slow-moving train headed into Dublin. He asked: "That one, yes?"

The Irishmen looked from one to the other and said nothing for a full minute. Then Sean said: "Why not?" The others laughed nervously. Rene, eyes sparkling, left the room and slammed the door behind him.

Looking from the window, I saw Rene walk across the road and set off for the railway. The whole area was deserted, nobody apparently wanting to be abroad on such a raw and blustery evening.

From where I stood in the Tara, I looked out over the waste land to the sea. Beyond the slow-moving train I could see the lights of boats making for harbour through the sea front and drizzle.

The Irishmen clustered round the window with me and we watched Rene disappear towards the railway line, head bowed into the rain.

He had been gone for about five minutes when Sean asked: "Do you think he will really do for the bloody train?"

The others looked at each other and then they all looked at me. "Well," I said thoughtfully, "that one has gone but he will probably have the next one."

Sean made for the door. "Christ" he said. "I never thought he'd do it." He made off down the corridor.

The others all started to talk together, one saying that it was all right because everyone would think the Ulstermen had done it and another said: "But they're our bloody people, Mother of God, I hope Sean stops him."

Just then there was the loud crump of an explosion and a flash from somewhere towards the sea. The windows shook and the Irishmen turned white and stood rooted to the ground. People appeared in the street and looked out to sea.

Rene and Sean came into the room, breathless. I looked at Rene and said: "Christ, Rene, you'll get us all bloody well arrested." He stood just inside the door laughing. Rocking back and forth on his heels. "I didn't do the railway, Leslie. It was a bang in the open," he spluttered.

"But you should see your faces."

The Irishmen unfroze and started to run together for the door, banging into each other in their panic to get out. I ran for my cases, throwing in the few things I had unpacked, as Rene made off for his room and said: "See you at the airport." He too was frightened now.

I was just about to leave my room when I noticed the two screwed up toothpaste tubes on the desk and I went back to snatch them up and put them in my pocket.

A minute or so later I was in the street and heading away from the area towards Dublin.

After walking for about a mile I telephoned Sean's number from a coin box and the phone was answered by the man himself. He came straight over by car to collect me.

At this time I had decided to forget about Rene in accordance with an agreement we had had from the early days – in times of emergency each would look out for himself.

Back at Sean's place on the outskirts of the city I found the other three committee men lacing into a bottle of whisky. They were red-faced and flushed with excitement. They were overjoyed at the bang we had caused and literally clamoured for a full shipment.

In the early hours of the morning I persuaded Sean to drive me to the airport after promising that I would contact them about their shipment. For about four hours I just hung around the airport lounge before catching the first available plane out for London in the morning.

As soon as I got into Heathrow I telephoned Homer and fixed a meeting at the Cumberland for later in the morning and, when he arrived, told him of the goings-on of the night before.

He had already heard of the explosion and was furious with me when I told him that it was all down to me. He rumbled on about international incidents for ten minutes and I waited until he ran out of steam before explaining that it had been the only way to prove to the idiots over the water that the stuff would really make a bang. He then saw the funny side of the incident and realised its value in establishing my cover as a dealer working on their behalf.

When we parted I went straight over to the railway station and made my way home, learning as soon as I got there that Rene had been trying to reach me for a couple of hours.

He called again about half an hour after I got in to tell me that he was at Heathrow and had had no trouble getting out of Dublin. I learned later that he had calmly walked down the road and booked into another hotel after he had left the Tara, only leaving again to catch a plane a couple of hours after mine.

The next day I travelled back to London to meet Rene and make the final arrangements for the plastic shipment. We decided to take advantage of one of our 'bent' Italian customs men and send the stuff by road for most of its journey. Rene's brother could liaise with the Italian and I would take over when the consignment crossed the border.

This method of shipment was, and still is, the simplest means of smuggling medium-sized loads through Europe. It worked in the following way.

Endo shipping the stuff out in a freighter for Naples sealed up in packing cases and marked as lighting equipment with a destination in France. On arrival in Naples the cases were put into a bonded warehouse and checked over by our customs friend who had just pocketed half a million lira. From the warehouse, after being broken down, the stuff was loaded into a specially built compartment, concealed at the end farthest from the doors, of a massive TIR container. This container was then loaded with legitimate goods for Holland, sealed by our customs man, loaded on to its trailer and sent on its way.

The TIR system is an agreement between countries that any customs official can seal a container or lorry and, so long as the seal has not been broken, it will be allowed to pass all control points unopened. Only at its ultimate destination will it be examined by another customs man.

On this particular trip, the legitimate cargo was furniture and, after making his way through into Holland the driver left his truck overnight in a side-street car park.

When he returned next morning he found that vandals had broken into it but had only stolen one armchair. After reporting the break-in to the police he then made his way on to Amsterdam, less the illegal cargo, which had been removed by me during the night.

There are hundreds of drivers more than willing to pick up an extra couple of hundred quid in this way and, in spite of the fact that the authorities know it goes on, there is no way of stopping it. Occasionally, very occasionally, there is a pounce by customs and goods are seized. This is always the result of an underworld tip-off and, even when the goods are found, the driver denies all knowledge of them. He is, after all, only a driver.

However, back to this particular load.

After driving the stuff to Amsterdam in a pick-up I took it straight to a warehouse run by the Bank and had it packed into forty-gallon oil drums which were then openly loaded on to a trawler about to leave on a fishing trip.

I paid off the skipper with £500 and gave him a couple of call-signs and a map reference off the East Coast of Ireland before flying on to Dublin.

Once there I arranged with the local laddos to have a fishing boat standing by in the area I had fixed with the Hollander four nights after he had set out and gave them their call signs.

Oh yes, I also collected £3,000 as the first stage payment on the cargo from the local IRA.

On the morning after the fourth night I watched the drums swung ashore at Dundalk and picked up the rest of my money. Leaving aside the expenses and £1,000 I picked up from Homer, Rene and I made more than £3,000 on the deal.

The Irishmen were delighted at first, but somewhat put out when they had to wait another two weeks for their detonators, which I had decided not to send through with the plastic. However, these duly arrived and I had a new and well satisfied client.

Over the next few months I arranged three more shipments for the same group, two of assorted rifles and hand-guns and one of grenades and ammunition. They all travelled the same route and all in all I made about £20,000 out of them.

Chapter 5

The Claudia Affair
December 1972

So far Homer and his bosses had been quite happy for me merely to establish myself as a trusted friend of the IRA, willing and able to feed their growing arsenal.

He was, however, becoming alarmed as the IRA terrorist activities gained momentum in Ulster. He decided it was time that we used my situation to bring off a major coup against them.

From German intelligence sources he had learned that a ship was loading arms in Hamburg, reputedly for legal delivery to a genuine customer, but actually destined for Dublin. At government level Homer arranged for the German authorities to unload the ship just before she was due to sail and her skipper, not wishing to have his vessel impounded, shipped out in ballast.

Thinking that he had seen the end of the matter, Homer wrote off the incident as a successful operation — until the same ship was observed by the Royal Navy off Malta with a new name painted on her bow and stern. The Claudia had been brought into existence and she was apparently underway for Libya.

Homer called me to a meeting in St. James's Park, London, where in true Bond manner, he fed the ducks as he briefed me on his concern over the Claudia.

That same night, I set off for Tunis where I hired a car as soon as I arrived to drive down to Tripoli. By noon the next day, missing out on a night's sleep, I was booked into the Libya Palace and had telephoned the Colonel's office. An hour later the Colonel himself was with me and I was discussing with him the probability of training more IRA terrorists at his Black September training school.

In doing this I was taking advantage of discussions I had already had in Dublin with Sean and his friends who had expressed their satisfaction with the Arab training scheme. I told him that, as far as I could judge, they had a fair amount of equipment but not enough men to use it effectively.

He agreed to take as many men as the IRA could send and our conversation then took a more general turn. The Colonel began to boast about the success of his terror school and of how Libya had become the prime supplier af arms and training for almost every anarchistic or insurrectionist organisation in the world.

With very little leading from me he went on to boast that at that very moment he was loading 40 tons of arms aboard a ship right in the middle of Tripoli docks. "They are for your Irish friends," he concluded.

This came as something of a shock. I had had no idea that the ship was already in harbour and, if what the Colonel said was true, she would be putting out at almost any time.

I guided the conversation back to the subject of the training and thanked the Colonel for his offer, turning down an invitation to dine with him that night on the pretext that I had business in Malta. He didn't know just how true that was. Somehow I had to get a cable off to Homer and there was no way that I would risk sending it from Tripoli.

As soon as the Colonel had left I telephoned the airport and booked myself on a late afternoon flight for Malta, arranged with the local Hertz office to leave my car at the airport, and packed. By nine o'clock I was booked in at the Dragonara hotel and off down to Charles' Bar to meet Endo.

I told Endo that I had a couple of cases of goods on the Claudia in the charge of the mate and without the knowledge of the skipper. I explained that, because of the unofficial nature of the cargo I was unable to keep in touch by radio and would have to assess the time she would arrive in Rotterdam, when the stuff would be put over the side for me to pick up.

It was a thin story but the best I could come up with at such short notice. And Endo, being a Maltese and a smuggler, was used to intrigue. For £200 he agreed to have his men keep watch for the Claudia as she passed Malta.

I then returned to the hotel and sent a telex message to Homer, using the code he had given me at the commencement of our business, telling him of the probable departure time from Tripoli and the extent of the Claudia's cargo.

In fact it was two days before the Claudia came through and as soon as Endo called me I sent off another telex to Homer, before quitting the island and returning to London.

When Homer visited me at my hotel the next morning he made a great show of thanking me and expressing his delight at the success of my mission, explaining that he was now having the ship tracked by Royal Air Force Nimrod aircraft and that she would be seized before she could offload. He gave me £1,000 and I set off for home.

The next thing I knew of the incident was when I heard on the radio that the ship had been boarded by the Irish navy and a comparatively small quantity of arms had been taken off her.

Later I learned from Homer that there had been a gigantic foul-up over the tracking of the ship and that most of her cargo had been jettisoned before she was stopped.

He explained what had happened. The Nimrods had kept track of the Claudia for most of her voyage with no problems at all, then, as she sailed up the Irish coast and darkness began to fall, she was picked up on radar by a waiting Royal Navy vessel. As ordered, the skipper of the navy ship kept well behind his quarry as she steamed on through the night but he didn't reckon on the cunning of the other skipper.

For hours the skipper, manning the bridge himself in the closing stages of his trip, watched the bleep on his radar screen at a constant speed matching his own. He became alarmed. Not only was he carrying an illicit cargo but he had already had a bad scare in Hamburg. With his 'drop' only hours away he began to zig-zag as he ordered his crew to jettison the cargo.

As case after case of arms went overboard the following skipper noticed the course changes and radioed for help from the Irish navy, who had already been put on stand-by.

By the time the Irishmen managed to locate and stop the Claudia most of the cargo was gone. What was left was impounded by the Irish authorities.

The whole affair was recorded at the time as a great success. In one way, I suppose it was – the arms never got through to the IRA.

But we had learned our lesson. It was no good trying to keep track of smugglers by over-flying and following. The only way to stop the trade in arms was to have sufficient information to pounce as they were being landed.

At a conference in London with Homer and two other men, whose identities I did not know, but who were obviously senior to him, it was decided that we would set up our own deal and therefore be in a situation where we knew from start to finish just what was going on.

Chapter 6

Sea Fox Fiasco

After the meeting with Homer and his bosses I was asked to get back out to Malta and right into the middle of the route between the Arabs and the IRA. Homer agreed that I should again use Rene, who still did not know of my real role as a double agent.

Rene, in his turn, was more than pleased to help with what he considered was just another profitable deal with the Irish.

We flew to the island and booked into the Hilton while we nosed around our old haunts, using Endo to introduce us to the few new faces on the scene.

By this time a lot of people had heard that we were in the 'big time' arms business and were not much interested in cigarettes. We were looked upon as local heroes by the smuggling fraternity.

After a couple of days I heard that the Colonel was in town and working from the Libyan delegation offices in Old Theatre Street, just off Kingsway. I deliberately had not tried to contact him when I first arrived as I was more than a little concerned that the Claudia affair might have made him suspicious.

However, it would have been unusual for me not to contact him if I was in the market for business and I decided to arrange to meet him. He came round to the hotel when I telephoned him.

From the outset it was obvious that he did not suspect me in any way over the Claudia business and he greeted Rene and me like long-lost brothers.

We sat in the lobby for about five minutes while we exchanged pleasantries and then I asked him if he had any work for us. He replied that he might have and suggested that we move on up to my room, where, once we were settled, he said: "I'm having the old trouble over ships, Leslie. You probably know that we lost one a short while ago and the skippers are getting nervous. Your British navy are not easy people to upset and get away with it. Can you help with one I want away in a hurry from home?"

He went on the explain that he had seven tons of arms ready for shipping to the IRA and that he had no way of delivering them. We discussed the matter for some time and I promised to look into it and contact him with a price. He replied: "No, Leslie, the other people will pay you on delivery. There is no prepayment now because they are losing their cargoes. They will pay only when you deliver. We are supplying the goods free of charge and really it is their job to arrange the shipping. But they are no damn good, Leslie. We have to do everything."

What the man had said didn't surprise me much but I did put on a show of reticence before showing him out of the door.

As soon as he had gone Rene said: "We don't want any part of this dealing, no? We can't risk our money for those stupid ones."

When I told him that was precisely what I intended to do he was furious. He started to shout and wave his arms around as he told me just what sort of bloody fool I was. In the end I promised him that I would finance our end of the business and that only my money would be at risk. He calmed down and agreed to go along with the deal.

At lunch we discussed the new proportion and Rene agreed to set-to later in the day and find someone who was prepared to carry the cargo. I would set off right away for Dublin to arrange payments and landing facilities and he would keep in touch by telephoning my home with any messages. I flew out for London that night and left a message at Homer's office as soon as I arrived at Heathrow, requesting that he contact me at the London Tara first thing next morning.

He didn't telephone me but came round as soon as he got into his office and received my message. He was with the Major.

I filled the pair in on the approach from the Colonel and Homer agreed to put up £7,000 in cash to finance the shipping deal on the understanding that I would repay him if I got any money from the Irish. Although I agreed with this plan I had no intention whatsoever of paying him. I reckoned that I deserved every penny I could lay my hands on for taking the risks involved in such a deal.

I told Homer that I intended to move on to Ireland and from there would play the whole thing by ear, only letting him know when we had all the details together. He left me to get on with my packing after arranging to have the Major hand over the money I needed as I passed through the airport that afternoon.

I called my home to make sure that Rene had not been on and lunched before taking a cab out to Heathrow, picked up the usual buff envelope full of ten-pound notes from the Major and hopped a plane to Dublin.

As soon as I arrived I telephoned Sean and asked him to meet me at the Skylon Hotel as soon as he could get over. He was with me about half an hour later.

I told him of the trouble the Colonel was having finding transport, and of our conversation regarding payment procedures, letting him know in no uncertain manner that I couldn't afford to finance their bloody army. We were in my room at the time and he asked if he could use the telephone. As nicely as I could I refused and he went down to the call-box in the lobby. I was beginning to dislike the whole Irish set-up and had decided that I would have to tighten my security in the country. It's all too easy for people to listen in on hotel switchboards.

Sean returned after about five minutes and told me that, because of my past work for them and the extreme regard in which they held me, he and his friends would pay me £8,000 for the shipping deal. They would also pay me half as soon as the ship was under way, the rest to be paid on arrival. He went on to explain that they were concerned about information which they feared was reaching the British and suspected that it was someone close to the Colonel who was selling them out.

I, in my turn, expressed my concern over security, pointing out that I would be shot out of hand if the British authorities got to know of my business with him and his friends. We had a mutual back-scratching session about what his cause owed us both and he left after promising to get the money to me that night.

True to his word he was back before ten with a jumble of mixed denomination English notes which counted up to £4,000.

I telephoned my home after he had left and there was still no message from Rene, so I rang the airport and booked out on an early flight for London the next day.

From the airport I telephoned Sean, told him to prepare plans for my delivery and that I would let him know when it would be, then boarded my flight.

On arrival at Heathrow I again telephoned my home, this time to be told that Rene had called and that he was having problems over the 'help' but would keep on trying.

This message changed my mind for me and instead of returning to Malta I booked the next flight for Amsterdam, arriving at Schipol in mid-afternoon.

I took a cab into the city and booked into the Europa hotel before setting off on what was now becoming my usual search for old smuggling friends. For some reason they were a bit thin on the ground and, apart from having a few drinks with junior leaguers I had a bad night. I returned to the hotel and turned in at about midnight.

The next morning, after sleeping badly and getting up late, I set off on a tour of the dockland pubs and eventually, around lunchtime, bumped into Greek Charlie.

After much back-slapping and utterings of "Hey you, you bloody Leslie, you," not to mention a couple of bottles of wine being poured down Charlie's throat, I began to get the picture. Charlie was out of work. I asked him if he knew of anyone who might do a week long eight-ton trip for me and he agreed that he would take it on. Gently I pointed out to him that he couldn't swim with the stuff – there was too much of it.

He replied "But with the money, you bloody Leslie, I can borrow the ship, no?" Could he? Of course he could. When? As soon as I wanted it. Where? Hamburg.

A quick phone call to the airport produced the information that we could fly out for Hamburg in a couple of hours and, pausing only to pick up the Greek's gear from the smelly flop-house in which he was living, and my cases from Europa, we made our way out to Schipol.

From Hamburg airport we took a cab straight to the dock area where Charlie found us a small and, unusual for him, clean hotel. Half an hour later, following ten minutes of telephoning by Charlie, I was being introduced to a smartly turned-out German by the name of Walter.

Walter, it turned out over a couple of beers, was part owner of a small coaster and he was prepared to charter her to Charlie for a couple of weeks for five grand in dollars. Charlie looked at me and I nodded. We had our ship.

Next morning I shot straight round to a bank and changed my sterling into dollars before returning to the hotel and telling Charlie to get his man round. By lunchtime Charlie had completed the paperwork on his deal and I had briefed him to get the ship over to Tripoli as soon as he could.

I was about to leave him to organise his crew and push off for the airport when I realised that I didn't even know the name of the ship he was going to use. I asked him. Smiling he replied: "By the time she is being in Tripoli she is called, er, well, yes, she is called the Sea Fox, yes? What she is being called now is no matter, eh?"

I couldn't see that it did matter and made a mental note of the name before taking a cab to the airport and booking the next flight out for Tunis. While I was waiting at the airport I telephoned my wife who told me that Rene had not contacted her again. I left instructions that he was to be told that I had arranged things and that he was to lay off at his end.

From Tunis I took the usual road through to Tripoli, again using a Hertz car for the drive. The reception manager of the Libya Palace welcomed me like an old friend, I was becoming a familiar face in the place. He gave me one of the best suites and I showered before calling the Colonel's local office. He was not in town but was expected the next day.

I wasn't put out by this news. I felt as if I had been travelling for a million years without stopping. In fact he didn't get into town for three days and I was able to relax completely, and although my insomnia was getting steadily worse, felt pretty well rested.

When the Colonel did arrive I filled him in on my arrangements for the shipment and told him that the Sea Fox should be in Tripoli within a matter of days. He told me that as soon as she docked she could load up and suggested that she did the turn-around as quickly as possible because he too was getting worried about information leaks.

Before he left the hotel he invited me to take a trip out to his training area with him the following day and, when I agreed, promised to pick me up at eight the next morning.

Precisely at eight he was on the telephone from the lobby and when I joined him he took me straight out to his Mercedes. I was expecting to be driven out along the Tunis road but, instead, we headed for the main Tripoli airport. There, we boarded an Aztec which flew us straight out to the camp. I remember thinking how overt he was becoming. It was obvious that his government had given up all attempts at hiding their training programme.

When we arrived at the camp I was amazed at the number of men around. If all the squads had been mustered I reckon the parade ground would have held a couple of full battallions.

Small groups of men were swarming in and out of the mock aircraft and there was a perpetual sound of small-arms firing from the range just over a small hill on the camp perimeter.

Occasionally a grenade would explode and twice I heard the solid thunk of heavy demolition charges. At one stage the Colonel pointed to a squad of about fifty men and told me that they were from the IRA.

I accompanied the Colonel on his quick tour of inspection but he left me in the mess-tent for an hour while he went into conference with the camp commander.

We left the camp after we had lunched with the senior officers and flew back to Tripoli. During most of the flight the Colonel kept telling me how pleased he was with his training camp and, as he was obviously seeking my approval, I agreed with him.

Back in the town I was left with nothing to do but mooch about the hotel until the Sea Fox came into harbour. After my previous experience in the Souk I was not inclined to venture out at night and only during the day on specific missions. I was glad when, after four days, the Greek brought his ship into Tripoli and the Colonel telephoned to tell me he had arrived.

Taking up the Colonel's offer of a lift I accompanied him to the docks and went aboard the decrepit old tub with him. Until then I had not seen her and, along with the Colonel, I wondered how she had made the trip.

However, when we raised the matter with Charlie he shrugged it off, saying: "She is a lot more trim than you would think by the look of her. She is the good ship for me, bloody good ship."

The cargo was slung aboard very quickly and the Colonel posted guards near the old tub while the crew and Charlie took the night off. Charlie promised not to get too drunk and to clean himself up so I took him into town and booked him into the Palace. It was the only thing I could think of to ensure that he got out to sea the next morning. However, when he insisted on going out to do the town I had to pretend that I was ill. He was so disappointed that I telephoned the Colonel's office, where I found the Major to be in, and asked for an escort to keep the Greek out of trouble on his binge. I just hung around the hotel until the pair returned at about one in the morning with Charlie dragging the young captain up the hotel steps.

I happened to be in the bar at the time and the night porter came to fetch me because Charlie was insisting on bringing the collapsed Arab into the hotel. When I got through to the lobby Charlie was at the top of the steps and he called to me as I approached the door: "Hey, bloody Leslie, they won't let me bring my good friend in for a drink, hey? You fix it, hey?"

I told him that his friend would get into dreadful trouble if he was found by his boss in the hotel and in the state he was in. At this Charlie turned around and tossed the Arab down the steps, laughing loudly as the figure bundled down onto the flagstones at the bottom. When he stopped laughing he stood with his hands on his hips and said quietly: "That won't get him into trouble hey, Leslie? I only wanted to bring him in because I thought we had to be nice to them." We moved through into the hotel.

Next morning over breakfast I gave Charlie his destination – Killala Bay on the west coast of Ireland – his radio frequencies and call signs. I also asked him to start checking in on his radio as soon as he came up with the Irish coast. We moved on to the ship and checked off the charts together as I told him that when he pulled into the bay I would have fishing boats ready to take the boxes into nets. He put out at about nine o'clock and I set off for Tunis by road.

I took the whole day over the hard drive and went straight to the airport on arrival. Unfortunately the best I could do by way of transport was a flight to London and then on to Malta. I checked in the car at the airport Hertz office and caught the plane, arriving in Malta in time for breakfast with Rene at the Hilton.

Poor old Rene was in a bit of a spin. I hadn't had the opportunity of briefing him on my arrangements and, although he had received the message from my home that I had fixed things, he didn't know what I had done. Then I had disappeared for a week, leaving him to chew his fingernails in Malta.

I calmed him down and told him everything that had happened. That shut him up. The whole deal was organised and he had done almost nothing for his share of the loot. He then remembered that Endo had offered him half a dozen rocket launchers at a knockdown price and again lost his temper because we could not now ship them. I recall that Endo only wanted fifty quid each for the launchers because they were not in very good condition. Rene had a good right to be annoyed, we could get £200 each from them in Ireland. We set off for Endo's office on the dockside.

Endo wasn't there when we arrived but his manager let us use his radio to call Charlie, who turned out to be only about fifty miles off the island. There was no point in losing out on Endo's deal so I asked Charlie for his position and told him to set a course to bring him into a situation where we could meet him with a launch about thirty miles off shore in three hours.

We then telephoned around until we found Endo and asked him to come down to his warehouse to see us. He arrived about ten minutes after we had contacted him.

I told him that we could do the deal if he could get the goods loaded PDQ and hare out to a point I had marked down on the chart in his office.

Nothing could have been more simple for Endo. Within the hour he had loaded the crates onto a launch he used to service ships lying off shore and he, Rene and I were on our way to the rendezvous.

We reached the approximate spot and circled slowly for about half an hour until Charlie chugged up over the horizon, spot on course as usual. The crates were slung aboard in nets so quickly that the larger vessel didn't completely lose way and, with a wave from the bridge, the Greek continued his journey. We put back into port.

I had told the Greek to take his time over his trip to Ireland and Rene and I decided to spend a couple of days in Malta. He had found one or two useful new recruits to the scene, he told me, and I thought I might as well look them over.

I wasn't particularly impressed with his new men but while we were drinking around I got wind of a massive shipment of cigarettes which had been put together aboard a coaster at Rotterdam and was bound for Spain. I considered trying to sell the information to the Spanish waterguard, but, although I found out the departure date, I couldn't discover the destination. I decided to forget the whole thing.

From Malta I sent Rene back to Paris, telling him that I would contact him there when the trip was concluded, and flew back to Dublin via London.

In London, while passing through Heathrow, I wrote down the whole plan for Charlie's cargo, including the call signs, frequencies and destination and then telephoned Homer. His sidekick answered the phone and I told him that I was just passing through and had a package for Homer. He asked which box I was in and told me to stay right there until a man came to me.

I put the phone down and opened the door, allowing a woman who had been waiting, to pass me as I left. It must have been only about a minute before two grey-looking guys in suits walked up and confronted me. I had a feeling I knew one from my first confrontation with their people but I wasn't sure. Anyway, it was the other who asked: "Homer's man?" I nodded. He held out his hand and I gave him the envelope in which I had sealed my note for the boss. That was all, the pair spun on their heels and left me standing there.

Back in Dublin I booked in at the Skylon and called Sean. He came over within thirty minutes and brought with him two of the men who had been present when we had caused the bang near the railway. We all went to my room.

I gave them the full details of the delivery and they agreed right away to have the extra rocket launchers at £250 each. The deal was getting better by the minute. I told them that to keep faith with the supplier of the launchers I had had to pay him £100 each for them to get them loaded. Of course I wanted the money from them immediately to cover my outlay. Again they agreed, telling me that they would pay me the following morning.

Sean told me that he would have a man on radio watch from five days time and would keep in close touch with the Sea Fox until it made its rendezvous. I suggested that he didn't go on the air too much until the last hour or so. Maybe he should just call every four hours on the hour. He and his friends thought that this was an incredibly good idea.

I turned in for another almost sleepless night after they had left and was up and about well before seven the next morning. It was a pleasant change to be able to walk abroad without having to look over my shoulder as I felt I had to in Libya and even Malta.

Sean came to the hotel with my £600 at about eleven and I set off for the airport as soon as he had left, having told him that I would return for my money after the drop. I was home with my wife in the early evening.

Homer telephoned me next morning to congratulate me on what appeared to him to be a certain "cop". Both he and his bosses, he told me, were delighted. He told me to rest up at home and he would let me know how things had gone after the seizure.

I asked him to leave the Greek out of his snatch or to ensure that he got away. He was a man who would be useful to both of us in the future. He promised that he would do what he could.

For a few days I kept my ear tuned to newscasts but there was no mention of an arms seizure off Ireland. Then, late at night, I had a frantic call from Homer. The French navy had informed the Admiralty that a large unlighted ship was reported making her way out of the Channel off Brest and apparently bound for Ireland. They had her on radar but were finding if difficult to close with her.

For whatever reason Homer had decided that I was double-crossing him and that the Sea Fox was just a decoy, with the larger ship sneaking in while the navy was searching for the tub.

I tried to explain to him that I knew nothing of any such plan but he wouldn't hear of it. He rang off after uttering dire threats about my well-being.

138

It took me about fifteen minutes to realise what was happening out there in the Atlantic. I immediately called Homer's office and was put through to his home. I quickly explained that in my opinion the ship the French were worried about was the cigarette ship from Rotterdam, making a large sweep into the Atlantic before coming back for Spain. In short he told me it was all bollocks and the HMS Ajax, which had been standing by to intercept Sea Fox had now gone to help the French with their problem. Then it was my turn to ring off in a temper.

Quickly I telephoned Sean at his home in Dublin to ask him how things were going. He was excited and wanted to ring off right away. They were in touch with the Sea Fox and she should be in within five hours or so. Would I please get off the line in case someone should want to call him.

I was more than happy to. I rang off and immediately called Homer back, telling him what the Irishman had just told me. He now seemed more reasonable and said he would pass the message on.

Whether or not he did so I don't know but it was not long after that that the Frenchmen caught up with the cigarette ship and called off their request for help. The Ajax immediately radioed the Admiralty and was told to get back on to the tail of Sea Fox.

By the time they had picked her up she was getting into Irish waters and uncomfortably close to Killala bay. They called in the Irish navy, who had previously been requested to stand by in the area, and the Irish navy turned out in its might and entirety, all three frigates of it.

Unaware of all the fuss he was causing the Greek headed into Killala bay, all the time chatting away with a verbose IRA man on shore who assured him that the collection fleet was standing by. Using his radar he picked up the pick-up boats and headed in amongst them, pulling his speed back to almost nothing at all. His crew started to throw boxes over the bundled nets of the fishing boats.

With about two-thirds of his cargo put over the Greek wandered back into the wheelhouse and glanced at his radar. He did a double-take as he saw the three strong bleeps put out by the rapidly approaching frigates, gave a quick couple of pumps on his siren to warn the crew and rang for full speed, making a lot of waves as he threaded his way through the fishing smacks still waiting to be loaded.

As the Irish navy pulled nearer, their radar men were thrown into confusion by the dozen or so boats threshing about in the bay as the Sea Fox zig-zagged for the open sea and the fishing smacks dodged about and headed for the cover in which they had been ordered to land their cargoes.

Not knowing which of the boats to chase, the navy missed the lot, Sea Fox making international waters and the fishermen making their harbours.

As he made what speed he could on his zig-zag course the Greek had the rest of his incriminating cargo slung overboard, but, in the event, he need not have done so. At first light the Ajax picked him up after an aerial recognisance flight but she did not even bother to board when she noticed that the Sea Fox was riding high in the water, having obviously discharged her cargo.

It might have been, of course, that Homer had kept his promise to let the skipper go clear, but I doubt that very much. He was like a bear with a sore head for weeks after the fiasco, wishing he had believed me about the other smuggler. I've no doubt he had his arse kicked well and soundly for having his men lay on an almost perfect gun-running foray for the IRA.

There was only one thing which spoiled the deal for me and that was the fact that the IRA guys only paid half of the money still due for the trip, insisting that they had not taken full delivery. I argued for a while but then gave in, telling them that if it was for the cause it was worth while.

They didn't, however, suspect me over the raid by their navy, even though they knew from their contacts that it was our Secret Service who had tipped both navies off on the whole deal.

It was just after the Sea Fox saga, when Homer had decided that he could talk to me again without blowing his top and shooting me, that it was arranged that I should take advantage of my ever-increasing stature with the Irishmen and sort out some local problems.

Previously I had made a couple of trips into Ulster with Sean when we were organising the early shipping, but I was now almost completely in the dark with regard to the real strength of the madmen who were creating such havoc in the North.

At a hotel conference Homer showed me a picture of a guy by the name of Kenneth Littlejohn and told me that the man was a Britisher who had offered to help and claimed to have a strong line into the IRA.

Along with the photographs he gave me an address in Newry and a telephone number for the man, along with a packet containing money for him for information he had promised. He also asked me to deliver money to two other men who were working under cover in the South and specifically to check out Littlejohn's contacts.

During our conversation it became evident that the man was becoming something of a pest, telephoning London with tit-bits which should have been passed anonymously to the local Special Branch, with whom he was not in direct touch.

To make a trip of it, it was suggested that I might find out a bit more about training procedures operating locally. Littlejohn, I was told, would be expecting me when I called on him.

I set off from London armed with another £1,000 for expenses and a lot of hope – as well as my thirty-eight – and flew direct to Dublin. Once there I called Sean and told him that I feared that things were getting a bit hot and that someone might have tipped off the British about my endeavours on his behalf.

In the past I had given him a lot of bullshit about my previous prowess as a mercenary and he had every reason to believe me. He suggested, as I had hoped he would, that I might find a niche for myself with his organisation .Would I work in the north either as a training officer or an organiser? I agreed to go along with his suggestion until my situation over the water became clear and then told him that I had ideas about getting stuff across the border which I wanted to discuss with his man on the spot.

Sean thought that this was a good idea and suggested that I saw a man in Newry, just over the border into the North on the East coast.

I hired a car and set off for Newry. My arranged meeting there with the IRA man would fit in nicely with my intended talk with the Littlejohn guy.

I had no problems crossing the border at Dundalk, my car wasn't even stopped, and I booked into a hotel just up from the Newry army post.

From the hotel I telephoned Littlejohn and asked him to come round that evening. I met him in the hotel lounge. My first impressions of the man were that I was with a first-class bloody idiot. He was flashily dressed and reminded me rather of a late forties London spiv. He was talking so loudly about his activities that I took him up to my room in case anyone should hear him.

I let him ramble on for a while and then asked him to introduce me to his IRA friends. (I had been told in London that he had thoroughly infiltrated the IRA and was actually leading a team for them.) He mentioned the name of his local IRA commander in Newry and told me that he would take me in to see him if I could convince him that I was on their side.

I laughed. The man he had mentioned was one of the names given by Sean. I told him this and although he looked rather down in the mouth he also found it amusing. He took me round to some building behind a garage and we were let in after Littlejohn knocked five times on the door in a three-two pattern.

In the workshop there were two men, one of them the man I wanted to see and the other a relation of his. Littlejohn introduced me and the number-one man was so pleased to see me that he hugged me, saying: "I have heard so much about you and you have done so much good for the cause." Littlejohn just stood with his mouth open. As far as he was concerned I was a guv'nor from London with some sort of contact among Irishmen. He didn't know of my activities over the past two years and no one there was going to tell him.

As I tried to talk with the two Irishmen, Littlejohn kept on butting in with things like: "Yeah, d'you remember when we did ..." He was nothing more than a loud-mouthed braggart. What's more it was obvious to me that the others in the workshop thought the same thing.

It was equally obvious that he had been working for the IRA in a real way, bombing and shooting right alongside them. This was a thing I had never done and, apart from my early deals, I had been working under the instructions of the Secret Service. This man, I had gathered in London, had gone to them after he had joined up with the terrorists and worked with them for a considerable time.

I wasn't so much worried about his morals with regard to killing and maiming as I was about the type of man he was. He was selling out anyone and everyone for money and I dreaded to think what a prat like that would do in a tight corner. It was a hundred-to-one bet that he would blow every friend he had.

I decided there and then to watch him closely and be ready to prevent him from blowing my cover by any means should we be picked up.

I asked Littlejohn to leave me alone with the man I had gone to see and, after he had left, I told the man about the latest drop in Killala Bay. He told me that some equipment had already arrived, taking me through into a small room with storage racks on the wall. He pulled forward one of the racks on its castor wheels and exposed a damned great box of acid detonators, hundreds of the bloody things. This was useful to me. I knew that he was a supply man but not that he dealt in such large quantities. I made a mental note that his place would have to be watched much more closely.

He rolled back another rack and exposed three cases of rifles and a box of ammunition as he explained that he had set up a training school of his own, using an instructor trained in Libya. That too was news to me and hadn't been mentioned by Littlejohn.

After about half an hour I left the man after he promised to call me at the hotel the next day. Littlejohn was still outside the workshop, doing his best to be picked up by a patrol if it appeared. There was nothing I could do but invite him back to the hotel for a drink but after only two I got so fed up with his boasting that I told him that I had to get to bed after a long day, and showed him out.

The next morning our friend at the workshop called me and asked me to join him there. When I arrived Littlejohn was already with him and they asked me to pull my car up into the workshop before leading me to a green VW and set off to the alleged training school.

As we drove, Littlejohn, sitting in the front passenger seat, pulled out a bloody great first world war type Webley revolver and started flashing it around. This alarmed both me and the driver. Deliberately I was unarmed that day and, I assumed, so was the other guy. We tried to persuade him to get rid of it and I even promised him a new one if he would simply throw the bloody thing out of the window. He refused. There was nothing we could do.

The training school turned out to be in Lurgan and was situated beneath another workshop. As we went down the stairs leading to it we were confronted by two men who were obviously guards and both were armed.

We passed on to a room behind the guards and I was surprised to find myself in a conventional classroom. On blackboards arranged in front of rows of desks there were four diagrams dealing with the making of bombs and showing how to insert fuses and arrange clock mechanisms.

On a table in front of the blackboards, apparently used by the instructor, there was a US army manual on bombs and urban guerrilla weapons.

A fifth blackboard, to the side of the room, had pinned on it a diagram, probably from the manual, of a fragmentation bomb – the type used by the Americans in Vietnam. This amused me and I did not tell them that this bomb was designed to be dropped from aircraft and explode about ten feet from the ground. I suppose they might have found some other use for it but I doubt it.

On a table at the side of the room there was a Sterling sub-machine with the strap used to attach it to the wrist of its owner cut away at the end farthest from the gun. It had apparently been snatched from the body of British soldier.

Through a door leading from the room I could see a small annexe in which there were five bunks, all with bedding. My friend from Newry explained that these were for people who needed to lie low in times of trouble.

Littlejohn followed us around during this tour and it was suggested that we all go over to a nearby restaurant for a meal. Littlejohn somehow just did not fit in with either myself or the other guy. He stuck out like a sore thumb with his swagger and oversharp suiting. I did not want to be seen on the street with him and I made this clear to both of them. There were a few heated words and instead of going for a meal we drove straight back to Newry.

Once there we went back to the original workshop where I had another long talk with our guide and another man he introduced me to who was in the workshop when we returned.

When we had finished our conversation, Littlejohn insisted on coming back to my hotel with me and when he did so I gave him the money I had for him.

He was furious that the sum was much lower than he had anticipated and demanded more. I had to tell him that I had no more money with me and, anyway, nothing he had told me was new and that he was being vastly overpaid already.

He spent some ten minutes telling me how brilliant he was and pointed out that I would never have located the school or the arms cache without his help. I had to put him right on that one, however, and pointed out to him that I already had an introduction to the workshop man before I met him. He didn't like this one bit but quietened down and eventually he admitted that he had not known about the classroom set-up and that he would never have seen it if he had not been taken there with me. To keep him quiet I told him that I would ask London to get more money to him if at all possible and promised to contact him in the near future, before asking him to leave, packing and booking out of the hotel.

On the way out of town I paid a quick visit to the workshop and told them that I was off back to Dublin before driving straight through to Belfast and booking into the Europa Hotel.

From there I telephoned a contact number for a man by the name of Ian and, finding him at home, arranged for him to meet me at the hotel the next morning, giving him my room number.

That night there was a mighty panic at the Europa when a bomb was planted in the hotel. We were all evacuated while the Army dragged it out with a Landrover, but I had a reasonable night's sleep after they allowed us to return.

Ian turned up as promised next morning and came straight up to my room to bring me up to date on the latest loyalist moves to organise resistance to the IRA. The loyalist efforts in this field are, of course, common knowledge now but at that time virtually no one knew of their plans.

He gave me a list of names of prominent men in the organisation and asked me to arrange with my bosses for the provision of arms for them. I promised to help him all I could and he left. As soon as he had gone, I packed and checked out of the hotel.

After driving back from Belfast to Dublin I went straight to Sean to report on my trip to Newry and tell him how impressed I was with their set-up before checking my car in and flying back to London.

I was furious with Homer for putting me in touch with Littlejohn and, at a meeting the morning after my arrival back in London, I told him so in no uncertain terms. He agreed that the man was a possible security risk and that he should in future report only to the army command in Belfast, thereby not risking more valuable operatives.

Over the next month or so, I made a number of trips to Dublin just to keep myself up to date with the plans of the IRA high command. On one of these trips Sean, who I knew by now to be an employee of the Irish government, told me that he thought he was under suspicion.

I checked this out with Homer and found that the idiot had tipped off the Irish Special Branch about Sean and that they were keeping him under surveillance.

I was furious at this indiscretion. It meant that my meetings with Sean had probably been observed and that the Irish Special Branch would now know of my existence as an IRA sympathiser.

They would more than probably tip off the IRA and that might well get my head blown off. I telephoned Sean and he told me that he knew that I was working for the British because the Irish SB had told him and that confirmed my fears.

This complete sell-out by Homer astounded me but Sean did not seem particularly upset. In fact, he invited me over to meet his own top men with a view to working as a double agent on their behalf. I asked him who these men were, thinking that he was only trying to trap me. He replied by giving me a number of names, one of which was that of a top Irish politician.

Knowing that if they had really wanted to do away with me they would have come over to England to do it I agreed to meet Sean's top man and travelled to Dublin to do so.

Our short meeting took place in a park and the man explained that he wanted me to keep his people informed of the activities of Homer's men in the Republic. He told me that it was not his intention to use this information against the British, merely to know what they were up to.

I relayed this conversation to Homer and he asked me to go ahead with the deal but instructed me that a further meeting should take place with the man in London. At this meeting they would fit me up with a tape recorder and take film which could subsequently be used to put pressure on the politician should this become necessary.

It was obvious to me that conversations between a British agent and a top Irish politician where IRA activities were discussed would be a most effective form of blackmail. I agreed to go ahead.

For a number of reasons this meeting did not come off. It was put back by the Irishman, until the whole idea was shelved.

Chapter 7

Contribution from South Africa

It was while I was hanging around in London waiting for the projected meeting with the Irishman that Rene came over to spend some time with me.

Soon bored with the London scene we looked around for a quick deal with which to keep ourselves amused and, eventually, decided on an approach to the Nigerians.

From past dealings at the time of the Biafran business we both knew that a former Nigerian diplomat lived in London, having decamped with arms funds at the time of the war. We made an approach to him and he invited us up to his Belgravia flat where he entertained us in the manner to which he had become accustomed since his fraud on the Biafran fighters.

In fact, this man no longer had any contact with his old friends in Nigeria, but he was in touch with a diplomat at the South African embassy. He gave us the name and extension number of the man and promised to call him and effect an introduction first thing next morning.

I called the number at about eleven the next day and the South African asked us to pop in and see him. He had already heard from the black and he was interested in some sort of arms deal.

We went to see him that afternoon and he expressed an interest in helicopter parts, Chieftain tanks and fighter aircraft. We told him that

148

we would try to arrange a deal for him.

Rene telephoned a contact of ours in Madrid who was a regular and respected arms dealer on the international scene. The man had the tanks and several French Mirage fighters, complete with spares, on an old airfield in Spain. We arranged with him to have his staff allow us to take a client over to see them, agreeing that if we could do a deal we would put our price on top of his to make our profit. He was more than happy with such an arrangement. He agreed to write to us confirming the deal.

Two days later his letter arrived and I straight away ripped off the letter-head and had it copied at an instant printing shop. I then used this notepaper to write out the specifications of the planes and tanks the Spaniard had told us of and promising the helicopter parts the South Africans required.

Rene signed the letter as the representative of the firm and we took it round to the embassy. Our man was delighted and asked when he could view the planes and tanks. We arranged to meet him and a side-kick at Heathrow the following morning to fly them out to Madrid for the viewing.

They turned up as arranged and we paid their first class fares for the journey. At the other end I had laid on an executive Mercedes – the big six-seater – to ferry us out to the airfield. The South Africans were obviously impressed.

When we arrived at the field, which was little more than a dump for old armaments with the runways left clear, we were all shown around by the manager. He had previously been told by his boss to give us every help he could and the South Africans got the full red carpet treatment.

They were quite happy with the tanks and the manager even had one ready to move – just to prove that they were in working order. However, both Rene and I were somewhat put out when they wanted to see a Mirage in the air. There were half a dozen of them in a hangar and I had a pretty fair idea that they wouldn't manage to get into the air. They probably didn't even have air-worthiness certificates. And, of course, there was also the problem that there was no one around who could fly them.

I quickly explained that we would be more than happy to put one up for them but that they would have to pay for a new set of tyres for it because the aircraft wore one out every time it took off and landed.

That had them. They decided that they weren't interested in seeing the plane off the ground after all. They would take our word for it that they were all in good condition. Their mechanics would check them out before delivery anyway. We left the airfield, drove to Madrid and then flew back to London. In the car back to the embassy we decided to meet the next day to finalise the order and paperwork.

We telephoned the South African from our hotel the next morning and fixed an appointment for the afternoon and then set to with a hotel typewriter and another sample sheet of the phoney paper. When we arrived to see them we were therefore armed with the final weapon in our confidence trick.

We sat in his ornate room and discussed the whole deal for about half an hour before reaching a mutual decision that the final figure would be agreed after his experts had seen the equipment. In the meantime, however, we told him that we would have to have a deposit of £14,000 to hold the deal open.

That he did not like one bit and he began to haggle.

Rene, arch con-man that he is, dropped the two pieces of notepaper on the desk. The first was an outline of the stuff we had on offer and the second was a receipt for the £14,000 "holding payment".

Rene pointed out, with my help, that we had, after all, flown them out to Spain at our expense and that we were obviously in a situation to do the deal. We then offered to squash the whole thing and push off, being willing to write off the business – which we could well afford to do.

That lot sold him and we waited for about twenty minutes until he had organised for the money to be sent up in cash, this because we had told him that we wouldn't trust a cheque as it would perhaps reveal to the authorities that we were dealing with the South Africans.

We left the embassy with fourteen grand to split between us and made our way over the road to Trafalgar Square where we sat on the walls of the fountain and laughed ourselves silly. The whole con had gone like a dream.

Chapter 8

Heroin Triple-Cross

It was pleasant to spend a week quietly at home after the South African con. There were no questions, no answers to give. There had been once, of course. There had been bitterness, tears and argument. But time had passed and even the irregularities of my life, the unexplained comings and goings had achieved a pattern.

The weather was good and the kids were kept off school under the pretence of some phoney illness. It was on the fifth day of walks, picnics and games in the garden that I got a telegram from the Bank through an accommodation address in Paddington which I had started using about six months earlier when I thought it would be a means of getting messages without Homer finding out. I was sure he tapped my phone.

There were no details, just that they had another job for me to do. I called that bastard Homer, I was learning to play by the rules. We would meet as usual. And I knew, however dirty the job, he would want me to go through with it. And, odds on, it would serve some higher purpose to let me down again.

I had cooled off over the last two days. The family knew I was going again and the house got quieter. As a style of life, this had all the trappings of a one-way ticket to nowhere. Already at the back of my mind was the question "Where do I get off?" So far, I had no idea.

The train pulled in through the depressing grey-bricked canyons that lead into the London rail terminals. I had dozed off on the journey and woke feeling uncomfortable in the fuggy warmth of the compartment.

The station was crowded with people setting off on homeward journeys. Nine to five? Other people perhaps, but not me. My trouble now was that I was beginning to feel more and more lonely in moments of self-examination. Who was I?

Working, I was tough, mean, a well paid civil service hood. Living in the lap of luxury in any city you care to name. But when the caper was over, so was I. Like the man whose stature measures up well inside his Rolls-Royce, but who on his own becomes nothing. Another of my troubles. I didn't even have a Rolls-Royce. And I was overdrawn at the bank – the one at home anyway.

I hailed a cab as it came down the ramp into the station and headed across the City towards the West End. As instructed by Homer I booked in at the Cumberland Hotel. It would be tomorrow before I heard anything from that plum-in-the-mouth bastard. Department men would be watching me in the meantime. I still didn't know what the job was about. And I wasn't going to worry.

True to form, there was an envelope waiting for me at reception. Inside was an already-opened letter collected from the accommodation address. It was under the business address of a Geneva import-export agency. I was to travel to Madrid where I would be contacted by two American "business colleagues" at the Alcala Hotel.

It was the first time I had come across mention of Americans involved with the Bank operations in Europe. This was a new dimension. It was something not lost on Homer either. Having helped himself to my mail it had obviously appealed to his warped sense of intrigue. He had enclosed £100 in fivers. Expenses to keep me happy.

This must be something, they were even keeping me happy. I will just mention in passing that it had taken Homer just two weeks to ferret out my accommodation address.

The hotel bar was reasonably full although you could hardly distinguish the numbers in the soft-lit gloom. There was one bird propping up the bar, a high class hooker if I ever saw one. I was half way through a whisky sour when she moved in. I knew she would. It was early and there were no other unattached males in the place.

Must have been a shortage of conventions in town.

152

"Hello," she said, peering at me from beneath heavy eyelashes that made her lids droop with effort. "Waiting for someone?" "Hello, how's business?" I replied, "getting tough?" She stiffened noticeably. "Cheeky fucker," she muttered, trying not to loose her cool and smiling for the world to see. "Interested in a trick or two?" "Who pays, you or me?" I asked, turning to look at her. Talk about burning eyes, like laser beams they were. "Get stuffed, clever boy," she said, trying to keep the decorum that enabled her to pass as a legitimate customer and non-professional. "Hold it," I countered as she made to edge away to look for an easier catch. "I'll blow your chances if you don't just cool it down. I've got an idea ..."

I called the barman over. He was beginning to take an interest anyway. "What's it to be, then?" I queried. She looked at me, "Gin and tonic, thanks," she said and added as an afterthought, "darling."

I gave her the once-over. She was certainly dressed to kill – and to escape the hawk eyes of the hotel staff. One thing hotels don't like is playing host to hookers on the prowl. Does reputations no good at all.

She had blonde hair of sorts, silvery blonde, straight out of the bottle. She was wearing a low cut black evening dress, slim fitting and just enough to be modest and alluring at once. Packaging is half the battle these days. She had a bottled tan, too much make-up and amusing eyes.

"Are you trying to screw me up, by any chance?" she said. "You're not the law, are you?" "Relax," I said. "I happen to have a few hours to kill, a few ideas how to kill them and the money to do it with. I thought you might fit in."

As much as I dislike the idea of paying, a girl's got to live and, I reasoned, we were both in a dirty business. So why not split the proceeds of the dirt money, I thought to myself? I could feel the reassuring bulge of the fivers in my wallet. There were ways and ways of keeping happy.

"What the hell do you think I am?" she said. "A tart with a heart of gold? I've got a working night ahead of me." "We could go upstairs and discuss it," I countered, staring hard at her. "Twenty five, take it or leave it," she said. "Any trouble and I warn you, I've got friends." I laughed. Friends? She didn't know what friends were. And if they tried their friendship on me, they wouldn't know what hit them.

"Room 214," I said. "I'll go up ahead. See you soon."

I took the lift upstairs. I had planned an evening on the town to see a few old friends in the West End, take in a meal and a few drinks, recycling a bit of the taxpayers' money. But now my fertile little brain was working overtime. I decided to let the lady earn her keep – and we would eat well on room service. Homer and his desk-bound mates could pick up that part of the tab for my fun and games.

There was a knock on my door, a gentle tap. I opened it. There she was, leaning on the door post, with a knowing smile. She walked into the room turning to kiss me on the cheek. "Tough guy," she grinned.

I clicked on the TV and took a bottle of Scotch from the bedside locker. Fetching two glasses from the bathroom, I poured a couple of fingers into each. "My name's Leslie," I said, passing her a glass. "Mine's Jean," she said, moving over to my side. "No argument over the price is there?" she said, nuzzling my ear.

I reached into my pocket, fingered through a few notes and counted out £50 which I passed to her. "Transaction completed," I said, "with more to come."

"Feeling flush?" she asked, not knowing whether to be pleasantly surprised or suspicious. "You are straight, aren't you?" "If you're clean," I said.

"Pure and ..." she said. Then: "You still planning a night on the town?" I put my drink down, put an arm round behind her and began undoing the zip. I said: "Try me." She stood up and let the slinky black sheath fall to the floor. I watched as she stripped off.

As I undressed, and not to be outdone, made a play of hanging my suit up properly in the wardrobe, I could feel her watching me from behind. I turned and we tumbled onto the bed. She was pale tanned, well shaped and verging on the plump. She was a true professional with hands, mouth and body, well practised in her own strange vocation. Good enough, in fact, to make me feel that I wasn't the only one enjoying myself.

I don't like complications in my life, or needless aggravation for that matter. Suited me that she was paid. A fuck in such circumstances was an enjoyable exercise and that, for now, was all that this great, bare-breasted bird was all about. Henry Miller, I've always thought, had a point. On the one hand, the guy was a nobody, a down-and-out

154

nothing, having none of the wealth and position of so-called successful men. On the other hand, he screwed his way into the affections of the girls those other guys had to pay to possess. It's the sort of absolute one-upmanship that I like.

The night passed enjoyably. We ordered and ate largely from room service, drank two bottles of wine and the best part of the bottle of scotch without bothering to dress. We tussled drunkenly from floor to bathroom and back to bed.

I slept late – as did my newly acquired business partner, short term contract or not.

At ten o'clock there was a knock on the door.

I opened up. It was Homer. He looked at the blanket I was wearing as a toga, and then over my shoulder at the bedroom.

My newly bought friend was lying uncovered and uncaring, legs akimbo, out to the world. The bedclothes were upside down, the room heavy with stale cigarette smoke and littered with the uncollected clutter of the night.

"You are," he observed, striding into the room, "a bit of a pig in your life style. No class."

He picked up the phone by the bed and called room service and ordered English breakfast for three, telling them very curtly to get someone up to clear up the mess immediately.

Jean had woken up, looking slightly less glamorous than at our first meeting. She clutched at the sheet to cover her ample breasts. "Who's he?" she said, as Homer settled into an armchair and began to read the Daily Telegraph as though this were the waiting room in a well-appointed railway station.

"A business colleague," I said. "Don't worry, he doesn't bite, just barks a bit. I do the biting for him."

Homer looked up from the newspaper. "Dear boy," he said superciliously, "why don't you and your charming piece of Bayswater delight freshen yourselves up before breakfast. Then perhaps you and I can get down to more serious matters."

Jean skipped into the bathroom. I followed. "Don't mind him," I said. "His finer sense of virtue prevents him from getting much – and he's been married to that for twenty-five years." We showered together. She was very naked, very alluring. I was very naked, hung over and didn't have the inclination or energy for sport. I dried her off with the large white bath blanket and made her promise to give me a telephone number. "A girl's got to live," she said, "but I'm always willing to talk terms."

When we emerged the room was cleared and breakfast was laid out on the table. Homer was already eating. Jean, restored to a sense of full awareness, made as much of a show as she could while dressing. I'll swear he only blinked twice.

We ate, making small talk like characters from some bloody stage play, and then I showed her to the door. I gave her the remainder of my expenses. She held the extra £50 and her eyes widened. "I don't know what line you're in darling," she said, "but don't stop, will you?"

She put the money into her bag, squeezed me gently around the zip fastener and walked off towards the lift. I watched as she went.

Homer's boy Frank was idling away his time further down the corridor and he eyed her as she approached. She blew him a kiss and wiggled her tight rear-end at him as she went into the lift. He blushed and began looking for a crack in the masonry to crawl into.

"I suppose you spent all the money I left you?" Homer asked. "Thank you," I said. "We enjoyed Her Majesty's money very much. Pity you couldn't have joined us." "Ha," he replied, attempting contempt. "Dear boy, briefing time." With that he lifted his brief-case from beside the chair, taking from it a number of documents.

"I think we're all going to enjoy this one ..."

What he meant of course, was that they had no idea what was about to happen. A few thoughts, a definite curiosity and me, buggerlugs, to play real live decoy pigeon.

Not too much was known about the Bank's American tie-ups. Or that was what Homer told me. Of course, they had their suspicions, organised crime and that sort of thing, and shared joint interests, laundering of dirty money and so on. Homer, of course, was a triple-faced lying bastard. But that I knew only too well.

We talked for about an hour and arranged that I would keep in touch with what detail I could. Wherever possible he would make sure I wasn't interfered with by local agencies. Madrid was probably only the first meeting place. The scene of the action would almost certainly be somewhere else.

I flew that evening to Madrid from Heathrow, picking up a "travelling" suitcase from Victoria Station on the way and leaving my "home" case behind.

I had got into the habit of keeping my operational gear, right down to the socks I wore, separate from my own stuff. I had a variety of clothes which I replenished frequently in various capitals. There were no labels to speak of on the clothing, nothing to identify me or my place of origin. A clean cut, anonymous sort of person.

In some of the cases I kept a small but powerful short wave transistor, my "other" passports, credit cards and all the essential aids to my trade.

The Iberia flight to Madrid was uneventful. I drank more than usual to lift me over the slow-headed feeling I still had from the night before. Stepping out of the aircraft at Madrid was like walking into a warm oven. As usual I had not enjoyed the flight.

But it was nice to be back in a warm country. I always felt more at home, freer about the body. There was no trouble at the airport. The Spanish make a great play of being thorough with a heavy hint of potential nastiness. I smiled my way politely through the formalities.

I took a cab to the Alcala Hotel, windows open, breathing in the foreign air of the wide Madrid streets, catching up on the sights and sounds of the majestic capital.

I checked into my room, showered and changed and was about to go down for dinner when the telephone rang. It was the front hall. Was I in for two gentlemen who wanted to see me? Yes, I told them, I was. And could they arrange for a drinks trolley to be provided by room service?

A matter of minutes later the two men reached my room. I had left the door open and was sitting in a high backed armchair facing the door. From outside a gentle breeze made the window-netting flutter. The sounds of evening floated over the darkening city roof tops.

My two friends were called Smith and Brown, or so they claimed, as if it mattered. Al Smith and Mike Brown. Their claim to import-export was equally dubious. American they were, by at least half a generation.

Formalities were few, none of us were newcomers. By the time the

157

drinks trolley had arrived such introductions were over and everyone was sure that we were who we were meant to be. We all stopped holding our hands over our holsters.

I handed out scotch with plenty of ice to my new playmates and stuck to neat mineral water myself.

Smith did all the talking. They represented, he said, a customer who had some merchandise which was in a trunk that had found it's way to Lisbon. There, it transpired, it was stuck. Mutual friends had suggested that I was the man to make sure it continued on its rightful way to an address in the U.S. My fee was to be £20,000, half then, half on completion. There was, of course, a one-sided guarantee to the deal. Should this modest trunk not find its way as arranged I would be shot very dead.

Smith, as he called himself, delivered this information as though he were discussing plastics, a trade which he claimed also to be in. It was all matter-of-fact and I was waiting for the trading stamps to be thrown in as a bonus.

Brown just stared aimlessly out of the open window with the apparent intellect of a punch-drunk booth-boxer.

I was thinking fast. A trunk worth £20,000 for a trans-Atlantic trip had to be nasty. Dope, probably heroin. The membership qualifications to the business world of these two hoods stood out a mile. If they weren't Mafia, then George Washington and Richard Nixon were soul mates.

I decided that on what I already knew I should back out – before I was given the facts of where, how, what, and to whom, which would make me bad news.

What I didn't know was that this was no offer. A "Yes" was the only alternative I had to waking up dead. As I found out later.

I stood up and stared out of the window across the sandstone hue of the city. Down below a traffic cop was having a ding-dong of a row with an excited taxi driver, presumably about a traffic law infringement. A small crowd was gathering to watch the real-life drama.

I turned to my unsightly guests and said simply: "Gentlemen, the terms you are suggesting don't sound like any sort of deal. I don't know what your consignment contains and I would rather not know. I

158

don't care for the possibility of dying, particularly when the cock-up could be someone else's. I don't know your organisation and how they play the game. And frankly, if you two goons are anything to go by, honour among thieves is an old Chinese proverb that went out of date way back."

The palms of my hands were sweating. It was not an easy speech to make. Smith smiled weakly. Brown looked like he wanted to erupt.

Smith stood up and made to leave. I said: "I'll contact the Geneva office and tell them this doesn't sound like my sort of line." My hand hovered at my hip-holster as I spoke. Their eyes were rivetted on the bulge under my loose shirt.

Brown followed Smith, scowling with Oscar-winning menace. Smith paused at the door and said: "Ah'll be in touch, stay around, O.K. brother?"

"O.K. mother," I replied deliberately using the wrong word.

I tried to wash the sweat from my hands and then went down to the lobby. I decided against the hotel dinner and made my way downtown for something more colourful. At least I would get some benefit out of the trip.

I found a cheerful little restaurant where the food was plentiful, the wine rough and the atmosphere friendly. Then it was invaded by a coach party of lusty Scandinavians which quite took the edge off my evening. They started, for some reason, singing Italian songs, my waitress got too busy to wink back at me any more, the brandy was appalling and I left.

I walked back to the Alcala, wishing that I had eaten there, and resolving to grab a good brandy or two in the bar.

I didn't notice anything sinister about the elderly black Citroen with whitewall tyres parked across the road.

It was quite late when I went up to my room. There were no messages for me at the lobby desk. I had just got into my room when there was a knock at the door. "Who is it?" I asked, walking quickly over to my suitcase and retrieving from the false bottom my Walther PPK. I had not taken the gun out with me as I had not felt in any immediate danger.

"Smithy, fella," came the voice from the other side of the locked door. I unlocked the door and took two rapid paces back. So-called

Brown hurtled into the room like an overweight Jumbo. I fired. Nothing happened. I scarcely had time to realise that it had been emptied when Brown hit me, full head in the chest. From then on I didn't have a chance.

I think I hit them both once effectively. Brown was an oaf, more stupid than most. I managed to roll out of the way of his second lunge and, as he made to pick himself up, I rammed the drinks trolley straight into his fat and ugly face without even getting off the ground myself. He subsided for a moment, cherry red Campari trickling down over his face and shirt front, and Smith kicked me right in the groin.

The pain made me double up. It also spurred the last ounce of energy out of me. I lunged upwards at him and as he toppled on to the bed I hit him as hard as I could manage in the mouth. Hard enough for a couple of teeth perhaps. But no way had enough.

I was picked up from behind by Brown and got a brief smell of Campari as he began, with peculiar delight, to make a cocktail out of me. I don't remember much else except the continued pounding accompanied by jarring pain, the taste of blood and the feeling of not caring in the end.

It can't have lasted more than a couple of minutes but the succession of punches and kicks seemed endless. It was a surprise when they stopped. I could just about see my two attackers as they straightened up ready to leave me, dusting down their suits.

Smith leant down and grabbed me by the hair. I didn't even have the energy to flinch. But he wasn't going to hit me. "See here, clever bastard," he growled, "we'll deliver the details when you've recovered yourself."

Then they went. I lay there for a moment or two and then dragged myself to the window. Through my swollen eyes I could just make the two men out in the street lights as they walked across the road and got into the black Citroen.

Just like a bloody movie, I thought to myself, as I began to drag myself towards the bathroom. I managed to get to the door of the room and lock it. I was still trying to get to the bathroom when I passed out on the floor.

It was mid-morning when I came round. With the beating and with being on the floor I was stiff. I couldn't move. I lay there for what seemed like an hour before I could move at all and the effort nearly made me black out again.

It took me a week to recover fully enough to leave Madrid.

I tidied up the room as best I could, ate and dozed on and off for nearly two days. On the third day Smith and Brown returned and briefed me on the assignment – which, of course, I agreed to go through with.

After that, helped by healthy doses of scotch, mixed liberally with cold showers, I pulled myself together. I began preparing for the job for which I had so willingly volunteered.

The trunk was being held in safe-keeping near the Lisbon waterfront. It was, I gathered, a reinforced and well-sealed version of a regular traveller's trunk. Its security for the time being was guaranteed.

I contacted a character I knew called Maha the Wise in Paris and arranged to meet him there to discusss a deal. I had no ideas as to how to ship the trunk to the U.S. and decided to sub-contract out to a professional in the trans Atlantic field. That way I stood a chance of being double-crossed. I also had a chance to stay alive.

It would cost me, but such things as staying alive make cost a lesser consideration. I could still come out with a few grand at the end.

Luckily the Alcala asked no questions. They let me be. Perhaps the Englishman is still known for his eccentricities. Perhaps someone was just watching and waiting, holding the hotel's hand. I don't know. Still looking slightly battered, I booked out after the week was up and flew to Paris.

I had contacted Homer in the meantime and obliquely told him what was afoot and that frankly, it stank. As if he cared. My flight to Paris was delayed and it was a bumpy ride all the way. No wonder I hate flying.

I took a cab from Orly and booked into the Scribe. It's a hotel I like for its old world anonymity and atmosphere. The rooms are old and solid, the bathrooms palatial if antiquated. I called Maha the Wise and invited him to meet me for a drink in the basement bar.

I changed and showered and made my way downstairs and to the news-stand around the corner from the entrance to the hotel to buy newspapers and periodicals. As I returned to the hotel a taxi drew up outside. From it emerged two stunning Eurasian girls, long flowing black hair, flashing eyes.

I followed them into the hotel. All eyes in the foyer turned as they stood chatting to each other in the middle, an eyeful of slim brown booted legs, leather coats and brown fur trimmings.

I smiled broadly at them and made my way down to the cavernous basement past the hairdressing salon and restaurant to the dimly lit wood-panelled bar. I walked straight to a corner table and was well into a scotch and the bundle of newsprint I had just bought, when Maha arrived.

Maha the Wise was so called because of all the smugglers into the US he was perhaps the best. He was first-rate if the pay was good. Shrewd and often vicious, he always delivered. And from his well groomed, smart haircut to his Gucci shoes he was a treat. Hand cut, hand stitched suits, silk shirts, were his uniform. Only the precious stones set into the gold rings on his fingers gave a slightly flash edge.

"My dear Leslie," he said, stretching out a well-manicured hand to greet me as I rose from my seat. "How good to see you again. You seem to have been having a problem or two ..."

I was about to ask him what he had been hearing on the grapevine when I remembered that my face still bore the obvious marks of the beating I took in Madrid. Cuts and swellings were still visible although most people had been too polite – or scared – to mention them.

"Oh, that," I said, feeling my still tender jaw. "I was outnumbered and outsmarted for once by a couple of meat packers."

Maha laughed. His laugh was evil, even if his appearance was not. "It is unlike you to be outsmarted, or to allow yourself to be outnumbered, mon brave," he said. "You should pay attention to details."

"Thank you," I replied, "but this time I wasn't making the rules. I was dealing with players from out of town."

We chatted further about mutual acquaintances, business as a whole, and were on to the third scotch when I noticed that the two Eurasian beauties had moved in at the far end of the bar. Maha, his back to the room, appeared not to notice my eyes wandering for a moment.

"What is it that I can do for you, my friend?" he asked. I outlined the deal to him. There was a trunk in Lisbon which I wanted delivered to the Eastern seaboard, no fuss, no questions. I had no idea as to contents, just that it belonged to an influential group of colleagues who were unable, because of other commitments, to fit it in themselves. He was looking straight into my eyes, smiling.

"There's £4,000 in it for you," I said, "half now, half on completion…"

Maha leaned back in his chair and looked abstractedly at the ceiling for a moment or two. Then he said; "From what little you tell me Leslie, this must surely be a consignment of drugs, heroin possibly? It can be the only explanation for the lack of detail as to the contents and for the obvious embarrassment of your associates in the venture. Of course I can arrange it with no problem, but it would cost you at least £20,000. That you must surely realise. Such things are expensive nowadays. Silence is golden, as you English say, and gold does not come cheaply." He rose to leave. "I should ask your colleagues for more money to play with Leslie, or not be so greedy yourself. Think on it, perhaps we can meet tomorrow."

He was obviously interested, his appetite whetted. For him the job would be easy. But even if he dropped his price it was going to be too much for me and what I hadn't told him was the one-sided deathly nature of my commission.

He left and I resolved to think on it for a while. There had to be an alternative. Perhaps I should have been more open with him, and explained the few options open to me. But the man was notorious for his lack of good nature.

I was sitting there, staring into nowhere, when I noticed that the two Eurasian birds were staring at me, giggling. My appetite, spoiled by the unsatisfactory turn of worldly events, began to improve. They really were something and they appeared interested.

I called the waiter over, ordered myself another scotch and told him to invite the ladies to join me. They made a show of shall we, shan't we, and then slunk over to my corner table.

Slunk sounds corny, but slink they did, making use of every feline movement knees could muster.

We talked and drank. These two were really something else. This was like a walking dream. But so natural that I didn't think too much about the why's and wherefore's. Perhaps I should have done. But if a man doesn't plunge straight in, what does he do? Rots while others do the swimming for him.

Anyway, it seemed these two birds had been stood up, in a manner of speaking.

No-one in his right mind would actually have stood these to up just like that. But it transpired that the man they were due to meet, a film type of some sort, had failed to arrive and was now not due in Paris until the next day. A fact which they found most upsetting. What were they going to do? They had cancelled all their other invitations and now it was already early evening. It was not too difficult for Aspin to step bravely into the breach. And it was not too difficult for them to accept my dinner invitation. Which is how I came, half an hour later, to be walking along the Boulevard Des Capucines with both arms full. We hailed a cab and took off in the direction of the Left Bank and St. Michel for something to eat.

My two companions were used to the high life. They decorated the table like hand picked starlets, toyed with their food and drank a lot – the best wines only, of course. I was one course ahead of the plate in front of me every time and when we reached coffee and brandy the anticipation was almost killing me. The innuendos were flying thick and fast and I was being told in delicately fractured English that I was as good as home and dry.

I paid the bill with the generosity of a man who has no tomorrow and we grabbed a cab back to the Scribe. As we crossed the river both ladies were being very friendly. My left hand knew exactly what my right hand was doing because they were both doing it.

My difficulty was going to be which of these angels was I going to entertain? The choice was going to be difficult. Until I realised there was going to be no choice at all.

We got back to the hotel and made a grand entrance. I would have preferred it to have been a quieter entrance, more discreet, but in no way was that possible. Waiting for the lift drew quite a crowd. We hit the room and I hit the bathroom. On the way out I caught sight of myself in the mirror. True, I was still puffy faced and battered from tussling with those two imported matadors in Madrid a week earlier, but no doubt it enhanced my manliness. Aspin, the cocky bastard, winked at himself in the mirror.

But I wasn't prepared for what I found in the bedroom. Only the two bedside lamps were on. And my two dinner companions, with whom I had expected at first to have drinks until one faded out, were lying on the bed and wearing about the minimum.

The one who called herself Tina got up and walked towards me. She still had on her thigh length leather boots, the brown of the leather contrasting with her flawless skin. She was wearing the briefest pair of pants, and one slim arm held to shield a pair of small, pert breasts.

She dropped her arm and drew me to her, kissing me with full soft lips.

The beds at the Scribe were built by a man with love in his heart. They are large, high off the ground, soft and plump. I lay in the middle of the chilly eiderdown. Four soft hands removed my clothes. I had fallen into the middle of a dream.

My two friends became my two lovers. They caressed me, they soothed me, they aroused me without raising the tempo above a waltz. When it was over I slept.

I don't know what woke me. Somewhere in the back of my head a small alarm bell rang. Something, I knew, was wrong. I woke up, blinking in the unaccustomed light, trying to see what was happening. Tina, luscious, naked and sensuous was sitting on the bed, her curved back to me. The other girl was squatting on the floor over by the wardrobe, slim buttocks resting on pale feet. She was searching my suitcase.

I leapt out of the bed and grabbed her by the hair. I flung her back towards where Tina sat, her eyes wide with sudden fear. I kicked the suitcase away.

The looks on their faces had turned from the soft melting pools of earlier seduction to coldness – terror. They both started to grab at their clothes which were piled together on the same chair. I stepped forward and slapped Tina across the face. Her head swung sideways and knocked with a thud against the other girl's. At first they made to attack me, standing like naked tigresses, arms and long nailed fingers at the ready, sweat beading on their trembling chests. But as I made to strike again they cowered, eyes pleading, back to the wall.

"For Christ's sake get bloody dressed and get your cheap arses out of

165

here," I said, angry at myself for having fallen so willingly into the honey-baited trap.

The two girls hurried into the bathroom and locked the door behind them. I checked my cases. The Walther was still concealed, still loaded.

I must have wakened at exactly the right moment. There had been time only for the girl to check through the clothing and find one passport, nothing else.

The notes from Madrid, with the details of the consignment and the contact numbers on both sides of the Atlantic were still under the mattress where we had been lying. I had been going to put them into the hotel safe down in the lobby after my meeting with Maha but had been sidetracked by bloody alley-cats.

I pulled my trousers on and was at the bathroom door as it opened slowly. The girls were terrified. One held a long stiletto type knife in her hand as they edged out and faced me. I grabbed her wrist and wrenched it round. The knife spun out and fell to the floor as her wrist gave. There was a cracking sound as I smacked her arm up to the wall and grabbed her chin with my other hand. "OK, Mata Hari," I said, "and who do you work for?" She said nothing. Tina was transfixed. I let go of the girl's face. There were finger marks on her chin where I had squeezed. As Tina made to back up to the door of the room I grabbed her with my free hand. She bit me, so hard that it broke the skin of my wrist. I pulled her over and cracked her head against the head of her friend. There was blood on her mouth – my blood. "Maha ..." gasped Tina. "He wanted you occupied and he wanted to know your customer."

"Shit," I said, dropping my grip on them. "The conning bastard." I made no move to stop them now. "Your trouble is that you put too much effort into your work. It's all give and no take, isn't it?"

The girl whose chin I had squeezed was holding her wrist like I had smashed it a trifle too hard on the wall. She turned at the door and spat. I sat on the edge of the bed, cursing to myself. I could hear their voices raised as they gabbled to each other as they fled along the corridor. Their exit was going to be a lot less glamorous than their entry.

I was going to run out of hotels at this rate. I called room service and ordered up a bottle of scotch and a pot of coffee.

I stood by the window and stared out across the skyline. Business, I thought to myself, was getting highly competitive. I must have been getting a reputation for being a bit of a soft touch. Or Maha was getting cocky. There was a time when he wouldn't have tried that one on me.

I drank half of the bottle of scotch and ignored the coffee. I ordered breakfast for mid-morning before crawling back under the sheets.

I took breakfast slowly, read the English newspapers available, and dressed with care. I called Maha and told him I thought we could discuss the deal again... He was, he said, glad there were no misunderstandings. "Of course not," I said, and hung up.

I took a cab to Maha's apartment at an address near the Boulevard Des Invalides in Paris 7. The cab battled its way across Concorde and over the river.

The apartment was in an ageing, but graceful building. I walked into the courtyard, nodded to the old lady sitting in the tiny room by the stairs, and walked up to the third floor, ignoring the services of the hand-pulled wrought-iron lift. The front door was opened by an equally old lady. The master, she said was in the salon.

I walked across the hallway to an open door. Maha was standing in the far corner of the room. It was a tall, elegant room, as perfect in its period furnishing, gilt chairs and marble topped tables, as he was in his dress.

He was shaking a cocktail in a silver mixer, smiling with his usual smooth charm. "My dear Leslie," he said, teeth flashing, "a martini would go down well, would it not?" I walked across the room. He put the silver mixer down and extended his hand to shake mine. We shook hands and I said; "I don't think I'll drink, thanks."

I was still holding his outstretched arm, pulling him slightly towards me. There was a momentary question in his eyes which did not have time to formulate. I kicked him in the balls with the hardest right-foot swing I could muster. I connected with crumpling impact.

His eyes opened so wide I thought his eyeballs would drop out. He was gasping for breath, the colour drained from his cheeks. I let go of his hand as he slumped, doubled up, onto the floor and began to vomit. I turned and walked slowly out of the room.

The old lady was hovering about by the door, dusting. She hadn't heard a thing.

The cab was waiting for me at the kerbside, the driver reading a tit magazine. We went back to the hotel.

I booked a telephone call to Endo in Malta and, as there was a two hour delay, took lunch in the hotel restaurant, which incidentally, has all the grandeur of an elderly Cunarder. The call to Malta came and I took it upstairs in my bedroom. Endo was refreshingly keen. Four thousand goes a long way over there, anyway. It was enough. No questions, just send the cash.

It made it all seem like child's play. I made a mental note to keep clear of the sophisticated dealers in the future. And over there on the dusty harbour-side across from Valletta, they knew some very simple rules. I did not have to spell out my reactions should anything go wrong.

Having told him on the telephone roughly what was to be done, I arranged to fill in a few details by cable, which, on their own, would make little sense. He was to provide the means of transport, I would actually have the trunk delivered to him at the time of embarkation.

I went to a post office and sent the cable, rather than send it from the hotel where prying eyes might later look. Then I called my own bank in Amsterdam and asked them to forward £2,000 to Malta by wire. So far, so good. I checked out of the Scribe, paid my bill and ignored the looks that the desk clerk gave me. I would hate to think of the story they had invented amongst themselves to fit the events, as far as they had known them, of the night before.

I flew back to London that afternoon, finding myself stuck with a British Caledonian flight to Gatwick. At least they treat you better than BEA, as it was then, which somewhat made up for landing in the middle of the bloody countryside.

I hired a car from Hertz, called Homer's office and left a message that I would be at the Cumberland again that night.

Homer called me at the hotel that evening. I was propped up on the bed, watching television, resigned to the fact that I might have to stay there for two or three days, hardly leaving my room, while the arrangements were made. He would come and see me, he said, when everything had been arranged.

Homer was always so busy with his dossiers on this guy and that guy that I thought it prudent for me to put the bubble in with the

Americans, just in case he forgot. That was always part of his trouble. This was the type of job that could end up as another ace up his well-educated sleeve to use against me in the future – if and when it suited him.

It was better for me to keep my own record as straight as I could. I rang the US Embassy and spoke to the Narcotics man I knew vaguely from Turkey a few years back. We arranged to meet the next evening at a pub in Shepherds Market.

I got a telephone call from Malta the next morning. I was told that the money had arrived and that a banana boat would be leaving Lisbon at the end of the week. I was given the name and the quay number.

Later in the morning a cable arrived. It contained the rest of the documentary details to fill out the jigsaw. All that was left for me to do was to contact chummy Smith or Brown in Madrid and tell them the time and place of departure and arrival. I kept the conversation with them simple. I got one-word Brown first, followed by a sneering Smith. By way of goodbye I told them to watch out for the next time we met as I felt there were a few matters unsettled between us. Bastards. I also gave them my accommodation address where they would send the first half of my payment.

The trunk was to be despatched, marked "Not wanted on voyage" in the name of a genuine passenger. I called Homer and arranged to meet him the next day. Breakfast together again. I set off from the hotel. A flat-footed friend of Homer's was lurking about in the lobby and followed me too conspicuously. I walked down Park Lane, making sure he was right along there with me, went into the Hilton and made a show of asking questions at the reception desk. Then I went to the lifts and slipped into one with a crowd of blue-rinsed American ladies.

I took the lift to the fourth floor then jumped a down lift to the first floor, before going down the wide steps from the first floor and out of the banquetting exit behind the lobby. I walked down the back streets of Shepherds Market. My tail was nowhere to be seen.

My friend from Narcotics was already in the bar, sitting in a corner. He was surprised to find us on the same side for once but didn't ask too many pertinent questions.

Without saying how I was involved I told him that the trunk was on its way and that, as far as I knew, his department would be interested in the contents. I also said I would prefer the tip-off to be uncredited. He could keep quiet about the source, earn himself promotion or a few more bucks, but he should remember in the future what a good boy Aspin was. We cut the meeting short, lest Homer's friend should happen to chance in on our cosy drink.

I walked back up to the Hilton and in through the back door again. Flatfoot was sitting in a lobby armchair looking angry. A Texan in a cowboy hat and red check shirt was asking him where all the action was. Flatfoot, who knew the environs of suburban Surrey better than anything else, was unable to answer him and was still trying to see if I was among the people leaving the cluster of lifts to his right.

I leant over behind them and said: "Perhaps I can help." Flatfoot nearly burst a blood vessel. The Texan was delighted. I told him to take a taxi to Raymond's Revuebar but that nothing London could offer in the way of action could match good ol' New York town.

As I left to walk back up Park Lane, Flatfoot was right behind me. I turned and walked back to meet him. The veins up the side of his neck were pumping double quick now. I invited him to walk with me and we strolled back to the Cumberland, he wasn't very talkative. We ate in near silence and I got him, slowly but surely, very drunk. He ended up sleeping in the bathtub in my room. He was still there, out cold, when Homer arrived next morning.

"For God's sake, man, get out of that bloody bath," hissed Homer as he saw him through the open door.

Flatfoot, dishevelled and unshaven, didn't know where he was. He shot me a glance from his blood-shot eyes that was meant to be a killer. I wished him well and left Homer to deliver one of the finest pieces of belittling oratory I had ever heard. Flatfoot went and breakfast arrived. We opened the windows and shut the bathroom door. The smell in there was terrible.

"And so, dear boy," said Homer, as though nothing untoward had happened, "What happens next?"

' 'You inform the appropriate authorities of the shipment," I said, suspecting that he wouldn't, "and I go to collect the remainder of my fee."

"Quite, dear boy," said Homer, wiping egg yolk from his chin.

"Do take the utmost care, won't you? We would hate you to have any, er, bother." He just didn't know the half. Or pretended not to.

A week later I got a letter from the Bank's outfit in Geneva telling me to go to Chicago for the pay off. I was given a telephone number to call on arrival.

I had to see it through otherwise I would have been giving myself away. But the thought of me and the trunk reaching US shores together held little pleasure for me. Both of us, in a manner of speaking, could end up with an unwelcome reception committee.

I flew Pan Am to New York. I was worried, drank too much, flirted unsuccessfully with the hostesses and listened to the tapes. The movie was some cloying romantic crap which I had no stomach for.

I was trying to work out the chances between being paid off, shot and dumped according to the contract, or just bailed out with no cash and no bullet. The more I thought about it, the less I liked it.

Every job has got its ups and downs. This had the makings of a real downer.

Out of boredom I tried to sleep, failed. We arrived at New York. The change-over to my Chicago flight was smooth, giving me just about time to soak in a bit of the American tempo, the up-beat pace.

I had time also to check in with Hertz and fix up a car at O'Hara, Chicago, and a route map. The first time I took a hire car out on an American city motorway system, it took me four hours to get back to where I started from. It's a great country, once you know which streets not to walk on and how all the machinery works. A couple of hours later I was feeling my way around the dashboard of a Galaxy 500.

I had called the number I was meant to from a booth at O'Hara. A non-commital voice told me to check into a hotel and call them the next day. I was given a new telephone number to call.

I checked down a list of hotels and picked out the Chicago Hillside on Highway 45. It struck me as being suitably anonymous.

I drove to the hotel without getting lost, checked in and grabbed a snack. In the coffee shop I picked up a woman who was midway on flight from a broken marriage to Reno to break it legally. She was fascinated by my accent – me by her tits. We both, for different reasons, needed some help to pass the time. She was called Sherry and had a bust measurement to match her age – 38.

171

I spent the night in her room, which struck me as sensible. I would rather have faced an irate husband than my potential paymasters trying to steal a march on me. The lady was very American and it was a change for her to be used the same way European men use their women. She'd got this thing about oral sex and shouted a lot when her mouth wasn't full. I got worried about the thinness of the walls. I slept, but kept on waking up. In the morning Sherry still had an appetite for more, which I hadn't. I ended up washing her thirty-eights in the shower while she cooed. Keeping in training is one thing, but this was going to leave me out of the championship stakes when it came to fisticuffs.

She was still lying all over me in no particular hurry to go anywhere when I called the number I was given. I told the same non-voice at the new number where I was, and again I was told to call back later while a meeting place was fixed. "Do you need a broad?" the voice asked in the same monotone, by way of parting. "No thanks," I said, "I've made a good friend all on my own."

"Sure, I'm a good friend" Sherry said as I hung up the phone. "Tell me about yourself." There had been no time for such formalities in the night which had just passed. "Me?" I said. "Oh, I'm a traveller, agricultural machinery, import-export, that sort of thing." "You don't look like a farm boy to me," she said, cupping both large white breasts in her hands, "don't feel much like one, either." I smacked her rump and started to get dressed. "I learn fast," I said, "thanks."

We took another snack in the coffee shop, a sort of brunch, with, as usual, too much food. The throwaway ratio in American eateries must be alarming. I gave Sherry my accommodation address in London, just in case she ever passed through between husbands. She said: "Thanks, fella" and left it at that. I began to know what it felt like to be a one-night stand. I paid the check and went back to my room. Sherry was already talking to a man at the next table sitting alone reading a financial journal.

I called the number again. The voice told me the payout was to be in the car park of a hamburger rest stop just up the Highway from the hotel.

I was given the name of the contact who was to introduce me to my Mafia paymaster.

172

The contact was a name that appeared every other day on the sports pages. An internationally known racing driver, one of the glamour set. I whistled mentally. Some people you can never tell by the company they appear to keep. I was reassured slightly. It sounded as though, for the time being, things were above board and if the Narcotics Bureau had seized the trunk off the banana boat, there was nothing about it in the newspapers yet. Perhaps my luck was holding, perhaps it wasn't.

I changed into slacks and a polo-necked jumper and wore a leather jacket which enabled me to use a shoulder holster for my Walther for the meeting that evening. I got the 500 out of the Hillside car lot and drove the short distance to the drive-in restaurant. It was getting dark. I hadn't eaten since breakfast and had passed the day watching old movies and bad chat shows. I walked up to the counter and ordered a burger. I had left the car at the far end of the lot, slightly back from the road. I didn't want anything to be too easy. While I waited for the burger to come up, I drank a chocolate milk shake, my nerves were tautening their way up for the climax.

The restaurant was almost empty. Apart from the short-order cook manning the charcoal, there was a guy doubling up on the till and counter, and two waitresses in smaller-than-mini skirts watching custom. There was only one other customer, a shabby looking fellow eating his way through a mountain of french fries and ketchup in one corner. He didn't look like a plant of any sort and neither did the staff. So far, I was safe.

The man at the till was shouting down the telephone. It seemed to be a conversation about having the house painted. He was shouting louder than his wife at the other end, that was for sure, and she was getting her own way.

The waitress who served me was a brunette with bad teeth that spoiled the effect of the smile she kept trying to flash. Her mate, leaning on the window near the door watching the car lot, was a peroxide blonde with over-red lips and a flat chest to match her flat feet. She had acne hiding beneath too much Woolworth make-up.

My burger arrived and I ordered a coffee. The burger was hiding under a double portion of french fries. I asked for a plate, shovelled the chips onto it and gave them to the waitress with my compliments. She looked at me as though I was mad.

I had been told my contact man would be arriving in a white Atlantic Fury. I was two bites into the hamburger when I spotted it, about a hundred yards away, drawing slowly towards the car lot and the restaurant. I stopped eating and watched. It was dark now, but the car was conspicuous, white with tinted windows. It stood out in the street lighting, but I couldn't make out how many men were inside. The car drew level with where mine was parked on the lot, and swung slowly in towards it.

When the occupants were close enough to realise the car was empty, it swung slowly round and rolled towards the restaurant. "Here goes mate," I thought to myself and, coffee in one hand and hamburger in the other, I walked casually to the door, pushing it open with my foot. There must have been about forty yards between me and the Fury. It had stopped, slightly sideways on to me, pointing towards the road. I walked slowly and, I hoped, coolly, on. The back passenger window began to slide down with the usual slow regular motion of an electrically operated window. I suddenly realised that from inside the shadows of the car, the blunt snout of a trimmed double barrelled shot-gun was being pointed at me.

Before I could move, there was a crash and flash as the first barrel was fired. The tarmac was alive with whining, rebounding pellets as I felt a searing pain in my legs. The coffee went flying up in the air, the burger dropped to the ground. I leaped to the right as hard as I could, banging down on to the tarmac and grazing the side of my face. As I rolled up into a continuing somersault the second barrel fired and then I was up, running, as fast as I could in an arc towards my car.

The Fury roared off with a screech of rubber, bounced over the sidewalk and headed in the direction of O'Hara.

There were tears streaming down my face, blood soaking my shoes and socks as I flung the 500 into drive and hit the accelerator. I sailed past the restaurant and out onto the road like a cat out of hell. The fat guy at the cash till was standing up, mouth wide open, phone still in one hand, staring in disbelief. The two waitresses were crouching down near the floor, looking as scared as hell. The shabby guy with the chips had knocked the plate onto the floor.

I got back to the Hillside and again put the car well to one end of the parking area. I stumbled out of the car and made for a service entrance to the hotel. I was in agony. It felt as if there were dozens of bits of salt in my leg. I reasoned that they knew they had failed, blasted off too soon, but I thought that they wouldn't be back for more so soon – not in my room already!

I still had my room key in my back pocket and made it into the hotel and to my room via the fire stairs. I locked the door and then pushed every moveable thing up against it.

I took my trousers off. My legs were a bloody mess. There were about twenty pellets in them, a fair ten apiece. But, thank Christ, the damage was not so serious as to lay me out. I washed and bathed my legs in the shower and then began to pick out the pellets one by one. It was a bastard of a night. I kept my Walther at my side and watched the door like a bloody hawk. Every sound, every noise and I jumped like a man on drill parade.

I had a bottle of scotch in my case and I used it liberally on my wounds. I stopped the bleeding with a towel and then after a few hours, dressed the wounds as best I could and bandaged them myself.

There was no one I could call, I just had to sit there and wait it out. I didn't even dare switch on the television. It was a night that lasted longer than any other I could recall.

Dawn came very, very slowly. I had finished off the scotch. My mouth tasted like my legs felt. Bloody awful. The graze on the side of my face had turned blue. I tried to shave, but the graze started bleeding and the face staring out of the mirror was a wreck.

I tidied myself up the best I could and telephoned O'Hara. The only jet I could get out of this hell hole was a direct flight to Amsterdam mid-morning. I reserved a place by telephone and promised the clerk to be there good and early to confirm it.

I went to the hotel lobby and asked the bellhop to collect my bags and call me a cab. The car I wasn't going to touch, the cases I couldn't manage. I hovered round the back of the lobby but there didn't seem to be any loiterers. I was paying the check by card when the blowzy Sherry walked by. "Hello, farmer's boy," she said brightly, "Looks like you should have stayed around and played with me longer." She put a gentle hand up to the brusied and grazed side of my face. I winced. "Thanks, Sherry," I said. "It's just that tractors is a tough market." "Tougher than I thought, sweetheart," she said, "You're a nice boy." And she hurried off to join the man who yesterday had been reading a financial journal who was coming out of the lift. He seemed to have extended his overnight stop.

The clerk gave me back my card, ignoring the state of my face. The bellhop came down with my luggage and helped me out to the cab. I gave him a twenty bill and asked him to check over my room and take care of the towels.

I had eyes in the back of my head all the way to the airport. And I didn't feel much better there either. So many people made me nervous. I picked up my ticket and, with the help of a porter, checked in my baggage straight away and went through to the departure area. From there I telephoned Hertz and told them to pick up the car.

I felt safer, but not much. For the moment, on reaching this comparative safety, I felt like ringing the voice on the telephone and telling him that he and his racing man still owed me. I thought better of it.

Still, there were going to be a lot of disappointed people. The Mafia link for one had showed their displeasure last night. Their trunk had gone astray, as planned, for sure.

My Maltese connections were going to be unhappy too when I told them delivery had failed. No more money for them. Partly, of course, because there was no more money for me either. Not only was I disappointed, I was sore as hell from the feet upwards.

I had played it easy with my Narcotics man, now I could do with the cash I could have asked for. On the whole deal, by the time all the expenses were paid, plus the two thousand I had already sent to Malta, there wasn't going to be much left for me.

The flight was called. The feeling of elation was incredible as the jet lifted up over the smoky city, cars flashing along the auto routes in the sunlight. One of them, I felt sure, was out hunting for blood. Mine. I scanned the fellow passengers on the flight. They looked straightforward enough. Anyway, how would anyone know I was on the flight? I booked last minute. You never could tell, however.

I was more relaxed now, but still nervous. When the stewardess offered me a drink I was half asleep, and I nearly jumped out of the bloody seat. I took a coffee, the nearest thing to breakfast for the day. I had the row of seats to myself and felt assured by that. I dozed almost all the way to Amsterdam, not even eating on the way. It's odd how I can sleep on planes, trains and boats but almost never in bloody bed.

Schipol was cool and refreshing. I transferred immediately on to a flight to London. By early evening I was back. I felt like a change of scenery and took a taxi to the Inn on the Park.

I wore dark glasses and made light of my bruised face at the booking-in table in the hallway, told the girl I had been in a car accident in Chicago the day before.

"Where did it happen?" she asked with pleasant concern.

"Oh," I said, "In a car park."

I got a single room at the back of the hotel on the second floor and called Homer's office. I told them I needed to talk to him urgently and would he call back.

I showered, put fresh bandage on my legs and some ointment I had bought at Heathrow, and went to sleep.

Homer arrived at about nine o'clock, dressed up like a stuffed penguin with a red carnation in his buttonhole, on his way to, or from, some dinner or other. He accepted a scotch because I didn't have gin and told me that I looked a mess.

"I think I need a doctor," I told him, showing him my legs.

"It will be arranged, dear boy," he said, producing a couple of folded telex sheets form his coat pocket. It was an Interpol message reporting the fact that a consignment of drugs, believed destined for a major drugs ring operation, had been picked up during a routine search of a banana boat shipping in from Portugal.

"Of course, you wouldn't know anything about that, would you dear boy?" he asked.

"I thought you would have told them," I said.

"Of course, of course," he said.

"Sometimes Homer," I said, "You are a lying rotten bastard." He smiled benignly and left.

An hour later the doctor arrived. He was a small man in cavalry coat with dandruff and bad breath. He poked and pushed at the mushy mess that passed as my legs and kept on tut-tutting. It took him half an hour to deal with me. We scarcely made conversation. I didn't feel any better.

I made a telephone call to Malta and broke the bad news to Endo.

He had already heard about the ship being raided and assured me that no one at their end had talked. I told them that I hoped they were sure, because when and if I found out who had told the Yanks, I would move in once, decisively. Endo was impressed. I felt secure as well, they obviously had doubts about their own operation now and money wasn't mentioned.

I spent the night with the television, had dinner in my room and dozed fitfully. In the morning I rang the US Embassy and spoke to my Narcotics man. "You got what you wanted," I told him, "and I missed my payoff. What's in it for me?" He hummed and hawed for a bit and said it was awkward. It was out of his hands and obviously to protect me no names had been mentioned. It had now become a political operation – by which he presumably meant CIA involvement – and simply there was no money to be had for me.

"I could manage a few hundred out of petty." He volunteered.

"Good" I said, "I can take a cheap holiday. By Christ, I need a rest."

Bastards. No payoff there either, I thought to myself. I must be losing my grip. I could end up martyred for charity at this rate.

The next morning, there was a hand delivered envelope containing 250 dollars downstairs. I used it to pay the bill, pocketed the change and left my baggage with the hall porter. Then I went for a long slow walk in Hyde Park, sat on a bench by the Serpentine and had a long conversation with the ducks. Ducks don't answer back.

It was while I was still resting up at home after the Chicago affair that Homer came up to see me on his own. For a couple of hours he and I walked, me still limping slightly, through the quiet streets of my local town. He impressed upon me the need for my continuing assistance and his fears that I was getting ready to pull out.

He was right. I had about had enough of his end of the business and I was worried about reports that other agents were getting into bother in Ireland. I asked him for his assurance that all would be well if I got into real trouble – that he would extricate me from any mess I got into.

He made all the right noises but didn't convince me that he was in a real situation to look after me.

What I really wanted was to get some official assurance from the

British government that I was working for them. Homer said that this was impossible.

After he had left I worried about this for some days and then went to a solicitor for advice on the matter. He suggested that, as I had a local policeman seconded to look after me and my home, we might make an approach to the Chief Constable in my area.

With nothing to lose, I agreed and, two days later, we met the Chief Constable by appointment. For what it's worth the following account by my solicitor records the Chief Constable's tacit acknowledgement of my work for the Department.

"Re; Mr. Leslie Aspin.

"Mr. Aspin called to see me yesterday, Monday. He had previously called to see me a few days earlier and was extremely worried then because he had been approached in a matter of what he considered to be of national importance and was fearful of the consequences.

"In view of his continued alarm and the fact that time was dragging on I thought that he should take some positive action very quickly, it became apparent that he wanted assurances from somebody in authority.

"I therefore telephoned the Chief Constable, arranged an appointment for me to see the Chief Constable with Mr. Aspin this morning at 11 a.m. I went to Police Headquarters this morning with Mr. Aspin, and saw the Chief Constable – there were the three of us alone.

"I explained that I only had a very rough outline and in those circumstances I wanted to know the details but I gathered that Mr. Aspin had some information which could be of importance and that he had been approached in order to participate actively in what might amount to a criminal venture. He was worried about the future in case it turned sour and wanted an assurance by somebody in authority that his position would be safeguarded and also if at any time in the future he required protection, this would be given.

"On the latter point, the Chief Constable explained the difficulties of protection but that most certainly, if Mr. Aspin were assisting generally, then such protection as they could offer would be forthcoming. So far as the former was concerned, the Chief Constable explained that under no circumstances could he sanction Mr. Aspin doing anything which might be construed as being illegal. There was some discussion and then I told Mr. Aspin that the Chief Constable had been very fair and I was not inviting the Chief Constable to comment on my remarks but quite clearly, although the Chief Constable was in no position because of his office, to sanction anything illegal, it was apparent to me that he was as eager as I was for Mr. Aspin to co-operate and I for my part would do what I could to assist Mr. Aspin if he came unstuck and doubtless, the Chief Constable or those instructing Mr. Aspin if he chose to assist, would do likewise.

"Mr. Aspin then asked to be left alone with the Chief Constable and I left the room and returned to my office. Mr. Aspin then phoned me at lunch time today and informed me that he was with the Chief Constable and two other persons for approximately 1 hour and he asked me to make a note of this interview – 1 (one) copy of which he would keep in a safe place. I therefore make this note immediately."

I felt just a little safer with that letter locked away and agreed to make a quick foray into Holland about a week later to check out rumours of Black September Arabs being seen around Amsterdam.

The rumours were true and I even found one who had been on the staff of the Colonel who knew me. Two hours steady drinking and old-times story swapping brought forth the information that he and half a dozen colleagues had been keeping a watchful eye on a couple of TIR containers which had been dropping off stuff right across Europe. Their final destination was Amsterdam and they were now filtering out one at a time.

I managed to confirm the drop points in Paris and Brussels, both of which I already knew, but he couldn't give me the details of a new one in Rome. But Rome occupied his mind more that the others, he gleefully told me that his colleagues intended to blow up a Pan American or El Al aircraft at Rome airport before the end of the month. This was in December, 1973.

Unfortunately he had no more details. If he had he would have parted with them to an old and trusted colleague like me. With nothing more to learn I left the drunken Arab, collected my bags and flew out.

At a meeting the next morning with Homer I passed on the

information about the Arabs and made a particular point of the Rome threat.

He promised to pass on this information to the three governments concerned.

I'm almost positive that he never did this and the thought that I trusted him to do so and did not make sure myself that they knew leaves me sick every time I think of it.

Before the end of the month a Pan Am plane was blown up on the Rome tarmac. I'll never forgive the bastard for that.

Chapter 9
Maltese Murder

Someone in Whitehall was obviously operating a stringent economy operation. Homer had told me that I was thought a lot of – I was on the payroll. And so what was I doing on an economy night flight to Malta, I wondered, if it wasn't that the fare was half the day rate.

"We are about," said the smooth airline voice up front, "to cross the Alps." The P.A. system crackled and I looked out of the window to my left.

There beneath us, like giant waves in the midnight darkness, were the Alps, blue, white and then sharply shadowed. One day, I promised myself a winter sports holiday there with the nobs.

The flight from Heathrow to Malta took a little over three hours. Getting through the two-bit airport at two o'clock in the morning took almost as long, it seemed. I stood in the queue for passport control. There were two channels but neither seemed quicker. They weren't – one man was operating both. I reached the window and he was busy working on his nose. He scarcely glanced at the passport.

There was another wait in the customs hall. The baggage came in driven on little tractors straight off the tarmac. By hand it would have been quicker.

Outside the customs hall was a scene like carnival time in Rio. For every man, woman and child on the aircraft, there were ten to meet them.

I elbowed my way through the howling brats and what looked like half the island's population. Luckily for my sense of security only one in ten came up to my armpits, useful if you're the type who gets uptight in crowds.

A gaggle of taxi drivers attacked me outside the exit. I chose the oldest looking guy thereby revealing the Englishman's inherent feeling for the lame duck. The guy was probably the richest. His car would more than likely be the best maintained in the fleet. He had an elderly black battered Chevrolet. The drive to Paceville and the Dragonara Hotel took an eternity as he coaxed each cylinder in turn. Having missed half the night's rest already, I wasn't too bothered.

He took the longer route towards St. Julian's following the Sliema front road. The streets were mostly empty except for occasional revellers. As we passed the Preluna Hotel on the Sliema sea front there was the usual late night crowd and the island's two sports cars were drawn up in front.

The Dragonara night club – the hotel bar by day time – was still in full swing when we arrived. I paid the ridiculous price the old cabbie asked for without query. Too true, he must have been the richest.

My room overlooked the sea. To the right the casino was lit up. The sound of cars starting up and people leaving occasionally punctuated the soft tumbling of the sea on the rocks beyond the hotel pool.

I ate breakfast in my room, sitting half out on the balcony. My brief was, as Homer called it, simple and straightforward. Which meant anything but.

The Claudia and Sea Fox affairs were worrying. Homer thought I would be able to use Malta as a base to continue watching the Libyan-Irish arms route and keep a general ear to the Mid-East scene. I was not so sure.

After the Claudia my reputation could be getting dubious. If anyone suspected, I could wind up in a nasty shape and have a snowball's chance in hell of getting in on anything useful.

The only way to go was head first, attack being the only form of defence this time. I rang the Colonel at his office in Valletta. The Colonel was still winning the Mr. Nasty title hands down. He held diplomatic status in Malta and with the close ties being developed between Malta's Premier Mintoff and the arch-maniac Ghaddaffi, that diplomatic status was not queried. While in Malta he worked out of the Libyan delegation offices in the heart of Valletta in Old Theatre Street just off Kingsway, the main drag.

Malta, at that time, was becoming even more important as the centre of European illicit arms traffic for all parties, with no little thanks to the Colonel and his mad master.

What stuff didn't pass through the island was contracted there. The Colonel was not at all surprised to hear from me. We arranged to meet at his office, at his insistence. I wasn't happy about it but he refused to come out to me.

The hotel had fixed up a hire car. Like at least half of the cars on the island it was a Triumph with a sunroof. And like three quarters of the cars on the island, it was well knackered.

The Colonel greeted me profusely. He did everything profusely, including sweat. We made small talk and I told him I was again on the look-out for business. He stared at me, long and hard, and then rifled through a stack of papers on his polished oak desk. It seemed I could be in luck.

The conversation touched on the Claudia and Sea Fox affairs. We agreed that nobody could be trusted anymore these days. Our particular barrel was full of rotten apples. None, of course, more rotten than the Colonel. He was sounding me out, for sure. Then he told me of a new shipload or arms, including rocket launchers, destined for the IRA. Perhaps he reasoned, I could act as link man. I was back in business, but had to be careful. I left the Colonel. He said he was going to find out more details, but I knew he wanted more time to check me out.

I left the delegation offices and walked to the bottom end of Strait Street behind the Law Courts were the car was parked. Turning the old banger out on to the lower road skirting the walls of the city and heading up towards Floriana, I realised I had company. There were two cars following.

Both followed, turning right to cut behind Floriana, past the front of the main police station and down to Sa Maison to link up with the Sliema road. It was the beginning of the tragi-comedy sequence of events in which there were so many minders that they couldn't help tripping over each other. Which saved my life.

It was an uncanny experience. But if there was ever safety in numbers, this was it.

The possibilities were plenty. Homer had probably contacted the British Embassy, or the cover operation, an import agency with offices just off Kingsway, conveniently near to the Libyan's office. Their brief would be to keep a guardian eye on me. Not so much to save my skin but in their own interests.

By going to the Libyan office I would also have alerted the Israelis to my being on the island again. And there were the Maltese themselves who, at police level at least, had no desire to encourage the use of the island as a brokerage house for terrorism. The Libyans themselves would also be careful to see how I behaved. There could even be a CIA man flexing his muscles in the shadows. He would get his information from either the Israelis or the Maltese police.

The cars followed all the way back to the hotel. I went up to my room and then, changing into slacks over swimming trunks, went down to the bar.

It was practically empty. Within seconds of the first drink half a dozen different lone drinkers with newspapers to read wandered in trying to look inconspicuous.

One by one they ordered non-alcoholic drinks and sat far apart. I went outside and lay by the pool, swam a few times and lunched in the sunshine. My fellow drinkers didn't budge.

After lunch a telephone call came from the Colonel. I took it in the bar. He wanted me to arrange for transportation of the "cargo" link with the "importers" at the other end and fix with them suitable payments for the crews. The cargo would be free of charge (a now regular part of policy to encourage terrorism in the West). The importer would pay transport costs as usual.

I agreed to the suggestions and wondered for a moment at the speed and ease with which everything was falling into place. Nodding a goodbye to the assembled company in the bar, I went upstairs, changed and went to the car. I drove off casually and watched with amusement as not two, but this time three, cars made hurried exits as I pulled out through the high walled gateway.

I drove up towards the Cable and Wireless office and, a good hundred yards in front of my pack of tails, cut sharp to the right just before the Cable and Wireless building, sped up the narrow road as though to join the coast road, the obvious route back towards Valletta. The other cars hit the small road as I reached the end of it. I turned left out of their view, but instead of taking the coast road U-turned back on myself. The three blind mice hit the coast road, crossing the intersection fast.

I drove back into Paceville, dumped the Triumph and went into a small car hire firm. When I left ten minutes later I was driving a white Ford Escort in which I took the Msida road to Valletta.

My first call was to Endo and when I left, a bottle of red wine later, a date had been fixed for that evening at Chains restaurant at the water's edge by Spinola Creek. There I was to meet the Greek skipper of a German owned tramp who would take on the deal.

I drove to the Phoenicia Hotel at Floriana, stuck the car in the car park at the side, and made my way through the gardens to the swimming pool which is set a couple of hundred yards from the hotel itself.

Drinks for me and the barman and a few quid and I was using his telephone. I sent a harmless enough looking telegram to Dublin, another to Homer's cable address and then called the Colonel. We arranged to meet at 10.30 p.m. the next night behind a church on a deserted stretch of the road between Valletta and the mediaeval city of Rabat inland. I remember thinking that the Colonel was getting more cautious. He had registered my objections about meeting at his office perhaps.

There were a couple of hours to kill now and I dozed and drank my way through them at the Phoenicia pool side. I had no wish to return to the Dragonara and chance stumbling over the missing nursemaids who, by now, must have been tearing their hair out.

I parked the car in a narrow side street up behind Chains and walked the few steps down to the restaurant. Dusk was falling and the creek looked like a picture postcard. The stone of the fishing cottages took on a reddish hue in the evening light. The multi-coloured wooden fishing boats lay still on the quiet waters and the old women selling fish from stone slabs half way up the hill on the other side of the creek were packing up to go home, their chattering voices echoing across the narrow strip of water.

186

The dinner was straightforward. The skipper agreed, with no fuss, to the deal offered. Smelling the money, he agreed to run my undisclosed merchandise from Tripoli to Ireland via whatever route he thought best. The nature of exports from Tripoli being what they were, and his tramp being no oil tanker, he obviously knew what was involved. We were too polite to go into detail. We arranged to meet later to decide on frequencies and codes and he left to recruit the extra guards he would need to protect this cargo in the event of trouble.

I left at about 11 o'clock, drove the short distance back to Paceville, and went into Sacha's night club. The English manager was still there, remembered me and let me buy him a drink. He made life sound like non-stop Chicago in the thirties, but came up with genuine non-fiction in the shape of a couple of local swingers with nothing but time on their minds.

The place was full of local eminents passing time with virtual juveniles away from the prying public and family eyes. The music was good, the drinks expensive — as always.

I found myself with a shapely little blonde girl called Angela who must have been half of my age at the most. We had a laugh and decided to hit the casino. She was drunk before we left. It was past one o'clock in the morning and the casino was only half full with an ill-assorted bunch of players losing their Maltese shillings under the dusty chandeliers.

Angela and I played roulette, took an hour to come up evens and left. I drove northwards up the coast road and pulled off the road where some rough sandy tracks led to the rocky edge of the water.

Half my age she might have been, but half my experience not. With this lithesome little creature I found myself involved in back-seat exploits that I had forgotten existed. We were halfway through the bout, me holding back for some hesitation about misleading a potential minor, she clawing away with the appetitie of a hungry cat.

She had a warm skin, dusky from hours of sunshine and a sweet smell of cologne mixed with human humidity, breasts that were full, firm and soft and perfect white teeth. As matter-of-fact as asking the way to the city centre she paused, sitting atop of me, and informed me that it was now after two o'clock and that she should be home by three. "Angela," I said feeling the tightness of her firm young backside on my thighs, "for you, anything." "Quick then," she said, smiling and humping away with a wild abandon that belonged on celluloid.

Somewhere, I thought to myself, something was wrong. Sex in the moonlight by the Med was one thing. When things are so easy I should have learned by then that the payoff line must have snags.

She came with a great gasp and shuddering, and I just lay there. I could have stopped the life-clock right there. It was like virgin honey, if there is such a thing.

Within minutes my Maltese Lolita was clambering over the car seat all naked limbs and abandon.

She began pulling on her clothes. "Besides," she said "we can't stay here too long, the police will come and check up." Talk about anti-climax. The mention of the police made me rigid with momentary panic. In Malta, of course, things were not always that easy. Morality patrols feature as a major piece of crime beating, particularly in the early hours.

I dressed in about fifteen seconds flat and swung the Escort back towards the road. Angela lived somewhere back of Valletta towards the island's main hospital, St. Luke's. We took the coast road. Under the tunnel that short-cuts the road through a hill ridge, there was a cluster of cars. It was a group of local speed kings holding time trials in and out of the lit up stretch of road in the tunnel. It's a regular cause of local juvenile fatality, they tell me. She ducked as we sped past the cars, to avoid recognition, and then guided me to her home.

Then I learnt what the payoff was all about. My sweet little Angela went to bed at ten o'clock, bid goodnight to her dutiful Catholic family, and then, half an hour later, clambered out of the window for a taste of the night life. Now all we had to do was get her back up into her bedroom window without waking family, neighbours, or chancing on a local police patrol. It was all I needed – to get run off the island on a morality rap.

I coasted the Escort down the slight gradient to the house which stood cramped between a row of others. Once under the protruding wooden window balcony, a common feature of Maltese houses and in this case, her bedroom, we stopped. Which is how at three o'clock in the morning, when I should have been minding my own business, I came to be standing half in and half out of the sun roof of a family saloon car, playing step ladder to a seventeen-year-old nymphette.

I sweated, she cursed foully under her breath and, with what I would have thought was enough noise to wake the dead, tumbled through the narrow side window on the balcony. The window shut immediately and I slid back into the driving seat, releasing the hand brake. As the car rolled to the next corner I saw in the rear mirror all the house lights suddenly come on. There was a lot of shouting and screaming.

I flicked the ignition on and the car sprang into life as the front door of the house was flung open. A balding man in vest and pyjama trousers came hurtling out of the door as I high-tailed it out of sight.

As I turned at the crossroads at the bottom of the side road I could see the irate papa standing at the top corner, blaspheming into the night and tearing at his thinning hair. The car lights were off and hopefully there was no chance for him to spot the registration number in the panic.

I cursed quietly to myself and, still sweating, headed back to the safety of my hotel room.

There were two men sitting on the leather settees in the lobby who both looked up sharply as I walked in.

"Evening all," I said, picked up the key and started upstairs. Both stood up and flashed lightning at me with their eyes. It was nearly four o'clock in the morning.

"Breakfast at midday, I think, don't you?" I said and turned my back.

I dozed fitfully through the night and spent part of the morning sunbathing on the balcony. Then I made some innocuous sounding telephone calls just to tie up a few loose ends. I called the Colonel and told him that our cargo would have to be shipped on a credit agreement, repayable on a C.O.D. basis. It would cost him £18,000 now, to include my fee and another five Gs for me on completion. He listened and agreed curtly.

I spent most of the afternoon by the pool. Predictably, my watchers turned up and if anything, there were more of them this time. One of the calls I had made in the morning was to a Lebanese Arab I knew on the island, a freelance friend of Endo's who posed as a shipping agent, who I had used before. I asked him to provide me an "escort service." He would also be useful visiting people on my behalf while I entertained the security circus who today would try hard not to lose me. They also knew by then that I had switched cars.

I ate at the hotel and towards the middle of the evening slipped into a lightweight suit, strapping on my Walther in a shoulder holster. I had a premonition that tonight might not be plain sailing.

Forty-five minutes before rendezvous time I drove out of the hotel driveway. Three cars disengaged themselves from the line of parked vehicles and followed me. I drove into Valletta and parked opposite the old Governor's Palace. I walked into Cordina's, the coffee house, using the side entrance by the car park. As arranged, Ricky, the Lebanese, was sitting at the bar drinking coffee. I walked by him towards the pay desk to buy a coffee ticket and slipped the car keys into his jacket pocket as I walked passed. I was choosing a cake from the other counter when he left through the front door.

I spent twenty minutes sipping my coffee before leaving and walking out along Kingsway, away from the car park. I cut down, walking part of the way along Strait Street ignoring its fat and toothy whores.

Behind me, the legion of tails were keeping a respectful but close enough distance. At the bottom of Strait Street I saw the Escort pull across and broke into a run. I could hear the others running behind me.

Then I was down on to the intersection. The Escort was cruising slowly, Ricky at the wheel. Behind him, honking its horn, was an elderly delivery truck.

I snatched the passenger door open and threw myself in. Ricky gave all the throttle he could and with a squeal of tyres we were away. At least one of the tailing cars, a Triumph, had had enough sense to link on to him when he picked up my car from the car park. That was now stuck behind the delivery truck which had obligingly stopped. We hit the road out through Birkikara towards Rabat, reached the rendezvous point five minutes ahead of time, parked at the roadside in the shade of a rare clump of trees and circled round to the back of the church in the shadows. I could not help but feel that the Colonel might chose this moment to pay me off in lead rather than cash.

Two minutes after 10.30 a brown Mercedes 220 SE drew up behind the Escort. Four men got out and walked up to it. I moved forwards quietly in the shadows with Ricky behind me. The Colonel had three muscle men with him but they seemed to be relaxed. I loosened the

Walther in its holster and worked my way round so that I was behind the group. The idea was that Ricky should stay behind me when I declared myself.

"Good evening, Colonel," I said, still in the darkness. The group swung round as one.

"I wanted to be sure of your intentions before we shook hands," I said, stepping out so that they could see me. Their hands remained at their sides, from inside me, my inner tension began to subside.

"Good evening to you too, Leslie," said the ever-courteous Colonel, his teeth flashing in the darkness.

"What would make you think anything so uncharitable? Our mutual interests are far too close to allow for any, hum, nasty misunderstandings."

I smiled, thinly and joined them. Yes, he agreed on the price and had some cash for me already. An envelope changed hands. In it I would find details as to the cargo and when it could be collected.

"I'm glad," I said, "that it is all so uncomplicated. It's good to do business with you, Colonel. I'm afraid I shall not be able to stay in Malta for long. My arrival seems to have stirred up rather too much interest. There are faces following me everywhere."

"As you wish, my men have told me of it. Hence this meeting out here," he said, scuffing at the earth with a pointed shoe. He seemed to find my popularity with other security agencies reassuring as to my trustworthiness, or untrustworthiness, which ever way you look at it.

We parted. Ricky stayed in the shadows and I lounged about by the Escort until the Merc had swung out into the road and headed back in the direction of Valletta. The night air was warm and quiet except for the clicking of crickets the trees.

To avoid any misunderstandings should the Merc be waiting round a dark corner, we drove on up to Rabat and took an alternative route down to St. Julian's.

Once there we went into Charles' bar in Spinola Road. I wasn't aware of being spotted, but somewhere along the line the tails must have linked in again. I recognised one of them as he looked in through the door and pushed off. The meeting with the Colonel over, I wasn't too concerned.

Ricky and I sat and discussed the deal for about an hour over a glass or three of scotch. He was to take over dealings with the Greek for me and act as paymaster locally if and when I left.

We were sitting at a table to the left of the door from the street. The blue neon-lit bar was to the right of the door. Behind us was the kitchen.

We had been chatting for about fifteen minutes when an Arab guy in a greasy ill-fitting suit and dirty, open-necked shirt, came in. He made a great play of picking out some records on the juke box and ordered a beer.

Ricky and I carried on talking. The Arab walked across the bar to the telephone in the corner of the room to our left. I watched him out of the corner of my eye. He glanced at us as he talked quietly on the telephone.

After the telephone call the guy walked back to the bar, finished his beer and left.

"I think that schmuk was watching us," I said to Ricky. He shrugged and said: "Leslie, you must relax. There are plenty of his type around. He just liked the colour of your eyes."

We left the bar. Opposite was a line of fishing cottages, now mostly converted into chi-chi holiday homes, standing between the street and the sea. Obliquely opposite was a slipway down to the water's edge.

As we came out, a car roared into life to our right about 60 yards away. In the glare of its headlights I couldn't see clearly but instinctively ducked and leapt behind a parked car. I crouched there between the car and the wall of the bar. Further along the pavement, Ricky was down as well, lying full length against the side of another car.

The oncoming car shot past and, about twenty five yards along, screeched to a halt. There was some shouting in Arabic and a slight figure darted out of the front passenger door.

He ran round the front of a black Mercedes back down the street towards us and then darted in between the parked cars onto the pavement. As soon as he got on to the pavement he started firing a hand gun. He fired between four and six shots and ran to within about ten yards of me. Ricky was lying absolutely still. I had the Walther out and was kneeling pressed against the wall, holding it in the two handed firing position.

192

I don't know what chummy was firing at exactly. There couldn't have been much to see, the street lighting was so bad.

Presumably he thought he must hit something in this direction. He was shooting on the run and there was no real danger.

Suddenly he turned on his heels and headed back up the pavement towards the Merc. He could have been out of ammunition, I don't know, but he was certainly retreating. What I do know is that after two rapid shots from my Walther the guy was somersaulting along the pavement, sideways into the wall of a house.

The Merc pulled away fast, rubber burning on the smooth tarmac. Chummy was slouched against the wall, half twisted with the force of impact, his feet and legs out behind him. There was blood coming out of the side of his mouth. his eyes were bloodshot, skin sallow and his face ripped open, probably from hitting the wall. He must have been about 30. It was the same guy who had been in the bar. He had nothing in his suit pockets to indicate who he was. There was a cheap plastic wallet with nothing but a few low denomination notes, some stamps and a chewed up snapshot of two young children.

He was dead, both shots had connected. Neither the Colonel or any of his men could ever put him together again.

The juke box inside the bar was still playing loudly. If anyone had heard anything, they weren't being nosey.

Ricky and I grabbed an arm each and dragged the failed assassin along the pavement, across the road to the slipway, down to the water's edge and flung him into the water with a splash. Who found him, or whether this mates came back and fished the body out, I didn't wait to find out. It was never publicly reported, that's for sure.

As we hurried back up the slipway I gave Ricky the car keys again and told him to return the car for me later in the day.

I walked quickly away. At the end of the street, on the far side of the road, was one of the cars that had been tailing me earlier. They had watched the whole shoot-out and done nothing. Bastards. But then, they would have been quite happy for either side to win the match. Surveillance is non-interference.

I moved quickly through the back streets, down past the Roundabout pub, across the front of the Hilton and slipped in through the casino driveway to get to the hotel.

In the lobby a guy I knew to be the security man was talking to a Maltese detective. They watched my every move as I picked up the key.

Three hours later I managed to make a stand-by seat on the night flight back to Heathrow. No one tried to stop me. Just in time, it seems. Soon afterwards I learnt that because of my "associations with undesirable persons" I was persona non grata on the island. I also had no further desire to play any more of the Colonel's strange games.

Heathrow at 6.30 in the morning wasn't very desirable either. I couldn't face waiting for the airport bus so I took a cab into town. Soon I would have to face up to Homer and report that my eye on the Maltese situation had been somewhat short-lived. If he didn't already know.

I took the taxi into the West End and booked in at the Hyde Park Hotel. After breakfast I showered and shaved before calling Homer's office. There was a call back within half an hour. We were to meet in the basement coffee shop of Simpson's, at 11.30.

As I walked along Piccadilly I spent ten minutes buying bits and pieces on the ground floor before going downstairs to the coffee shop. Homer, considering that he had probably heard of my balls-up, was in a reasonable humour.

I told him roughly what had happened in Malta. The narrower my escapes, the more amusing he found it.

"And is the deal still on, do you think," he asked "or was the Colonel merely playing around with you?"

"He wanted me dead, all right," I told him, "but the deal should still be on. It's set up and it's cost him cash already. He was just willing to have me out of the way once the ball was rolling. They don't trust me any more."

Homer thought for a while, fingers arched under his chin. "Then you can pretend to give him the benefit of the doubt as to his responsibility in the matter and continue with the deal, can't you?" he said, thin lipped, eyebrows raised.

"Christ, Homer," I said. "You have got to be joking. That mob are like bloody poison ... You can stuff it."

"Hush, dear boy," he said, glancing round the restaurant, "Please

194

remember where you are. I can't see what you're objecting to. If you bounce back as large as life, there is always a chance that they will assume a lack of guilt on your part. Anyway, they're not very good at their job are they, old chap?" He paused and then added: "I'd hate to read the riot act to you. I really think you ought to take my suggestion very seriously."

I looked at him, at the old school tie neatly knotted into the crisp cut of the starched collar, at the lumpy Adam's apple protruding from above it. How I wished I could strangle the guy then and there.

"You don't give me any choice, do you," I said and he just smiled that clever boy smile of his. His long-time threat still stood. He would shop me to everyone I had ever worked with.

My brief now was to operate on the deal out of London and we were to meet again at the end of the week. Homer gave me a parting gift.

He paused after paying the bill and said: "I received a message from our chaps in Malta just before I popped out to meet you. Seems two of our Libyan diplomat friends left the island in some sort of disgrace this morning. Some sort of instant recall after local government displeasure."

We parted on the pavement in Jermyn Street. Homer hailed a cab and I played doorman, which just about summed up our relationship.

The next few days were quiet enough. By telephone and cable I kept the whole deal moving and warned Ricky to take good care of himself. The Colonel's office reacted as though nothing had happened and I sent them a cable with banking details for the rest of the money.

Instead of seeing Homer again at the end of that week, I checked out and flew to Paris on an invitation from a guy I had introduced into the Black September training cadre. He had telephoned my home and left a message to call him. Regretfully, remembering recent episodes, I though it prudent to avoid the Scribe and instead took a room in a small hotel back of the Arc de Triomphe.

It was a small place that I had used once before quite by chance. Stuck in the side street with a lobby the size of an egg box, it had telephones in each room, telex, and the bedrooms were done up by some guy who must have been apprenticed as stage designer at the Lido.

This Black September man I was meeting had an office just off the Rue Kleber, a reasonable walk away.

I was suspicious, the deal following so soon on the heels of the near-catastrophe of the Malta assignment, but I had no choice but to play it along. There were no complications. They were shipping more arms as part of the urban guerrilla terrorism in the West policy, and wanted them brought across Europe for later distribution. Again, the source was Libya. And the arms were to be stored by Libyan legations at "safe" houses, notably in Brussels where they maintained a number of buildings.

Truthfully, I don't think the Black September man knew anything of the attempts so far to kill me. If he did, then he was playing a stage role with no flaws. He was working on his own initiative in asking me to help him, he claimed. We talked about the Europe deal, agreed fees and pinpointed the collection point in Marseilles.

We started drinking, a bout which lasted from early afternoon right into the early evening. I drank more water than scotch and he drank more scotch than water so that when I was merely feeling warm he was well drunk.

We started talking about mutual acquaintances in the strange world we occupied. Fighting men, some stirred by patriotism, others by love of bloodshed and hard cash. And others, like me, who had just drifted into it.

When we parted he was almost unconscious through booze. Me, I felt a little queasy, nothing more. But he had told me some interesting data. Like, for instance, a squad of guys I knew of from the mad Ghaddaffi's terrorist training school in the Libyan desert. These men, of mixed nationalities, would any week now, be dispersed through Europe's capitals to lead local hot-heads and arm them from the weapon caches. It was told like a throwaway line, a bit of bragging. It sent a chill down my spine and all the alarm bells ringing.

I spent the night in Paris and flew back to London the next day after sending a message to Homer. He was at Heathrow with a driver to meet me.

Dashed inconvenient, it was, he said, to come hurtling around after me on a Saturday. He was wearing what he called his week-end togs and looked to me like a well-dressed version of a West Country farmer.

I told him about the new deal that had been put up to me – and the threat of increased trouble right through Europe. He got very serious as the car headed into town and made a lot of notes.

Firstly I was to transport the arms as requested. No, he would not intercept them, but follow them through and pick them up and their would-be users at a later date.

That was the point of dispute I always had with him. He would never pick up the stuff before delivery, always wait and hope to catch the users, by which time a lot of stuff disappeared.

Homer dropped me off in the West End, thanked me and promised to meet my demands for more expenses the next week. I decided to stay in London for a few days before returning home for a week. When the new shipping deal was taken care of, I could concentrate on the European venture.

I needed to relax. The recent nearness of death made me keen to live a little. I broke one of my old rules and called the number that Jean, the call-girl, had given me.

"Oh, it's you," she said, sounding not unpleased – "I didn't think I'd ever hear from you again."

"I didn't think you would, either," I said. "It's Saturday afternoon and I have to dream up some way of passing the time until Monday. Any ideas?"

"I might have a few. I wish you'd given me some warning. I'll have to cancel a date or two."

"You won't lose out, sweetheart," I promised.

She gave me her address. She had a flat in a luxury block along the Edgware Road near Little Venice. It was called a luxury block and charged for it. It looked identical to the council flats quarter of a mile up the road and wasn't built much better either.

I bought flowers, chocolates, two bottles of champagne and some perfume. London must be the only town that takes real detective work to buy goodies in the West End on a Saturday mid-afternoon.

Jean was dressed for tea when I finally got there. The sort of things whores wear for teatime. Thigh length black leather boots, and a blue combed wool mini dress that hardly covered her backside, with a high buttoned neck.

The two-roomed flat was warm, furnished out of a cheaper version of Ideal Home, and the bedroom was the centrepiece. The bed nearly filled the room and with the curtains open, afforded a view all across West London. behind it the wall was mirrored with smoked glass. There was mirror on the ceiling too.

"It's a business deal," I said when she opened the door, "I don't want you to starve."

"Try me," she said and kissed me. One thing you don't get when you pay for it is kissed. Sunday suddenly looked very bright. Not that I remember much of Sunday when it came. We spent the Saturday evening drinking and extending a guided tour of the flat which got slightly out of hand when we first reached the bedroom. We started off making love in the bedroom, tried again in the bathroom, then tussled on the kitchen floor, which was all right except that the lino was chilly.

Even her picture albums had a catch. Other people have smudged up family groups and out of focus landscapes. Hers were of a different variety and what a variety.

Monday morning and I crawled out on all fours into the carbon monoxide that Londoners laughingly call fresh air and nearly collapsed at the impact.

I was headed for Victoria to swap suitcases and make for the country, planning to stop off at the accommodation office on the way.

Which I did, and that changed my plans.

There was a cable from the Bank. They were sending this guy Ventura over to London. He needed my assistance, they said. The cable also contained a number for an incoming Geneva flight. Their Mr. Ventura was all I needed. Like poison personified. Known for nothing but his ability to rub out, hard, fast and with no mess. He was the hit-man of the organisation. So now the Bank was getting windy about the failure rate of my business ventures, my possible friendship with the right side of the law perhaps?

The prospect was alarming, and I should have known that it had to happen.

I gave up the idea of Victoria, sent a post card to the kids, hired a swank Jaguar 4.2 from Hertz at Marble Arch and decided to play it straight with Ventura.

I contacted Homer, arranged a hotel room, complete with observation, for me and the guy when he arrived the next morning and went back to Jean's. She was in mid-client.

I sat in the hall way and when he came out of the lift I went up.

"Change of plan, lovely," I told her.

She let me in and I followed her to the bathroom and sat on the toilet seat while she showered.

"I could sit here and watch you all day," I said, by way of conversation.

"Five years and you'll be a dirty old man," she said. 'What's up, anyway?"

"Remember, Sunday that I had to kill? I've got the Monday to get rid of as well."

She looked at me like I was nuts and said "OK. But today's on me. I fancy the movies. Every working girl's got to relax some time."

I borrowed her kitchen table to clean up the Walther.

I was feeling that much at home and it had to be done.

She walked into the kitchen, saw what I was doing, and said "Now I know you're some kind of freak. What are you doing with that bloody thing in my house?"

"Relax, lover," I told her, "just a tool of the trade. I'm not a tea-leaf or anything like that though. I don't go in for stocking masks either, OK?"

We spent the afternoon watching some dreary film with a sad ending. Tough lady that she was, Jean cried. We ate popcorn. I didn't watch much of the movie. I was formulating a plan. If Ventura was going to get me, he would take it slowly, wait for an opportunity.

My idea was to slide one in on him before he had time to come up with one of his own. I had to frighten him off permanently – or kill him. You can't run from the Bank for ever. If I chose the time and the place I would have a slight advantage and a chance to get away. But I would need an accomplice.

I asked Jean if she could drive. She could. I told her briefly that I wanted her to take my car the next evening from the Royal Garden Hotel where Homer had fixed the rooms for me and Ventura. She was to wait for me behind the Albert Hall, parked by the steps.

"Don't worry," I told her. "There's no law involved, this isn't villainy." Well, it wouldn't be, not in so many words.

I dropped her off at the flat later in the evening and refused an invitation to stop over. I was getting nerved up again, wouldn't be able to sleep and needed to work it out of my system a bit.

I fancied spending the night in a Turkish bath or something similar and made the mistake of trying a sauna place in the West End.

It was so plush and centrally situated that I couldn't believe that here, a stone's thrown from some of the more respectable clubs and ministries, I would find a rip off joint. I really wanted a sauna.

A sauna I got, then a massage from a healthy looking blonde girl with a German accent. It was good and I was relaxing, pores refreshed and tingling, then the girl made her play.

I was lying on my stomach, towel across my backside, when I noticed the massaging had stopped. I lifted my head and cast an eye backwards.

The bird was down to her bra and briefs.

I turned over and she grabbed my balls.

"Shall I carry on?" she whispered, and was about to make a few more suggestions when I got up from the table. I grabbed her round the waist, threw her across the table, ripped the back off her pants with one hand and slapped her across the backside so hard that it was red before I took my hand away. The girl screamed.

I said "Pussycat, when I want massage, I want massage. The high life from you I don't want."

I grabbed my clothes hanging on a hanger from the door. A little guy with glasses and a red face burst into the room followed by a sturdy woman in a white coat.

"He hit me," protested the girl in a rising, guttural voice. I put my clothes on while the woman calmed her down. The little guy looked nervous.

I had a shouting match with the big woman, refused to pay and threatened to call the police. She told me that I wouldn't dare and added that she would have me seen to – worked over by the boys.

I pushed the little guy aside and stormed out into their reception room. There were two cavalry twill types reading Country Life with their bowler hats still on.

"They don't give you sex over at the club, I suppose," I said and they both went very red without looking at me. "So long suckers."

I slammed my way out into the street and ended up spending the night in the car.

I listened to the radio and treated myself to a large and lengthy early morning breakfast with a pint of freshly made orange juice, at the Cavendish.

I met Homer's buddy in the Red Lion pub in Whitehall, just after opening time that morning, and told him what was up.

He was as dry as ever and said something to the order of "We hope you get by, old chum."

As an understudy to Homer, he was learning fast. He had the cheek to query my demand for expenses. Now I had an idea who was booking their airline tickets for them.

"Send me on an economy night flight again, Captain," I said, "and I might box you up and send you somewhere romantic like Rio, via air freight."

All he could muster was: "Very droll" as he leaned back in the corner of the dive bar between the men's room and the cellar door. I could have smashed him right through the wall. I didn't. Instead I just turned and left him sipping his tomato juice.

I met Ventura in Terminal two at Heathrow in mid-afternoon. He was travelling light with only one black leather grip. He was not planning to stay long.

I told him we were both booked in at the Royal Garden and suggested checking in there before talking over a drink or two.

I told him I didn't know what he had in mind, but perhaps we could take a meal together later.

He was very quiet as I gunned the Jaguar back along the motorway into West London and it was only when we met up in the hotel bar later that he became more friendly than I would have thought possible from his reputation and got to the point.

"There is some concern, Leslie, that you may be getting pressured, shall we say, from unwelcome sources." He was direct, at least.

"What do you mean?" I asked, all innocence.

Ventura narrowed his eyes.

"The management feel that you have had an alarming run of bad luck, Leslie. They wondered how much of it was a coincidence. It is quite possible, of course." He paused. I said nothing but let the cocktail pianist fill in the interlude.

"I just, or they just thought, that I could help you straighten out any problems you might have. Perhaps you should take a short break, lie low for a while."

There was no menace in his voice. Which was unusual. Here was a guy who could make "good morning" sound like an invitation to the knacker's yard. My fears were confirmed – he was out to finish me.

We talked, going over the events of the past few months, notably the Claudia and Sea Fox. They had also heard a full acount of Malta and among other things, obviously knew about the trunk that got lost out of Lisbon.

I played hurt and surprised. My business loyalty was not to be questioned, particularly not with a firm of the Bank's standing. It wouldn't really have mattered. Even if it had have been true, Aspin had become highly dispensable.

The talk was just dialogue, padding between now and then. Then being when he would try and chop me.

I was relieved when he accepted my suggestion that we take a taxi to the Serpentine restaurant for dinner.

"It's not far," I volunteered. "We could even walk back through the park."

He either thought his acting was good, or that I was stupid. I think he seriously believed I thought everything was all right.

The car keys were in an envelope at the reception and Jean would pick that up after I had left.

We had a fair dinner at the Serpentine restaurant, during which I drank a lot and pretended to get slightly drunk. I talked about what I would do with a long holiday, go sailing, take a remote farmhouse in Scotland with my kids, that sort of thing.

Ventura smiled a lot, drank practically nothing and even showed me pictures of his pet dog. A Dobermann, would you believe? By the time the meal was over it was dark. He thought the walk would be a good idea. Kensington Gardens was closed now, but we walked slightly away from the direction of the hotel into Hyde Park, and then cut up through the trees towards Knightsbridge. There were a few shadowy figures about, walking dogs, or each other.

We strolled through a group of tall trees approaching the ride which runs through to Hyde Park Corner, just before the football pitches which flank Knightsbridge Barracks, near to the bowling green.

We had stopped talking and I was pretending to have difficulty lighting a cigarette. My nerves jangling and blood pounding in my ears. I had never been in such danger.

Ventura was behind me somewhere. I heard the spring and faint click of a switchblade as he eased it into the locked-on position. I swung round. He was one pace from me, knife in hand held low and pointing upwards.

"Goodbye, Leslie," he said, with real pleasure and made to swing forwards, hoping to tumble me with the weight of his body as the knife continued its upward path towards my stomach. I turned round, half right into the weight of his move, stepping slightly backwards. He came forwards and I caught his wrist as he tried to turn at the last moment to counteract my sudden move. My knee came up and met his free hand as he tried to punch me in the groin.

We both fell off balance into the grass, me desperately holding his knife wrist. It was stalemate and he had the knife still.

He rolled backwards and leapt up, wrenching his knife hand free and, as I tried to follow, he kicked me. The shoe glanced the side of my face and ripped against my ear. It spun me round but it made him change course with his next lunge.

The knife ripped through my sleeve and I felt it cut, but not deeply, just as I caught him with my elbow in the sternum. He gasped, momentarily winded, but my kick to his head missed and hit his shoulder instead. He was knocked off balance and hit the ground.

Lying on the ground near him was my cigarette.

I stooped over, grabbed it and screwed it into the side of his left ear as hard as I could.

The burning tobacco lodged there and he screamed. His solid six foot frame shook with agony as he held his head in both hands. I had just had a one-in-a-million lucky break and had to follow it up quickly.

His back was to me, the knife lay on the grass. I kicked him with all my might in the region of his right kidney and he jack-knifed sideways as I aimed another one at his head.

He went limp. For good measure I upped one of his arms, twisted it and turned it behind his back and then let the limp form fall backwards onto the ground. There was a sickening crack as the 12 stone dead weight crushed the twisted arm. He was out cold.

Ventura wouldn't forget me for a long time. I began to run for my life.

I ran to Knightsbridge and the hundred yards along to the Albert Hall. Jean was there, sitting in the Jaguar, bless her overworked little heart.

I tore open the door and flung myself into the car and shouted: "Go for Christ's sake, go."

The Jaguar purred forwards and she turned down the circular road behind the Hall, turned left and then right into Exhibition Road and headed for South Kensington.

We stopped in Thurloe Square and she looked at my arm in the car courtesy light. The jacket was torn but there was only a slight scratch on the flesh.

She didn't ask what I had been doing. I don't think she wanted to know. I was whacked, she was scared.

We drove back to her place in virtual silence and once in the flat she dressed the cut. I sat for a while and stared out across the bright lights of Paddington and thought about the world. I was gathering too many enemies and too few friends. Things weren't working out the way I had planned.

We climbed into her cool bed and within minutes I was asleep. I don't often sleep well, but I slept. The combined effects of the previous night and the nervous and physical exhaustion of the evening were sleeping draught enough. I left in the morning. She looked strange, there was a sad look in her eyes.

Before I left she said: "I always pick them, Les, I thought we might have something. It would have been nice to see a lot of you."

I thought for a moment that there was a trace of a tear in one eye. Perhaps I was imagining it.

"Bye, Jean, and thanks for everything," I said, and walked out of the flat.

I called Homer and told him I was going home for a few days and that I would call him before I set out for the European jaunt. I drew some cash and stopped off at a post office and sent off a money order for £100.

She was, after all, a working girl.

Chapter 10
Brussels Bloodshed

I had decided to throw my hand in with Rene and his friends over the trans-Europe arms deal. There were increasingly few people I could trust any more. They worked primarily for cash, and there is a dubious but strong loyalty among mercenaries.

With people motivated by political passion or some finer sense of national loyalty, anything, it seems, goes to further the end of their cause.

But with the loot and plunder brigade, the terms are spelled out hard in black and white and the true professional knows that seeing the job through provides the reference and conduct report for the next assignment.

We agreed to meet in Paris to plan the operation. Getting the guns and rocket launchers, grenades and pistols off the ship would not be too much of a problem. Getting them across into Belgium might not be too easy – quite a few TIR containers had been opened up at about that time.

I travelled to London for a final meeting with Homer before setting off. It was brief and to the point. He was pushing me harder and harder to involve myself when I knew my usefulness, at least where the Bank and the Libyans were concerned, was at an end.

They wanted me dead and they would, between them, try again. Homer must have been aware of this, but he was getting more documentation from me on the personalities involved in the international world of arms smuggling, the whys and wherefores of how they were inter-linked, then ever before.

To replace me, he would have to go through the whole charade of finding a suitable candidate for the blackmail he used on me; go through the whole complicated procedure of weaning him into departmental ways, feeling out some sort of working understanding.

I felt I was, for the time being, a spent force. He wanted to wring every ounce of blood out of the stone.

My outbursts of what he saw as truculence disturbed him. Would his patience wear thin? Perhaps.

I took the train to Dover and a cross-Channel ferry to Calais. I like trains, have always thought it a civilised way to travel. The jet gets you from A to B. With a train you feel your way, see the countryside change mile by mile.

It was a long time since I had been on a cross-Channel ferry. A couple of quid spent on a private cabin and meal at "High Sea" was once my idea of luxury.

The crossing was uneventful. I enjoyed it but it wasn't my idea of luxury any more.

The car I had hired was waiting for me at Calais docks. It was a Mustang convertible provided for me by an old acquaintance. I drove through to Paris without stopping. For a couple of hours at least I felt free. I made the most of the road.

Rene and his cousin Pierre met me as arranged at a bar on the corner of Rue Le Petit Pont. They were in a free-drinking, free-spending mood. To subsidise liquid expenses they had booked us into a ropey "characterful" Left Bank hotel run by a former crony.

The other guests seemed to be mostly professional ladies of friendly inclination and mercenaries in transit. There was a good atmosphere and I felt safe in the climate of double-cross and uncertainty which now surrounded me. It was years since I had found myself in a dosshouse like this place, let alone the antique communal chambre en famille that it turned out we were sharing.

It was furnished with elderly beds and gigantic wardrobes and it smelled, like the whole of the building, of garlic, oil, dust and cheap perfume.

There were no telephones in the rooms, but the small office at the base of the stairs by the street was turned over to us.

I went to see the Black September man in Rue Kleber once, he seemed less friendly than the last time we met.

The ship loaded with the arms was due into Marseilles in a week. He told me its name and berth. We would not be involved in unloading but would collect the merchandise direct from the warehouse.

He was quite keen to know how the goods would be transported but I cut him short. To set up the drop off points I was given a telephone number to call in Brussels. I didn't want them to know anything about what happened in between. We were getting a £8,000 "start fee" and the other half on completion.

I had my own skin to look after – and the other boys' money too. The money, in dollars, was handed over without trouble but I still didn't like the atmosphere hanging around the Kleber meeting. My suspicions were increased when later in the week I tried to contact the man again. The offices had been vacated, the telephone disconnected.

It was a good week in Paris. The calm before the storm, you might say. I lived rough with Rene and Pierre, dressing casually, eating in the Left Bank cafés with the student types, getting drunk in the evenings and sitting up late with the windows onto the decrepit balcony open.

The sounds from the narrow street outside filtered up, the whores calling to each other and swapping gossip, while we talked about old times when the living was dangerous but at least we knew who the enemy was.

Rene had worked out a plan to shift the arms up from Marseilles using three TIR lorries, with trailers, ostensibly shifting chemicals under which the gear would be hidden.

He and Pierre were going to drive two of the lorries. I volunteered to drive the third but we decided it would be better if I drove them down and then headed back up the road and set up the Brussels end ahead of them.

It was also safer to have us split up – at the wheel of a multi-tonner I would have been vulnerable to a phoney hijack.

The night before we were to leave, the patron of the seedy establishment thought it was a good excuse, the paying of respect to his old buddies at arms, to throw a junket. I had been happy to have had, until then, no more than a nodding-on-the-stairs acquaintance with what the patron called his little family.

With the exception of one plump young country girl only recently arrived in the city, his little chicks, as he called them, were scrawny old fowls with little to commend their femininity.

Two or three had boyfriends whose sole motive in life can only have been self-protection, a state of mind coupled with stupidity. But as parties go, it wasn't bad. There was a spade guy from Guadeloupe with a flat nose and a scar across the bridge of it, who owned the records and danced with himself. Rough red wine flowed like water and one of the whores produced an enormous Salade Niçoise and broke the bread with her own fair, scrawny hands.

The transit mercenaries were not invited.

I got drunk enough not to mind the hygiene aspect of the eating arrangements. By the time midnight arrived we were even dancing with les girls, a feat which, in sober retrospect next day, nearly put us all off lunch. I remember washing three times in the morning.

The three of us left the party in full swing at about one o'clock. The patron got very emotional, flung his arms around Rene and said it was like the old days with the boys going off to fight. We might never meet again. How he had loved them like sons. Big tears ran down over his unshaven chin and mingled with the sweat on his squat, fleshy neck.

Except the memory of dancing cheek by jowl with the grade four princesses, the morning, when it hit us at ten o'clock, seemed quite fresh. The excitement of the campaign robbing heavy heads of their hangovers.

We packed our cases into the Mustang. Pierre had given it the once-over mechanically and reckoned it was rally-perfect. It stood impatient at the kerb, shining like a jewel in that masonry junk heap.

We took the toll road south out of Paris towards Lyons – a beautiful road. Heading out of Paris on the network of flyovers and unders, it was like plunging into a wide movie screen of lush woodland and fields.

A couple of hours out of Paris, the Mustang purring like a warm cat, we took a meal break at one of the snack halts. We sat watching the cars speed underneath and it was like holiday time. I was in the mood for driving and took the wheel all the way to Lyons, nearly getting lost through the city.

It was well into the evening when we reached Aix-en-Provence. We were hungry, ahead of schedule. I turned the Mustang off the autoroute into the maze-like one-way system of the old town. Driving the one-way system in that town is enough to turn a guy into a raving lunatic. One wrong lane and you find yourself going the rounds again. After a lot of cursing from the other two I managed to navigate the way to the centre and we picked on one of the big cafés by the roundabout for a meal.

We ate in near-silence. The bonhomie was slipping away into tension, the job about to start. We ended up sleeping in the car on a lay-by just outside of the town and woke in the cold early light of the morning, cramped in our metallic foxhole with condensation streaming down the windows.

We descended on a small petrol station, washed and brushed up in the back, hosed down the dusty car and took in the fresh southern air. Rene used the phone, got very agitated and cursed loudly into the elderly mouthpiece.

We sat in the deserted forecourt of the garage and held a council of war on the bonnet of the Mustang.

We had almost lost the job. The boat had come in during the night and nearly run foul of a French naval reception committee which had been hiding around the islands off Marseilles. They had been waiting for another ship and ours had had the misfortune of running into their little ambush at the right time, right place.

Unable to run for it, they had been on the point of being boarded by a search party when, miraculously, the ship the navy were really after hove into sight. Then, at the last minute before discovery, the mini-flotilla scrambled itself together to give chase to the suspected drug runner, leaving the arms carrying ship to politely carry on its own way into the docks. Unloading had then been done. So nervous were the captain and his crew that the usual precautions had not been taken. Now our contact man was afraid that the on-shore operation might have been spotted through carelessness. He wanted the warehouse cleared as soon as possible, in daylight if need be.

Rene said that he and Pierre should meet with their other driver and

210

three co-drivers outside of the city, I should head back up through France and not be involved. They knew the city like the back of their hands. If anything went wrong, they could duck out and hopefully disappear. I might not enjoy the same privilege.

Rene took to the telephone for another half an hour. If the gear was to be shifted ahead of schedule, then the Customs fix had to be brought forward to have the lorries sealed. They had a hard day ahead of them.

We drove to St. Antoine, on the fringe of the city, and had breakfast in the café where Rene and Pierre were to be picked up.

We had been there for about an hour when a battered Peugeot pulled up behind the Mustang and a large swarthy guy came into the café to join us. He left the three co-drivers in the car.

He was obviously agitated by the night's events. They talked but the patois was beyond me and I could only understand a word or two of the conversation. Paul, the swarthy man, was to be the third driver. He wasn't happy. The omens, he thought, were bad.

We split up. The farewells were like real good-byes and I told them to cut it out. Wasted emotion, I said, and I'll see you all in three days or so. I hoped.

I drove back towards Aix-en-Provence and rejoined the N.7 to follow the route to be taken by the lorries back up through France. We had decided that they should take the old route to Lyons and then the N.6 up the long hilly stretches of countryside via Dijon, on to Rheims and then across into Belgium.

I pulled into a Routiers for a snack lunch just short of Montelimar.

The car park was empty except for three mangy-looking dogs and a kid on a bicycle who watched me with staring gypsy eyes. The food was reasonable. The café was empty except for the surly red-lipped and ruddy-faced woman who served. We had a row about the bill as she attempted to subsidise the lack of custom with my tourist ignorance.

She shouted and I refused to pay the excess. A man with a meat axe came out of the bead curtains hanging over the door to the kitchen. He agreed to knock off a few francs and I gave him the money as per the menu.

I walked out into the car park towards the Mustang. The woman was still cursing her head off. There were two young men with curling black hair and yellow skin leaning on the bonnet.

211

"You no pay," said one with eloquent clarity, rubbing one hand in the other. His mate had his arms folded. From a distance the kid with the gypsy eyes leant scowling on his bicycle. Some family, this one.

I stood in front of the two youths and then made to move forward to open the car door. They both moved. But as the first leg came homing in towards what I regard as very private, personal and valuable, I shied away, taking the foot with me. The weight of the kick carried the youth with its momentum as I pushed the outstretched leg up. His other leg gave way and he fell backwards, his skull connecting with the windscreen pillar. I let go the leg with a twist just in time to get a flurry of blows in the kidneys from the other youth. We traded punches and I went down twice. He was big and fancied his looks, but he wasn't that effective. Mamma and Pappa, he still with the meat axe in his hand, stood by the doorway of the tumbledown café fifty yards from us. God forbid if he decided to exercise any simple butchery in my direction.

Then I cheated. I ran towards the little boy with the bicycle. The two youths, now both up and angry, were after me, ten feet behind I ran past the boy, grabbed the bicycle and circled back towards the car. Papa, seeing that the fight was about to become unequal, now that I had been unmanly enough to arm myself, was moving out towards us.

I reached the car and swung round, lifting the bicycle to shoulder height. The two heroes kept on coming and I laid into them both with my bit of armoury, plastic mudguards tearing flesh and bicycle chain oil mingling with blood as I changed the backwheel gear on the leg merchant's nose. The two youths were on the ground, shaken and trying to disentangle themselves from the bicycle. Papa was homing in, but they lay in the way and it gave me the seconds I needed to open the car and get in.

Papa was already on the door handle when I got the ignition on and slammed the car into reverse. The Mustang shot backwards as the meat axe smashed into the tonneau cover in a vain attempt to do some damage.

The backwards thrust of the car left the man up-ended near his sons, one of whom was now on his feet, gesticulating wildly. I slammed the car downwards and roared out towards the road. The skidding rear tyres made a shower of dirt and dust and, as I sped past the battered trio, the back nearside wheel caught the bicycle by its back end. There was a crunching of metal and it half lifted the battered pedaller into the air and brought it crashing down on to the still prostrate form of one of the youths.

I hit the tarmac with a squeal of rubber and spun the car round towards Montelimar. In the rear mirror, through the clouds of red dust, I could see the menagerie trying to dust itself down and drag the gear change victim towards the ministering arms of mama.

Not a tourist spot to be recommended.

I pulled in at a petrol station in Montelimar and filled up. There was an ugly gash in the rooftop near the driver's door. I resolved to leave quickly before pride forced the motley family to pursue me.

Postcards for kids would have to be sent later.

Apart from that little incident, the journey was uneventful. I spent the night in a small hotel en route which was cheap but had a kitchen enough to make a gourmet cry. I ate too much, chatted with the woman who ran the place and tried, unsuccessfully, to sleep, my belly fit to burst.

The next day I drove across the border into Belgium, noticing with satisfaction the ease with which commercial lorries were crossing with little attention.

I drove through the centre of Brussels and up to the Europa Hotel. It would be a change to hit the five star circuit again after roughing it for so long. I promised myself a night on the town and no aggravation at least until the next day when I should make contact with the Libyans.

The hotel was full of slant-eyed Easterners. Europe is over-run with Japanese business men and tour parties. They are very polite, but sometimes, through an alcoholic haze, I have reasoned that in fact it's all a subtle plot and that take-over is on the way. Thousands of Red Guards disguised as yen-wielding business executives. I'm not racialist but I wouldn't know the difference.

I showered and noted the bruises, souvenirs of Mid-France, coming out nicely.

I took dinner in the old city, wandered round the square and then took a taxi to Pol's, the jazz club that for me is the city's highlight.

Sitting at a table on the gallery I passed the night drinking scotch and listening to an American trio that I had never heard of.

213

The next morning I took breakfast in my room overlooking the EEC administration buildings before calling the contact number I had been given and arranging for one of the Libyans to meet me in the hotel.

He came shortly before lunch time, all smiles and sweaty, limp handshake. We took a car ride in his BMW to two houses in the suburbs, owned, I gathered, by their diplomatic legation. At the second, a back access would allow the lorries to off-load without arousing too much suspicion locally. I was to call the man when we were ready for the handover. I had heard nothing from Marseilles which meant, as far as I was concerned, that everything was all right.

That afternoon I got a telephone call from Rene who was on the road in France. Everything was A.O.K. although the start had been a bit hairy and very hurried.

I arranged to be with the car on my side of the border at lunchtime next day. With luck we could get the shipment off-loaded during the afternoon and the lorries to their proper destination in the city by the end of the day.

All that had to be done then was finish up the deal with the Libyans, go through the inventories and take the cash. Which I thought could be the trickiest part of the operation. There had been no attempt yet to jump me, but I couldn't believe that my popularity had suddenly risen from zero.

I took the next evening quietly, ate at the hotel and got into conversation in the bar with a party of visiting journalists from London and the States. On the English contingent's instigation, we took a ten minute walk up the hill, passed the EEC buildings, to an English pub where we taught the Americans how not to play darts.

I tried to go to sleep early, failed and sat, at three a.m., eating a room-service steak, drinking scotch and staring out of the window.

I cleaned my Walther, polished it minutely until it gleamed and then cat-napped fully dressed.

Morning came. I ordered breakfast and some newspapers and stuck my head out of the door to retrieve my shoes. They were gone. I padded out into the corridor, into the service area behind the lifts. Empty – no shoes.

I called the front desk. "I have no shoes" I said.

"Call the housekeeper" said the desk.

"No" I said, "you call the housekeeper."

Moments later the housekeeper rang. I told her my shoes, which should by now be sitting polished outside the door had been hi-jacked. It was not possible, she claimed. I was very patient. Today, I told her, I was wearing a blue suit. I wanted my black shoes. She promised to mount a search and it was an hour and a half and four phone calls later when there came a knock on the door.

In came a demure black-dressed girl smiling with apologies, my shoes in her hand. They had been found by an aggrieved Frenchman on the third floor. Now they were hunting for his shoes. The black dress was a simple affair that enhanced her ample 18-year-old breasts. I felt guilty for fancying her on the spot, but the days are gone when hotel guests can ravish the wenches as and when they please. I got up and sorted the girl out a couple of francs for her trouble. She turned to the wardrobe and bent over to put the shoes on the rack, exposing stocking tops and white pants on a broad Flemish bottom. I came closer and gave her a playful pat on the inviting rump. She straightened up double quick, blushed deep scarlet and said a very rude word as she fled for the door. However, she did manage a smile on the way out. I waved as she went and thought to myself, careful Leslie, my boy.

I set off in the Mustang for Charleroi, reached the town and pulled up just outside on the main road. It was two o'clock when the convoy of lorries, white cabins and blue truck bodies, came along the road. Rene was up front in the first of the three. He drove past with a great blast of the klaxon.

I trailed behind them until we reached a truck stop and petrol station. Rene was in fine form, though tired from the long, slow haul.

"It was a pity you had to choose such a bastard route Leslie, you bloody man," he said grinning.

"Your trouble," I told him, "is that you want it too easy, mon bloody vieux. And don't relax, because now we've got the hard bit."

I telephoned the Libyans and told them to expect us in two hours. That way, I reckoned, we could arrive early in case there were any funny ideas of relieving us of the cargo on the cheap. At my request Rene and Pierre strapped on a gun apiece. We hit the road for Brussels.

We arrived, as planned, before my contact of the day before. He didn't look too surprised to see us already there and had with him two

215

car-loads of assorted "attachés" who were to help shift the crates.

We worked in near silence, unloading one truck at a time, shifting the genuine crates and containers to reach the armament boxes. It was dark when we finished. There was enough armament under that place to blow the quiet neighbourhood off the map. And it was all destined for urban guerrillas somewhere in Europe or the U.K. who would use it to smash apart someone else's neighbourhood during the coming months.

I hoped that Homer could be persuaded to change his evil little mind and scoop this lot before the hand-out started.

My contact was still smiling a lot. He obviously loved his work, or felt the power of destruction he now had in his hands to give out goodies for the disruption of law and order. I hoped one day to have the opportunity to shove his smile backwards into his face.

We worked on the inventory, smiling-teeth and I, until he was satisfied that there had been no rip-off along the line. Then he handed over a manilla envelope containing the remainder of our cash and we left, each watching the movements of the Arabs lest anything should go wrong.

The way we had planned it, we walked far apart so as not to present a bunched target, although it seemed unlikely that they would risk a noisy gun-fight there as we still had the lorries to get rid of. An hour and a half later and I had Rene and Pierre back with me in my room at the Europa, laughing and jostling like a successful rugger team, as they washed the grime of the road and tired sweat from their backs.

We sat down in the room amid a pile of discarded clothing which made the place look like Oxford Street in a summer sale, split a bottle of scotch and the money. I gave Rene the extra cash to take care of any remaining pay-offs in Marseilles.

In the meantime, he had hired a Renault 16 through a local car service and planned to set out with Pierre for Paris during the night.

It was force of habit, one that I should have taken notice of, not to linger on the scene of action longer than we needed. All I had planned was to have an easy night and leave at a leisurely pace next day to return to Calais, preferring the longer land route and the shorter crossing instead of heading for Ostend. And, anyway, I had to return the car.

216

We ate downstairs in the hotel coffee house. Pierre took his small grip and hopped a cab into the city to meet some old friend or other and Rene decided to stay drinking with me for a while. At one o'clock he decided it was time to call it a day. We promised to keep in touch and, as usual, that our next meeting would not be just because of a job. The way things were that's all it would be for.

Or we would meet by chance when we were both old and grey, if we lived that long, and greet like friends who had seen each other only a week before. It's the kind of bond that develops, although the sentiments are not expressed.

We took the lift up to my room so that Rene could fetch his bag. He collected it and I offered to accompany him back down to the lobby.

The lifts, two of them, are in a block arrangement facing the corridor of each floor. To each side of them are passageways and behind the shaft, linking the two side passageways, is the service room for each floor. I scarcely noticed that the light in the side passage nearest to my room door had been extinguished and that the passageway was dark. It hardly contrasted with the dim, subtle lighting of the main corridor. I was looking back down the corridor as we waited for the lift. Suddenly I saw Rene stiffen, but in the moment of realisation, the attackers were on us. The lift had arrived and coming from it, eyes startled, was one of the men from the unloading – behind him was another. They were the only people in the lift.

The first guy was just pulling his hand out of his pocket as I saw him. The wide blade of an "afro" fighting knife flashed at me.

I realised that they had been on their way to do me a mischief when we had surprised them. Instinctively I wrenched myself away. The man with the knife lunged and I side stepped, Rene caught him over the back of the neck with a side handed chop sending him down with a groan.

The second man, wild-eyed and with the advantage of surprise gone, leapt out of the lift at us, reaching into his pocket. The lift shut behind him. I punched him full in the face and kneed him in the balls. He doubled forwards but grabbed me in some sort of attempted bear hug. I smelt his hot, spicey, foul breath and tried to free myself from his grip. Rene came up behind him and started punch-bagging away at his kidneys. Just then the other lift arrived, the doors opened and I grabbed his outstretched arm and swung him round with his own weight into the lift.

He whacked into the back wall of the cabin with such a crash, his eyes almost bursting with the force of the impact, that I thought we'd screwed up the lift between us. But the doors closed, leaving me only time to see the guy dropping slowly down on to his backside, sliding down the wall so that his jacket was riding up over his head. Rene made for the fire door and the stairs and I turned to follow suit. As Rene disappeared through the doors I realised that the knife-man was up and about again.

I turned and tried to kick the guy. He feinted to one side as I tried to duck backwards and bulldozer into him. There was a sudden burning sensation and the knife plunged into my left shoulder. The knife-man tripped over himself and I ran for the fire exit. The knife was lying on the floor.

I got to the stairs and began jumping my way down them, four at a time, right hand clasped to my left shoulder – wet with the blood which was oozing out. I was bouncing off the walls to get round each turn and came out of the bottom fire door into the lobby like a spinning top.

I ran across the lobby. Behind me I could hear the Arab hot in pursuit. Rene had started up the Renault and was pulling out from the parking area in front of the hotel. I managed to open a rear passenger door and flung myself into the car, trying to pull the door shut with my good arm as the car gathered momentum. But the Arab, a tenacious little sod, was wrenching at the outside of the door and running with the car, almost off his feet. We must have travelled a good 30 feet like that when I couldn't take it any longer and the guy dived in onto the back seat with me. He started punching away and I tried to hit him back. None of it meant much because within the confined space and lack of energy in the punches, it was like mosquito bites both ways.

Then the bastard got right on top of me with his hands round my neck and started trying to choke the life out of me. He was wailing some bloody curse and I was shouting and then gasping for every breath as his fingers groped for my balls. Rene, pushing the little Renault for all it was worth to get us off the main road, swung around a corner, sliding the car on the greasy, wet surface.

The back door was not fastened properly, only held closed by the forward movement of the car. The force of the turn and the skid pushed the Arab back and I got one arm up to force him up and off me. He felt the cold rushing air behind him and started snatching at the back of the seat and the front seat nearest to him so as not to fall out.

It took every ounce of energy I had left in me. I doubled up one leg and kicked the guy in the chest with every bit of strength I could muster, smashing him through the door. He hit the road with a sickening scream, one leg caught for a moment between the door and the car body, dragging him for a few feet.

I hung over the back of the back seat, gasping in the fresh air. The car door smashed against a parked car and sent pieces of shattered glass showering everywhere.

"Are you all right, Leslie?" shouted Rene, above the roar of shattering glass and the rush of air. "I hope you kill the fuck-pig," he shouted, not letting up speed for a moment.

Out of the back window, along the street, I saw a Mercedes and a BMW pull up under the street lights where the Arab was lying. There was a lot of gesticulating, and the men who had jumped out of the cars were making to pick the broken body up and load it into one of their cars.

If they had any sense, I remember thinking, they were going to leave me be for a while. That innings I was certainly winning.

Rene circled around and came up to the roundabout above the hotel on the one-way system. He wanted to get me back to the hotel and see to me, but I told him I would manage. He had to rendezvous with his two mates and then get out. It was me these chummies were after and there was no need to complicate matters.

I emptied my jacket pockets and took it off with his help. I had no further need for it now. It was blood-soaked, ripped and beyond repair. I borrowed a towel from his bag, wrapped it round my shoulder, and slung his jacket over my back. In this way, I hoped, I could get into the hotel without attracting too much attention.

In five minutes I was outside the hotel, after stumbling along the downhill incline. I combed my hair with my good hand and walked up to the doors. There was a porter type fellow outside. I gave him the equivalent of about a fiver and asked him to help me cross the hall-way. I told him I wanted him to take me up in the lift, come back for my key once I was up, and to help me try and look normal. I didn't want to start keeling over in front of some cop in the lobby. I didn't know whether or not the fight had been reported.

We were in luck. A fella with a stunning bird walked in out of a taxi at that moment and managed to distract the few people around as we made our entrance.

Minutes later I was in my room.

The porter type looked at me.

"What's your name?" I said. He must have been about my age. He kept looking at my shoulder. I realised blood was seeping through to my shirt front.

"Tony," he said going whiter.

"Tony," I said, feeling tired, "I need some medicaments and some bandages and perhaps someone to help me fix them, but not a doctor." I pulled out another fiver's worth of Belgian francs from my hip pocket and said: "I'd better swap rooms as well if we can do it tactfully. Someone might come looking for me soon and I don't want to be found in this state."

"OK boss," he said, beginning to relish his new role as gangster.

He disappered for another ten minutes and came back with another key. He helped gather my stuff together and led the way up the stairs behind the fire door to a single room on the floor above. I spotted blood, my blood, on the steps leading down. The door of my new room was open. Sitting inside was the girl who that morning had returned my shoes. She blushed on catching sight of my face when I entered.

Then, when recognition had been achieved and she spotted the red seeping across my shirt front she gasped with concern and hurried to help me into the room.

Tony had brought the scotch bottle from my old room and I anaesthetised myself happily as she stripped away the shirt and began to wash the wound. It was deep, bleeding heavily and hurt like hell. I gritted my teeth.

Tony had left the room and the air was heavy with concern. She ran in and out of the bathroom with wet towels like a mother hen.

Her name was Maria. She was still wearing the little black dress and her white bosom heaved with deep breaths as she tried to clean up the gash in my shoulder. She plastered the wound with some proprietary ointment or other which cooled it for a moment. She wiped my sweating brow and I looked into her large brown eyes and full, serious mouth and wished to hell I didn't hurt so much. "You have bad friend, I think," she said softly when I was bandaged up.

"They're not friends, love," I said.

She was very close to me. I kissed her. She let me kiss her and blushed again. With one hand I slipped open the front of her shift and felt the warm bulk of her breasts. She pushed me back onto the bed and said I must rest. I half closed my eyes. I was tired, God I was tired. Particularly tired of bloody Arabs trying to shoot, knife or otherwise maim me. This time had been a close call.

My shoulder hurt like buggery. Maria kept on wiping my brow and I lay there as she sat beside me, mesmerised through half open eyes by the sight of her breasts which hung now temptingly from her opened dress. I passed out.

It was mid-morning when I came to. The room was empty, everything neatly arranged. I called room service and ordered an English breakfast. Under the telephone was a scribbled note bearing the name Maria and an internal number. I dialled and told her I was leaving the hotel.

"You must let me change the bandage," she said.

I breakfasted, dressed and washed in the best way I could and then Maria came to the door.

I let her change the bandage which she did with the care of a mother bathing a new baby. This time she strapped my arm to my chest for me so that I would not jar the wound.

She stared at me with her big eyes when I told her she was a sweet kid. I gave her £50 in francs and she looked like the heavens just fell open.

I made my way downstairs, paid the bill under the suspicious eye of the desk clerk and I left the Mustang keys in an envelope with the cashier saying they would be collected. Then I left the hotel and took a cab to the airport. The clerk was on the phone looking furtive as we drove away.

I got a seat on a London flight without trouble and had time to telephone the Calais garage before I left. I promised a bonus payment and explained that I could not return the car, they would have to fetch it.

When I reached London I felt lousier than during the night. I called Homer's office from Heathrow and told him I was hurt badly, before hiring a car to take me all the way to my home.

Homer came to see me that evening. He was as charming as ever. "My dear boy" he said, "aren't we getting popular?" Sarcastic bugger, even with me in that state.

"I've been making a few discreet calls out to our chaps in the field," he said, helping himself liberally to the grapes he had managed to bring with him. "It seems your name is mud in certain quarters. It seems you wouldn't be very welcome at certain Arab embassy cocktail parties at the moment."

"Thank you for finding out," I said. "I think I knew that already. Remember? I told you that before we embarked on this last caper. What are you going to do now, pension me off and leave me be?"

Homer looked surprised and feigned hurt.

"Dear boy, no, not that. You're much too useful. No, I think you'll find we have plenty of work to suit your special talents. I think you might take a little paid holiday first though, get the old frame back into trim."

He leant forward as though to commiserate with me and patted me gently on the shoulder. The bandaged shoulder.

"Watch my ARM you bastard!" I shouted as the pain seared down the left side of my body.

"Oh my dear boy," he said, "so sorry . . ."

I looked at him. "Holiday?" I said. "You mean, paid time off, just like real human beings get, two weeks to do what you will, live day to day with your kids and learn what the basis of female neurosis is all about?"

"Something like that," said Homer.

Then he added, standing up to go: "I had something more like a couple of months in mind. When you've got a bit better of course."

He left and I stared out of my bedroom window at the clouds scudding across the moon. I was ready to pack the whole thing in.

222

Chapter 11
Assignment — Kill Littlejohn
March, 1974

I had spent most of the night tossing and turning in my bed. What little sleep I had managed to get had been torn apart by visions of that knife coming at me in Brussels. My sheets were damp from the perspiration I had exuded during the night. I had no idea what time it was, but I wasn't sleeping, just lying, hands gripped into balls of knuckle, tensing at each throb from my injured shoulder.

It was daylight but cloudy and there was very little light coming through the heavy curtains at my window. Just enough for me to see the telephone on the side table as it cut my head in two with a screaming ring.

Unthinking, startled, I reached out for it with my left hand, only to drop it back into its cradle as I screamed out with the pain from my injured shoulder. I lay back, sweating and cursing as the pain subsided into a just bearable throb. The telephone rang again. I decided not to answer. Obviously my wife was out or she would have taken it the first time. It was probably for her anyway. Homer knew I was injured.

Christ, the bloody thing wouldn't stop. I knew that if I just unhooked it Homer would send round his local man. I picked it up with my right hand, nearly dropping it again because my palm was wet with perspiration. If it's possible to groan in a whisper that's the way I answered: "Yeh?"

The voice on the other end was familiar, chirpy, disgustingly bright to a guy in my state. "Is that you, Leslie?" It was Homer's secretary. "No, it's my bloody ghost. Wadyawant?" "The man wants you, hold on."

In preparation for the shock that had to be be coming, I eased myself back against the sodden pillows and rested my aching head on the top of the head-board. I looked for the glass of water I kept on the bedside table − it was empty so I drew what moisture I could into my dry mouth and throat.

Then came the prissy voice of Homer: "Leslie, how are you, dear boy? Better, I do hope." What could you say to a bastard like that? Only four days before I had been stabbed, kicked and beaten trying to fix a job for him and here he was with the 'dear boy' act.

I decided to tell him just how I was: "How the bloody hell d'you think I feel, you senseless bastard? I feel as if I've still got that bloody knife in me and my whole body is a furnace heating up the boiler which is pumping steam out through a million little holes in my skin −"

Homer cut me short: "Oh, do shut up and listen! We're not all lazing about at home you know. Oh, I'm sorry that you were hurt and aren't feeling too good and all that, but it's imperative.

"Pull yourself together and see me at the Cumberland this afternoon at three. OK?"

"No, it's not bloody OK," was all I could think to reply. "It's not bloody OK at all. I'm sick, tired and no use to you or me in my present state . . ."

I couldn't go on. My shoulder felt as if it had a red-hot poker in it and someone with a meat cleaver was still trying to split my head assunder. I looked down at the blood oozing through the dressing on my wound. I thought of a dozen things I'd like to say to the smooth bastard and said: "OK, three o'clock."

He just rang off. I let the phone base fall to the floor from its precarious perch on my stomach. I couldn't even drag myself back down and into the bed and I must have stayed in that half-sitting, half-lying state for about half an hour.

With my mind frantically searching for the reason for this summons to Homer, I paid less attention to my body and my sundry pains seemed to subside. It had to be urgent. It was in Homer's best interests to get me well again and into the field as soon as possible. Even he wouldn't mess a wounded man about without good cause.

I dragged myself out of bed and throbbed my way to the bathroom to snarl at the grey face with the slit, red-rimmed eyes which I saw in the mirror over the handbasin.

Sitting on the edge of the bath I turned both taps on full and tried to let the plug in the hole by dangling it on its chain. With the water swirling round I couldn't do it and had to turn the taps off and start all over again – plug first, water later.

Then I filled the hand-basin with cold water and plunged my head in. It didn't help the headache but it made me feel a little fresher.

I threw in a handful of salt, sat on the edge of the bath until the water looked about deep enough and I had got it to a reasonable temperature. Then, shrugging out of my wet pyjamas I let myself in using only my right arm. I soaked for about twenty minutes gritting my teeth as the salt water bit into my wound, before crawling back over the edge as the water started to turn cold.

As I ran my shaver over my bristled chin and cheeks I remember thinking that the whirr of the motor was soothing and actually helped my aching head. Quite the reverse of shaving with a hang-over headache, when the motor sounds like a pneumatic drill.

Shaved, I felt better. The face in the mirror had dropped to something near my own age – still grey but more relaxed.

Back in the bedroom I called Homer back. I am unable to explain the complicated procedure of question and counter question with switchboard operators used on these calls but because of my state of mind I muffed it and had to have a second go.

This time I got through. We were both more reasonable now and I promised that I would be at the Cumberland Hotel at the time he had give. He, in his turn, was apologetic about having to bother me in my wounded state. I asked him what it was all about but all he would say was: "Your old friend Ken – he's escaped."

That was enough. It was important. Both to the Department and to me. Homer was talking about Kenneth Littlejohn.

Ever since my first meeting with Littlejohn I had not liked him. But it was only after his arrest for a bank robbery that his full history emerged. It appeared that he and his brother, Keith, had been an embarrassment ever since they were recruited in 1971.

At that time, on the run from the British police who wished to question him with regard to bank robberies, he had been hiding out in Eire. With a strong record of robbery he naturally made contact with local criminals on the fringe of the official and provisional IRA. He decided to capitalise on his new friends.

He travelled to London and through his brother arranged a meeting with Pamela, Lady Onslow, a prison visitor and voluntary welfare worker who had tried to help Keith following a sentence for robbery.

The brothers told her that they wished to pass on important information to MI6 and she arranged a meeting at her home with Mr Geoffrey Johnson Smith, Junior Minister for the Army. They explained to Mr Smith that they were in a position to inform on the provisional IRA and could pass on information with regard to gun-running. They wanted immunity from prosecution in Britain.

They were introduced to senior officers in the Department and returned to Eire to start work. Their first move was to set up a business in Farranfore by the name of Whizz Kids Ltd., specialising in women's hot pants. Nobody can recall them ever selling anything.

They then moved on the Clogerhead, Co. Louth, just on the Republican side of the Irish border. In October 1972, they led a raid on the Allied Irish Bank in Dublin and stole £67,000.

After this raid they fled to London and warrants were issued by the Republican courts for their arrest.

The Department were furious with them. This was the sort of scandal they wanted nothing to do with. They always claimed that the robbery was freelancing on the part of the brothers and not covered by their orders, which were to act as informers and agents provocateurs.

The Department, who of course knew where they were living, had them arrested by the Scotland Yard Flying Squad and extradition proceedings were started to enable them to be sent back to Eire to face the courts on the bank robbery charges.

Their arrest had come as no real surprise to me but I was later horrified when I heard that the Irish trial was to be held in open court. Surely this would mean they would blow the lid right off the Department.

The extradition proceedings, which were held in London, were heard in secret so that was OK. But when they were sent back to Dublin the shit really hit the fan. In open court it was explained how they had been sent to Ireland to obtain information and, in the role of agents provocateur, to stir up trouble for the IRA.

Kenneth recounted his meetings with the Junior Minister and named his controller and Inspector Sinclair of the Special Branch in London. In fact he had expected Sinclair to have him released after his arrest but an officer who telephoned the inspector was told to take back the message that the Department had washed their hands of him and his brother.

At the Dublin trial Ken was jailed for twenty years and Keith for fifteen. But only seven months later, they both escaped from Dublin's Mountjoy prison, Keith to be re-arrested almost immediately and Ken to get clear. He has since been re-arrested in Britain and sent back to finish his sentence in Ireland.

I drove to the railway station in my red Rover 2000 and caught the mid-morning train for London. As I sat back in the first class compartment, which I had to myself, I opened the newspapers I had picked up at the station bookshop. They were full of the escape story. The Daily Mirror splashed it all over their front page: "SPY BROTHERS BREAK OUT". No wonder Homer was agitated. There had been sufficient embarrassment at the trial to last the Department for the next hundred years, and now this threat that Ken would start it all up again.

I lay back and closed my eyes as I tried to bring into my mind every little thing I knew of the brothers. I must have fallen into a light sleep because I was half-way to London when the ticket inspector threw open the door to demand my ticket.

I felt better. My bad night had really knocked me up. When I arrived in London I picked up the evening papers – the Littlejohn escape was still hitting the headlines. I read them as my cab threaded its way through to Marble Arch and the Cumberland Hotel.

With Littlejohn on the run and probably wishing to tell everything, something obviously had to be done. He had to be persuaded to return to the fold, like the little black sheep that he was.

From a telephone near the reception desk, I asked for Homer's room using the cover name he had used when booking rooms at the hotel in the past. When he answered he gave me his room number and I took the lift to his floor.

Never given to over-spending, he had taken only a small room on the fifth floor for this afternoon assignation. The door was opened by my deputy controller, Frank, who waved me on into the room with his left hand as he held the door wide with his right.

I moved forward cautiously, expecting the next move which was almost routine. As I passed beyond the shutting line of the door Frank kicked it shut and put out his left arm across my front. This placed his back against the wall on which the door hinged and his left palm hard up to the bathroom wall. With his right hand he frisked me, found my Smith and Wesson 38 in its belt holster, left it alone and then let me through. He had only wanted to make sure that I was not wired for sound. Not very trusting, my masters.

Homer sat in an armchair against the window, legs crossed carefully so as not to rumple his impeccable blue pin-stripe. He had removed his jacket and wore a double breasted waistcoat with a fob. He didn't speak even to greet me. I stood by the foot of the bed and said: "Well?"

For some 30 or 40 seconds he just stared at me, hands in praying position with his forefingers lightly touching his lips. Then eyes glinting, he said: "You look fine to me old chap, what's all the fuss about?"

I sat on the corner of the bed. There was only one other chair and by this time Frank was in it.

Homer went on: "We won't waste time, Leslie, we're in trouble. Littlejohn is on the run, as you know, and he's got to be prevented from making another embarrassing situation. He's caused enough trouble already.

"You know him. He's not the usual calibre and he hasn't got the sense of people like you. There're not many like you, Leslie."

He relaxed visibly, having said his little piece and flattered me a bit. He seemed to be waiting for me to say something. I wasn't going to rise to his bait, however, so, after a long pause, he continued: "We think we know where he's heading for and we want you to get after him."

"Why me?" I asked.

"You know him."

"So do you."

"Don't be bloody silly, Leslie."

"All right, so do a lot of others."

"He trusts you and will take advice from you, then."

"There is no reason why he should trust me, I've only met him a few times, haven't I?"

"But you're the same sort of operative, you know what I mean, much better but the same sort."

"No, I don't know what you mean, he's a snotty-nosed amateur and a crook with it ..."

"Quite, Leslie, quite. And he knows you well enough to blow your cover into a million little pieces. He is either in, or about to go to, Amsterdam. He's got to be made to see reason."

I lay back on the bed and said nothing for about a minute. I had to think. Homer was right. But Homer was also letting me in for something I wasn't going to like. Not ever was I going to like this one.

I said: "I don't think for one minute that he's going to listen to me – or anyone else for that matter. You've had him. Why not cover up and try to face up to the fact that he's going to spill the lot. I'll pack in my running deals and get out altogether. That'd suit me anyway. Several bites at my throat so far this year have got me thinking about quitting already. I'd be quite happy to get on with my own business again."

He lay back in his armchair and looked intently at the Wedgwood blue wardrobe in front of him. Just looked straight ahead, his head nodding slightly, eyes slitted as though there was a strong light in the room.

Homer tapped lightly on the wooden seat edge of his straight-backed chair and I took my pack of Marlborough from my shirt pocket and lit one. The smoke lay heavily in the unventilated room. Then he shouted: "LESLIE."

For the first time ever Homer had shouted in my presence. He swung round at me and continued in a soft, ever so soft voice: "You, Leslie, are going to go for Littlejohn. You are going to find him and talk with him. If he will not listen to you, you are going to deal with him in such a way that he will not talk to or listen to anyone else. You, Leslie, are going to do that. You!"

I still lay back on the bed, smoke drifting lazily above my head. I had to think.

Of course, I could refuse the order, get up and walk out. That was option number one. As option number two, I could agree to do it but not go through with it. The possibility of this was slight. Homer would have me watched every inch of the way. Anyway, if I refused or loused up the deal deliberately Homer could and probably would activate his old threat of telling several of the outfits I had been double-crossing over the years, all about me.

I put my right hand to my wounded left shoulder and winced as I sat up and swung my legs off the bed. Homer turned to face me and for a few seconds we just looked at each other. Christ, how I hated him. Frank blew his nose loudly and mumbled something about the smoke in the room. The spell was broken, I had decided that I would have to go ahead with the deal.

Still looking straight into Homer's cold grey eyes I said: "You know that I've never killed anyone except in self defence. I'm not sure that I can start now, no matter what the threat to me, or you."

He replied: "Leslie, dear boy, now who said anything about killing?"

"But you said to 'deal' with him."

"Yes, but not kill him, Leslie."

"Just what do you mean then, Mr. Bloody Homer?"

"Just deal with him Leslie, just deal with him in any way you think best on the spot. The provos have had their chance. They have had long enough to do it but they haven't managed it. Now it's ours and, therefore, your turn Leslie."

My head was aching again and my shoulder throbbed as I shrugged my acquiescence. He noticed my wince and threw his glance to my injured shoulder. "Do you need specialist attention on that? You can have it, you know, just for the asking, all on us, old boy."

I turned down his offer of help and wrapped up the conversation by walking out of the room, slamming the door behind me. The job had to be done and I was the guy put up to do it. There was no doubt that the bastard could cause a lot of damage and had to be stopped. There was also no doubt that Homer intended me to kill Littlejohn.

I caught a cab back to the station and returned home to make my arrangements.

Checking my local travel agent, I found that there was a week-end package trip deal for Amsterdam which could get me into the country as an ordinary tourist. I decided to take advantage of it. What better cover for such an assignment? I booked on to it.

That was how I entered Holland on the night of Friday, 22nd March, and arrived at the Alpha Hotel in Amsterdam centre. Actually I did not stay at the hotel because there had been some mix-up over bookings. They transferred me to the American Continental instead.

From the Continental, I set out on a tour of my old haunts and friends. All that first night and into the dawn of the next day I asked around for Littlejohn. No one had seen him. I returned to the Continental and my bed, not sleeping but resting my body.

At about 10.30 on the 23rd, my telephone rang – it was an old friend by the name of Peter. He told me that Littlejohn was staying at the Esso Hotel in company with a couple of left wing anarchists and an IRA deserter.

I telephoned the Esso and checked but there was no one registered under that name. This didn't surprise me, of course, but the man was such an idiot one never knew what he might do.

Having showered and dressed I armed myself and set off for the Esso arriving at about eleven-thirty. A quick tour of the bar proved negative and I settled myself in a corner to wait for him. For three hours I kept watch on the comings and goings of the hotel but there was still no sign of him. I gave up and went out of the hotel for lunch at the Continental.

In the evening I returned to the bar of the Esso and placed myself in a corner where I could keep my eye on the whole place. I was beginning to think that the tip had been wrong when he had not turned up by nine and went out for a stroll.

While I was out I called in at the Pink Elephant bar and there was Littlejohn standing in a huddle of men, laughing and drinking. All I then had to do was wait for him to go alone to the toilet or leave the bar.

But for two hours or more he never left the company of the other men and when he did move, he went straight out in the middle of the

231

huddle of men and climbed into a car.

There had been no chance of getting at him.

At eleven the next morning I was back in the Esso after keeping observation outside fom 8.30 and not seeing my man.

It must have been at about noon that I saw the renegade IRA man approaching the corner of the lobby in which I was sitting. He came right up to within about fourteen feet of me and just stood looking at me. I just sat and looked back for about 30 seconds and then looked down at the magazine I was leafing through.

Over the top of the magazine I watched him turn on his heel and make back for the lift. I knew that this man had only seen me twice before, and then only in company with a dozen of his friends, but I was sure that he recognised me. He would not, of course, know my real identity and he thought I was an IRA sympathiser. However, if he described me to Littlejohn, the game would be up.

With no intention of cutting loose from the assignment now that I had found my man, I made the decision to sit it out. Maybe the guy had not managed to recall where and when he had seen me. Some chance.

About five minutes later Littlejohn came over from the lift with two heavies and stood right in front of me: "Hello, Leslie."

I looked up into his face and said: "Hello, Ken." Nothing more was said for a full minute as we just stared at each other.

Then he said: "What are you doing over here?" I replied that I was putting a bit of business together and asked him how he was managing with his "troubles".

"I'll be all right – if no one shops me." He stared hard at me, lifting his eyebrows.

I looked straight back and said: "Not me, chum. You're none of my business. How about a drink?" He replied that he had no time and moved off with his bodyguard. I shrugged, got up and left the hotel, I would try again later.

As I walked away from the hotel I noticed a burly guy in a brown raincoat and tyrolean hat standing about twenty yards from the doorway. I don't know what made me take notice of him, but it must have been some sixth sense because ten minutes later when I stopped to cross the street, he was following me.

Not quickening my pace, I walked on and made a few quick turns as side-streets made themselves available. The guy behind stuck like glue. I was definitely being followed.

By this time I was scared. It was obvious to me that the Littlejohn company had realised that I was up to no good and had decided to take the initiative.

I doubled and back-tracked for about two hours, always keeping in crowds and trying to throw the tail. I found this impossible, but I did manage to keep a fair distance between us — I had no intention of allowing him to get into a situation where he could damage me with either knife or gun.

Finally, after all the ducking and dodging, I found myself outside the Continental Hotel. This was by no means by design — I had been so intent on keeping the man behind at bay that I hadn't cared where I was, just so long as I was among people.

I darted through the door, catching my injured shoulder as I did so. The pain nearly made me faint.

In my room I threw the few things I had unpacked into my case and telephoned down for a cab to be waiting at the door. As soon as the porter called me back to tell me it was there I called the desk and made sure that I had nothing to pay — being on a package trip — and left my room. The reason for checking with the desk was that I was afraid that if I tried to make off with my case and owed money I might well be delayed while payment was demanded. This could well have given my pursuer the opportunity I was sure he was looking for.

After taking the lift down to the ground floor, I moved quickly across the lobby to the waiting cab, noticing that my tail was standing alongside the reception desk, chatting with a clerk. I don't know whether he saw me because I didn't look back as I flung my case into the cab and followed it in, telling the driver to get me straight out to the airport.

Once there, I checked on the next possible flight out — it was to Paris — and booked onto it. Forty minutes later I was in the air and four hours later, having connected with a London flight at Orly, I was at Heathrow. About half an hour after that I was booked in at the Tara and lying on my bed as I tried to pull myself together.

There was only a duty man on Homer's telephone and he promised to have him telephone me as soon as he could contact him.

Homer didn't call back, but his side-kick, Frank, did. He told me that Homer would see me at the hotel next morning at ten. He urgently wanted to see me. I agreed with this arrangement and he rang off.

I hardly slept at all during the night. My shoulder still throbbed a little but that wasn't the main cause. I just couldn't relax at all. And every time I woke from a short doze and checked my watch I started to think how lousy it was to be an insomniac. That didn't help me relax, it just made things ten times worse.

By the time Homer and Frank arrived next morning I was pretty much washed out and hadn't even bothered to shave. Certainly I was in no mood for the ripping off which Homer started in on as soon as he had sat himself down.

He led straight in with: "Leslie, dear boy, you have made a right balls of the thing, haven't you. You didn't even make a serious attempt at it ... You flew out with you tail between your legs as soon as they looked you in the eye. You're useless, Leslie."

I started to reply but he cut me short by saying: "You even ran away from the man we had covering you ..."

It was my turn to cut in: "The man YOU had covering me? Do you mean to tell me that the guy who frightened the bloody life out of me was your man? If he was then why didn't he identify himself? You silly sod, you silly bloody fool ..." My tirade ended as I ran out of words. There was no way to describe how I felt about Homer at that precise moment.

He picked up the telephone and ordered coffee for three and then just sat waiting for me to stop pacing the room and to calm down.

But the last thing I intended to do was calm down. I was bloody furious and accused him of intending to have his man shoot me after I had attended to Littlejohn.

It was only a short while before that another agent, albeit a junior league man, had been found shot in a Surrey lane with all the evidence pointing to the fact that the Department had done it. I was quite ready to believe that I would end up the same way if Homer and his bosses decided that they were finished with me. In fact I still do think that way, especially now that they've learned how I've used them to set up

234

my own deals with the Arabs and the Irish.

In reply to my accusations Homer merely shrugged and lifted his eyebrows. I moved to the door and, taking my thirty-eight from its belt holster, nodded them both out of the room as I opened it: "Piss off," I hissed, "now."

"They both got up and silently walked past me through the door just as the waiter arrived with the coffee. I quickly shoved the gun into my pocket before the waiter could see it and took the tray from him. Then, nodding to Homer and Frank, who were still standing in the corridor, said: "They'll pay." I slammed the door.

After drinking a couple of cups of coffee I showered and shaved before checking out and catching a train for home. I had decided that I was finished with the lot of them.

Chapter 12
Quit or Die

Back at home I rested up for about a fortnight, enjoying being with the family. The only contact I had with the Department was via my local liaison man, sent round by Homer to find out how I was getting on and to tell me that the Department understood that my recent behaviour was the result of tremendous pressure.

I listened to the guy patiently – after all, it wasn't any of his doing, and then asked him to leave. I told him that I just didn't want to know.

It was obvious to me that I was not going to be left alone at home and I had a real fear that Homer really would prefer it if I had an 'accident'. He had been all too ready to have me attend to Littlejohn when he became an embarrassment. Why then shouldn't he have someone do the same to me? I decided to quit the country, pull in my money from my various deposits, and pack it all in.

Taking no luggage at all, I caught a train for London and spent half a day playing tourist as I made sure that any tail I might have acquired was left behind. I then picked up my operational suitcase from Victoria, took a cab to Waterloo and caught the Paris boat train. Getting out from under as far as Homer was concerned was as simple as that.

From Paris I took the night train down to the South and spent the next couple of months using Nice as a base as I pulled my mind and belongings together. Using Rene, who I called in to help me, I removed my reserve suitcases from eight points throughout Europe during this period and gathered what information I could about my status with the various groups I had worked with.

Rene soon found out that the IRA, the Libyans and the Mafia people in Italy were all very anxious to have meetings with me. There was no threat from any of them but they all had urgent work which they wanted me to undertake. I made up my mind that I would quit the business altogether, or at least give myself a few months to establish a new identity and appearance.

Eventually, fed up with hanging around the flesh-pots of the South of France, and hearing from Rene that the Mafia and the Bank were both after my blood, I decided to make one more trip to Ireland to collect money I had deposited there and quit for good.

There were no problems on the trip, which I made by air on my Irish passport, and I even had a couple of meetings with people I could trust in the Republic who I thought might help me in the future in one way or another.

That was what led to my cover being completely blown. I don't know how they did it, but the Irish Special Branch got on to me during my short visit and, finding they had let me slip out again, leaked what they knew of me from their own sources and their Homer-type friends in London to the Irish People, a Republican newspaper.

On September 6th, 1974, they ran an article which read: "Kenneth Littlejohn is alive and active. And the man who had replaced him as the British Government's chief provocateur in the 26 Counties is on lunching terms with a 26 County Cabinet Minister.

"The Littlejohn replacement is Mr. Leslie Allen Aspin who travels at will on British and Irish passports. His passport numbers are H316974 and P812059.

"But Aspin is not without his bothers.

"Aspin's main worry is a Libyan task force who are on his trail since he scuttled the Libyan-Provo attempt to land arms on the Claudia more than 18 months ago. Since then two Libyan agents have died mysteriously and the Libyan authorities blame Aspin for both deaths.

"The British agent's most recent excursion to this country occurred three weeks ago. Reason for it was a meeting with a 26-County

Cabinet Minister. The British spy and the Minister met at Dublin's Skylon Hotel. The receptionist at the Drumcondra Road premises confirmed on Monday last that Aspin was at the hotel two weeks ago but when an Irish People reporter enquired as to whether he had left a forwarding address, the receptionist, after a delay, disclosed that Mr. Aspin had never been there. Her earlier confirmation of his presence was a result of his name "ringing a bell".

"Enquiries to the British Embassy in Dublin as to whether Mr. Leslie Aspin was on their staff met with evasive replies. An Irish People reporter who telephoned 695211 was, after some time, advised to ring 984911 and from there was advised that a telephone call to 62334 (without the essential 7) might be helpful.

"It is the Libyan European Office in Brussels, however, which has the most up-to-date information on the movements of Mr. Aspin. Although the office is officially silent on the existence of the British spy, reliable sources are in possession of highly significant dates on his movements.

"The Libyan office dossier shows that Aspin was in Libya over Christmas 1972 when final arrangements for the Claudia shipment were being made. He left Libya on the departure of the arms ship and the dossier next records his presence in Malta while the ill-fated successor to the Aud was in transit.

"A gap then occurs until an insertion notes that he was in Dublin, again at the Skylon Hotel, in late February of this year. His whereabouts on March 16, when Kenneth Littlejohn escaped from Mountjoy jail, are not recorded but the dossier does name a hotel in Amsterdam where he was seen with Littlejohn on March 22.

"The Aspin trail returns to Dublin where it is recorded that on 22 June he met a leading opposition politician just six weeks before he was sighted there conversing with the National Coalition Minister.

"No indication is given in the dossier of why Aspin had the Skylon rendezvous first with the Fianna Fall man and then with the Minister. What is certain however is that Libyan intelligence was not far behind him. His dangerous double game as British agent and provisional-Libyan sympathiser could have ended dramatically on either occasion."

It was the publication of this article which led me to agree that an account of my Secret Service activities could be published in the Sunday People, a British newspaper unconnected with the Irish People. It was natural after that that my mind should turn to telling the whole story and that is what I have now done.

I have earned a lot of money at the game but most of it has been frittered away on a playboy existence – the old easy-come, easy-go principle.

I have had the fast cars and my own private plane as well as some very beautiful women. And there is no doubt that I have had my full measure of adventure.

But at 33 I am a washed-out wreck with a price on my head. I am an insomniac with the sort of nightmares one gets when one has killed a few people.

With regard to killing, I must underline the fact that I have never killed a man who did not threaten my life in some way. I am by no means proud of this side of my activities and I am certainly not a natural assassin. By a peculiar quirk of fate I have never shot a man except in the back and I don't think I could look a man in the eye and pull a trigger.

Since I started to write this account, I have bought a share in a business in the United States and, left alone by the men who are still seeking me, I intend to work quietly there and die of old age.

However, I have had two offers of work passed on by Rene from a government who know all about me but for whom I haven't yet worked ...